D1563897

DISCARD

One Voice

Rabbi Jacob M. Rothschild presents a custom-made, engraved Steuben bowl to Dr. Martin Luther King, Jr., at a landmark Atlanta dinner in 1965 honoring the Nobel laureate.

One Voice

*Rabbi Jacob M. Rothschild
and the Troubled South*

JANICE ROTHSCHILD BLUMBERG
with a Foreword
by Coretta Scott King

MERCER

ISBN 0-86554-150-7

All books published by Mercer University Press are produced on
acid-free paper that exceeds the minimum standards set by the
National Historical Publications and Records Commission.

Library of Congress Cataloging in Publication Data
Blumberg, Janice Rothschild, 1924–
One voice.
Includes bibliographical references and index.
1. Rothschild, Jacob M., 1911-1974.   2. Rabbis—
Georgia—Atlanta—Biography.   3. Civil rights workers—
Georgia—Atlanta—Biography.   4. Afro-Americans—
Civil rights—Georgia—Atlanta.   5. Atlanta (Ga.)—
Biography.   I. Title.
BM755.R63B57   1984   296.8'346'0924 [B]   84-22723
ISBN 0-86554-150-7 (alk. paper)

CONTENTS

FOREWORD

"The ultimate measure of a man is not where he stands in moments of comfort and convenience, but where he stands in times of challenge and controversy. The true neighbor will risk his position, his prestige and even his life for the welfare of others. In dangerous valleys and hazardous pathways he will lift some bruised and beaten brother to a higher and more noble life."

These words from Martin Luther King, Jr.'s sermon, "On Being a Good Neighbor," could be applied as a fitting tribute to my husband's good friend, Rabbi Jacob M. Rothschild. Like Martin, Rabbi Rothschild was deeply committed to justice, equality, and brotherhood. He was an early and strong supporter of the civil rights movement, who gave generously of his time and talents to the struggle.

Rabbi Rothschild shared in Martin's Dream as a basic tenet of his own religious teaching. He had the courage to proclaim his belief publicly long before it became expedient or even physically safe to do so in a Southern city.

Through his wisdom and dedication, he was able to influence significant numbers of others to pursue the course of racial justice. He was in great measure responsible for the Atlanta dinner honoring Martin as recipient of the 1964 Nobel Peace Prize, an occasion that heralded a new era in race relations in our city.

Janice Rothschild Blumberg has movingly evoked his story, for she too shared the Dream. Her memoir is an eloquent reaffirmation of the bonds of solidarity that unite Jewish and black Americans as well as an inspiring story of commitment and brotherhood during an exciting, creative period of American history.

Coretta Scott King
Atlanta
September 1984

ACKNOWLEDGMENTS

Initially the credit for this manuscript should go to the subject himself, for he provided not only the inspiration but also much of its actual content. His civil rights sermons, widely quoted herein, reveal in his own words the means by which he helped improve race relations in Atlanta during the decades of greatest turmoil throughout the South. He once considered putting them into book form under the title "Sermons from a Southern Pulpit." Ralph McGill encouraged him and wrote the introduction to it, but the idea was soon abandoned for lack of interest on the part of commercial publishing houses.

That the idea was abandoned was undoubtedly due also to lack of interest on the part of the rabbi himself. At about the same time—the late 1960s—he and others of his age group were asked to write or tape brief autobiographies for the American Jewish Archives. He delayed for so long that I suspected he would not do it at all. When I mentioned this neglect to him, he suggested that I write the autobiography for him. Accordingly, I brought along a tape recorder on our next long trip and while he, a captive subject, drove the car, I interviewed him about the first thirty-five years of his life, those that I had not shared with him. I intended to wait until he had retired from his congregational duties, then use the material I had documented as a basis for a collaborative effort to

write of his life and work. When he died, three years before his scheduled
retirement, I determined to write the book myself.

Initially I sought advice from his dear friends and mine, rabbis Jacob
Rader Marcus and Levi A. Olan and Dr. Benjamin E. Mays. Their encouragement led me to begin quickly, first gathering all obtainable files
of Rothschild correspondence as well as sermons and other writings. I am
deeply grateful to Robert Lipshutz, president of the congregation at that
time, and his board of trustees for granting me access to them, and particularly appreciative of all that Rabbi Alvin Sugarman did throughout
these ten years of incubation to facilitate the birth of this book. His first
great contribution was to relinquish the time of his newly arrived young
assistant, Rabbi Edward Paul Cohn, who helped me put the papers into
workable order. Rabbi Cohn provided not only time and expertise—there
was also much joy in associating with one so enthusiastic over the task at
hand.

That the project came to a screeching halt when I remarried, in May
1975, was by no means due to the wishes of my beloved husband, David
M. Blumberg. A longtime friend and admirer of Jack Rothschild, David
urged me to continue working on the book without interruption. My
judgment and his schedule, which I chose to share with him, dictated
otherwise. Consequently, I postponed resumption of my writing until
such time as our lives became more settled, more conducive to long-term
concentration.

The postponement might have lasted forever had it not been for a
second enthusiastic young scholar, who is not a rabbi but a professor of
history at Valdosta State College in south Georgia. Dr. Louis Schmier
first approached me in 1982 with a request on behalf of the Southern Jewish Historical Society to prepare a paper on some aspect of the Rothschild
rabbinate for a forthcoming meeting of the society. In accepting the challenge I mentioned that I intended "some day" to write a more detailed
account of Jack's life and work. From that moment on Louis Schmier became my personal teacher and guide, giving freely of his time and knowledge, cheerfully shoveling through early drafts of the manuscript to edit
and advise, patiently and candidly treating it as if it were the doctoral dis-
sertation of a promising Ph.D. candidate. No words are adequate to express my appreciation to him.

Others also gave devoted service by providing editorial advice on
early drafts of the manuscript. For this I am extremely grateful to my

daughter, Marcia D. Rothschild, my son, William L. Rothschild, and daughter-in-law Dr. Hava Tirosh-Rothschild, my sister-in-law Jean Rothschild Levinson; and dear, dear friends Rebecca Gershon, Adelaide Eisemann, and Marjorie Goldman. Likewise, good friends Dr. Malcolm H. Stern and Bernard Wax responded helpfully when approached for their advice.

Research assistance came from many sources. Conversations with Fred Beerman, M. William Breman, Miriam Freedman, Abraham Shurgin, Charles Wittenstein and others helped immeasurably in sparking and verifying my own recollection of past events. Max Gettinger, Mark Jacobson, and Dianne Ratowsky aided materially in obtaining documents necessary to my research, as did various members of the staff of the Atlanta Historical Society and the Robert W. Woodruff Library of Emory University. I owe a very special word of thanks to Lee Sayrs, of Special Collections at Emory University, for her help with final details.

A neophyte author soon learns that completing a text is by no means the end of one's task in producing a book, nor even of the favors one must ask of friends in that regard. I am deeply indebted to the Hebrew Benevolent Congregation of Atlanta and the Southern Jewish Historical Society for providing the support necessary for publication of this volume, and to Coretta Scott King for so graciously consenting to provide the introduction to it. In view of her schedule during this summer, it is an even greater testimony to her friendship for her to have done so. My most sincere thanks to her, as well as to her administrative assistant, Delores Harmon, and her staff assistant, Stephen Klein, for their helpful cooperation throughout.

Much as I appreciate the efforts of all who have helped in the process of producing this work, I cannot close without a final word about my husband, David Blumberg. It takes an extraordinary degree of character to withstand three years of a wife's concentration on her life with her former husband. David did it, cheerfully and enthusiastically, and for that I thank the Almighty.

PROLOGUE

Forty-five minutes before the scheduled time for Jack's funeral Marcia, Bill, and I were held up by traffic at Brookwood Station, half a mile from The Temple. We couldn't understand why that part of Peachtree Street was so busy in the early afternoon of an icy, wet Wednesday, 2 January. Most of our close friends were still away on winter vacations. Surely all those cars couldn't be going to The Temple!

We soon learned that The Temple was indeed their destination. It took us another fifteen minutes to reach the entrance ourselves, and then we had difficulty getting up the driveway even though police were facilitating our entry by turning the other cars away. Television crews blocked pedestrians crossing from the parking lot into the building. I couldn't believe what I was seeing. "If only I could tell him," I thought. "He wouldn't believe it either."

Inside, the pews were packed as if it had been Yom Kippur, the Day of Atonement, except that many of the faces were not Jewish. Even a cursory glance as we walked to our seats revealed many whom we didn't know, and others whom we recognized but would never have expected to see. Among them were then Governor of Georgia Jimmy Carter and First Lady Rosalynn. We were told that the entire executive staff of Coca-Cola attended also.

Dr. and Mrs. Martin Luther King, Sr., were seated alongside the Carters in places of honor just behind us. As I sat down, Daddy King patted me comfortingly on the shoulder and whispered, "Coretta will be along soon." She had gone to the airport to pick up Congressman Andrew Young, who had flown in from Washington to attend the funeral. His plane had been delayed by bad weather. By the time they arrived the pews were filled; the only space available for them to sit was on folding chairs, which had been hastily set up just inside the entrances.

It wasn't only the crowd at Jack's funeral that surprised us. The attendant publicity seemed equally amazing. Both the *Atlanta Constitution* and the *Atlanta Journal* ran front-page stories, editorials, and photographs about him for two days. Even in the black community, where for some years it had been fashionable to reject the comradeship of white liberals, publications joined in the chorus of condolence. The *Atlanta Inquirer* devoted as much of its front page that week to the death of Jack Rothschild as it did to the inauguration of Maynard Jackson—one of its own—as the first black mayor of a major Southern city.[1]

Sitting in that front-row pew gripping a hand of each of our two children, themselves already adults, I began to think of Jack's life and what there was about it that caused so many people to mourn his death. He had never thought of himself as a Very Important Person, and while he was certainly important to us we had not realized he was quite so important to the public as this avalanche of attention indicated. To us he was human, brighter and braver than most but by no means immune to common frailties. His insecurities ran deep, in fact, but he never permitted them to shake his confidence in doing what he believed was right. Nor

---

[1]Art Harris and Colleen Teasley, "Temple Rites Today: Rabbi Rothschild Dies," *Atlanta Constitution*, 2 Jan. 1974, p. 1A; Art Harris and Colleen Teasley, " 'Always Brotherly': Rabbi Rothschild Mourned by Religious, Civic Leaders." *Atlanta Constitution*, 2 Jan. 1974; Raleigh Bryans, "Rothschild's Funeral Held," *Atlanta Journal*, 2 Jan. 1974, p. 1A; "Rothschild Praised as Unifying Voice," *Atlanta Journal*, 2 Jan. 1974, p. 2A; Editorial, "Jacob Rothschild," *Atlanta Journal*, 2 Jan. 1974; "News this Morning," *Atlanta Constitution*, 3 Jan. 1974; Art Harris and Colleen Teasley, "Rothschild Paid Final Tribute," *Atlanta Constitution*, 3 Jan. 1974; Editorial, "Rabbi Rothschild," *Atlanta Constitution*, 3 Jan. 1974; Billie Cheney Speed, "All Faiths Mourn Rabbi Rothschild," *Atlanta Journal*, 3 Jan. 1974—copies in Jacob M. Rothschild Manuscripts, Special Collections, Robert W. Woodruff Library, Emory University, Atlanta, Georgia (hereafter cited as JMR MSS).

did they lead him to become pompous, self-righteous, or sanctimonious. Perhaps I helped in that respect by never consciously trying to feed his ego. It had simply never occurred to me that he might have needed such artificial nourishment. His self-deprecating sense of humor—which sometimes proved too sharp for those interpreting the barbs as aimed at themselves—succeeded admirably in keeping him in balance with himself. It evidently influenced us in a similar fashion. Otherwise, we might have been more prepared for this public reaction to his death.

What was it exactly that made it so? If he had excelled as a pastor he surely did not realize it. That, actually, was the one area of his profession with which he felt somewhat uncomfortable, and not without reason. People often complained about his brusqueness of manner, his—as they expressed it—"lack of spirituality." I could imagine the sheepish, incredulous grin that would have crossed his face had he seen some of the letters we now received, letters that said, "His thoughtfulness and many kindnesses to me and my family . . . will always be a cherished memory," or "I really loved Rabbi Rothschild as did thousands of other people. . . ." I don't believe he ever thought of himself as a rabbi whom people loved.[2]

Neither in his own mind nor in the view of others did Jack Rothschild fit the standard image of "a man of the cloth." But though he never wore the "hairshirt" of religiosity, he did deeply and truly believe in a Divine Spirit—a portion of which he believed exists in every human soul—and in a central plan for all of creation. He had often said that religion was not "merely a way of looking at certain aspects of life but a certain way of looking at all life." His Judaism was that of the biblical prophets, a religion "of deed rather than creed," of right rather than rite.

Jack knew he was not a scholar. Although some people believed he was and flattered him by saying so, he knew better than they what it meant to be one and was aware that his friends who were themselves scholars would not have applied that term to him. His colleagues in the Reform rabbinate apparently found other qualities in him to admire. They wrote to us about his integrity, his courage, his forthrightness, his "sharp realism, keen wit, eloquence in brevity." One referred to him as

---

[2]Ann Schwartz Glick to Janice O. Rothschild (hereafter cited as JOR), 14 January 197[4]; Susan Simon to JOR, January 1974, JMR MSS.

"a rabbi's rabbi."[3] Another, a younger man who had once served as a summer replacement at The Temple, said "he was my most practical teacher."[4] Another comment most succinctly and vividly described him as having "guts, integrity and a vision of himself not on Sinai, but in the valley where the action is."[5]

The most important item on Jack's agenda for himself had always been the needs of his congregation, and after those, the needs of his community. For that reason he would have been especially gratified to read the words of a young woman the same age as our daughter who, reminiscing about her years in his religious school, wrote, "He caused me to equate Judaism with civil rights and fighting for justice—actively, not just in thought or through monetary contribution." To teach that idea, above all, was what he had tried to do.[6]

More than once in those later years Jack had said to me, "I don't know what I would have achieved in my career if it hadn't been for the issue of civil rights coming to a head when it did, or if I had been anywhere else but here when it happened." His may have been too harsh an assessment. I believe he would have pursued justice with equal vigor whatever the issue and wherever he was. It was true, however, that he had come to exactly the right place at exactly the right time, for himself, and perhaps for his city as well.

Evidently others thought so. "Baldy," editorial cartoonist for the *Atlanta Constitution*, expressed the sentiment in his announcement of Jack's death. In the foreground he drew a huge book entitled "Brotherhood" open to a page where the name "Rabbi Rothschild" appeared to have been written with a freshly dripping pen. In the background he drew the skyline of Atlanta.[7]

Both the skyline and the book had changed radically in the twenty-seven years since Jack had come to Atlanta. The city had grown from a

[3]Rabbi Robert Samuels to JOR, January 1974, JMR MSS.

[4]Rabbi Philip E. Schechter to JOR, January 1974, JMR MSS.

[5]Rabbi William Sajowitz to JOR, January 1974, JMR MSS.

[6]Aileen Jacobson to JOR, January 1974, JMR MSS.

[7]Editorial, *Atlanta Constitution*, 2 Jan. 1974.

Deep South state capital of fewer than a half-million people to a cosmopolitan center of more than a million and a half. It had emerged from a
reputation for Bible Belt fundamentalism where the Ku Klux Klan held
sway to that of a sophisticated metropolis respected for many reasons, not
the least of which was the memory of a native son—a black man—who
had led America into a new and better concept of itself. It had almost
erased the marks of lynch mobs demanding, "Death to the Jew!" by declaring itself "a city too busy to hate" and by striving sincerely to live up
to that claim. Jack had devoted his ministry to helping make these things
happen. The people were telling us that they knew.

    Only to do justly, to love mercy, to walk humbly with thy God . . . (Micah
6:8) These words of the prophet Micah were among those most meaningful to Jack throughout his life and most descriptive, to me, of how he
had lived his life. As I sat there in the sanctuary of The Temple, surrounded not so much by the crowds and music and doleful eulogies as by
images of the past, I thought of them once again. It had been a long walk,
not in terms of years but of distance traveled.

C H A P T E R • O N E

NOTIONS
OUT OF CINCINNATI

"**W**hy did you want to be a rabbi?"
I asked Jack this question on one of our first dates, as soon as I thought I knew him well enough to be blunt. He fielded it in a manner developed over the ten years since he had entered the rabbinate, with a quick quip designed to divert the thought. He understood, of course, that what one really meant by the question was "How could anyone who seems so 'normal' choose a profession that seems so 'abnormal'?"

Jack answered my query by saying, "Because I like to sleep late and I wasn't born rich"—the implication being that clerics didn't have to get up early and punch a time clock to earn a living. I soon learned that while it was true that clergymen usually could choose when to begin their day, their open-ended workdays and seven-day weeks often made them wish they did have a time clock to punch.

I also learned that there was a kernel of truth in his implication that he might have chosen another profession had he been born into a wealthy family. He was fascinated with law. News items and dramatizations about court cases drew his attention above all else. He relished using legal examples to illustrate his sermons. Had his parents been able to finance it, he might very well have opted for law school rather than rabbinical seminary. Had he chosen law, however, he likely would have had to do so over the vigorous objections of his strong-willed mother.

Jack's mother told me of the family history. She, Lillian Abrams Rothschild, was one of three daughters born to an American mother widowed while her children were still very young. They were of Lithuanian Jewish origin, lived in a small town upriver from Pittsburgh, and adhered to the Reform interpretation of Judaism. In order for Lillie's mother to be able to earn a living for herself and her three little girls, she placed them in a local convent to be educated and supervised by the nuns.[1]

While this exposure to Catholicism in no way diminished young Lillie's devotion to her own faith it did add to the jaundiced view of her taken by her prospective in-laws when Meyer Rothschild presented her to his traditional, Eastern-European-born parents. A beautiful, stylish, fair-skinned blond, thoroughly Americanized, with an ebullient personality, and no knowledge of Yiddish—what kind of a Jewish girl was this, they asked. "They behaved as if he were marrying a Gentile," she told me. "And as far as they were concerned, that's what I was. To them Reform wasn't Jewish."[2]

Perhaps the legend has grown with time but Lillie's version of it bears retelling because of the effect it may have had on Jack's decision to become a rabbi. According to her, she was so indignant at the way the Rothschilds had treated her that she vowed revenge—appropriate revenge, that is. She determined to give birth to a son who would become

---

[1]Conversations with Lillian Abrams Rothschild, 1946-1962; with Jacob M. Rothschild (hereafter cited as JMR), 1946-1973; and with Jean Rothschild Levinson, 1983.

[2]Ibid.

an outstanding *Reform* rabbi. She did, on 4 August 1911. To emphasize her intentions she named him after an especially pious and much revered ancestor of the Rothschild clan whose name was Jacob, and then persisted in calling him "Jack," a nickname inconsistent with an image of piety.

Meyer Rothschild was one of twelve children. In 1917, while Jack was still a child, Meyer's sister Gertrude married a Reform rabbi, Samuel S. Mayerberg, thus taking the edge off Lillie's alleged revenge. Meanwhile, however, she had succeeded in winning the friendship of the elder Rothschild, himself a wise and learned rebbe, who by that time must have decided that his son Meyer had found himself a jewel.

Jack liked and admired his Uncle Spier, as the family called Mayerberg, and in one respect followed his example as a rabbi. Mayerberg was the "pistol packin' rabbi" of Kansas City, so called because during the years he had led the campaign to rid the city of the corrupt and infamous Pendergast machine he had had to carry a gun for self-protection. While Jack, during his fight for civil rights in Atlanta, never felt threatened to such a degree, both he and I at times had reason to believe our lives were in danger.

Mayerberg served as a fine example to his young nephew, but it is likely that another, Dr. Samuel S. Goldenson, rabbi of Pittsburgh's Congregation Rodeph Shalom during the years Jack attended religious school there, gave him his earliest insights into a ministry devoted to social action. "He was fearless," Jack told me, recounting a famous incident of his childhood. "When the coal miners were starving—and there were members of his congregation that owned mines—he gave a scathing sermon about the mine owners and defended the miners' right to strike. Two of his wealthiest members resigned. He was that kind of guy." Clearly he helped Jack become the same.[3]

The Rothschilds lived in Pittsburgh's Squirrel Hill area when Jack was a child. According to Lillie they were the first Jews to move into this now heavily Jewish neighborhood. She also recalled—apochryphally, perhaps—that the neighbors came from blocks away to visit her when Jack was born because they had never seen a Jewish baby.

At least one story of his precocious childhood is documented. During the summer of 1918, when he was seven years old, he learned that a

---

[3]JMR, interview with author ca. 1970. Tape and transcript in JMR MSS.

local Anglo-Jewish newspaper was appealing for donations to a Milk and Ice Fund for indigent children. He persuaded his neighborhood friends to have their mothers bake cakes for them; he and his friends then sold the cakes for fifty cents apiece. The proceeds—a whopping $18.50—were then sent to the Milk and Ice Fund. To show its appreciation the newspaper published a picture of Jack and his friends in the rotogravure, along with the story of their remarkable enterprise. Though the amount was inconsequential compared to what he was later to raise for the United Jewish Appeal, it was a worthy and auspicious achievement for the seven-year-old.[4]

Jack recalled that his was not "an upper crust" social group but "a very close-knit coterie of friends that grew up together." One of them became a physician, another a lawyer, another—in addition to Jack—a rabbi. By the time they graduated from Schenley High School in 1926, Jack had already received a scholarship to the Hebrew Union College (HUC) in Cincinnati. He didn't use it that year, however, because his mentor, Rabbi Goldenson, counseled the elder Rothschilds that their son was too young—having finished high school at fifteen—to make such a weighty commitment. Instead, Jack entered the freshman class at the University of Pittsburgh and devoted as much time as he could spare from his other subjects to the study of Hebrew. Since the language was not taught in Reform religious schools in those days he had a lot of catching up to do before he could be confident of maintaining the standards set for rabbinical candidates at HUC.[5]

The following summer, a few weeks before Jack was scheduled to leave for Cincinnati, his father suffered a severe stroke that left him paralyzed. Jack decided to cancel his plans for school, remain at the University of Pittsburgh, and get a job that would enable him to help support the family.

Lillie wouldn't hear of it. She sent him packing, opened a dress business in her home, and supervised the care of her husband while she worked. Jack's ten-year-old sister Jean came home from school each afternoon to serve as nurse-companion to her father.

---

[4]"Jack's Big Cake Idea," *Pittsburgh Jewish Chronicle*, Summer 1918, photograph and clipping in childhood scrapbook, Rothschild family private collection.

[5]See note 3 above.

Meyer lingered in that condition for five years. When his father died, Jack again told his mother he intended to stay home, get a job, and help her pay off the enormous debts that had accumulated from his father's illness. Again she said no. The course of study for rabbinical candidates at that time lasted nine years: the students earned their undergraduate degrees from the University of Cincinnati at the same time that they trained for the rabbinate at HUC. Jack had two years yet to complete and Lillie refused to let anything interfere.

Jack was known as "Racky" to his friends of those years. One of them, Rabbi Sidney Berkowitz, then a small-town boy just out of high school himself, later described his impression of Jack when they first met, the day they both arrived at HUC:

> I was drawn to Racky for his self-assurance, his friendly outgoing manner, his leadership ability, his clear, logical mind, his ability to articulate the most intricate of thought processes in precise terms. . . . But there were other more important bonds that inspired my admiration. . . . He had been to a Major League baseball game in Pittsburgh. He not only knew baseball and basketball, but he played them. There was no athletic skill in which he failed to demonstrate some prowess. . . . He may not have known some obscure Hebrew paradigm, but he certainly knew the batting averages of the top major league players. He gave me a new concept of the rabbinical student.[6]

Even when Jack ceased to participate in those energetic activities this image remained with him. At school he quickly won a reputation as a good card player—both at poker and at bridge—and often was invited by certain professors and their wives to provide a fourth at bridge. He served another of his professors—archaeologist Nelson Glueck, who later became president of HUC—as a partner for horseback riding.

Contact sports, however, remained his favorites throughout his college days, in spite of the few broken bones and the amended profile he acquired while indulging in them. It is said that the nose he was born with did not have a curve to it, but that its shape was a result of his ignoring a blow dealt him during a college basketball game. His mother, whom he claimed was so fiercely protective that "whenever it was raining

---

[6]Rabbi Sidney Berkowitz, Sermon delivered at the celebration of JMR's twenty-fifth anniversary as rabbi of The Temple, Atlanta, 23 April 1971, JMR MSS.

in Pittsburgh she would call me in Cincinnati to tell me to wear my galoshes," not only approved the activity but on one memorable occasion even joined in. (The incident was so often recounted by his colleagues in my presence that I am inclined to believe it.) On the night of their ordination, Jack and his friends left the reception in their honor to play ball on the lawn of the college. Lillie, still dressed in her party clothes, played on one of the teams. With her as an example, it was hardly surprising that Jack remained "a regular guy" despite his profession.

"I frittered away a lot of time," he admitted, adding, "I made adequate grades, though. Enough to keep up my scholarships." It was all the more praiseworthy that he did so, for he was forced to work at part-time jobs in order to support himself. He waited tables in a nightclub, sold boys' clothing in a department store, worked in the school gym, and taught Sunday school. Often he returned from his Saturday-night job at the nightclub with barely enough time left to shower, shave, and catch the trolley to the synagogue where he taught Sunday school. Summers in Pittsburgh he ran an elevator at the William Penn Hotel, clerked in Kauffmann's department store, "companion-tutored" sons of a wealthy family, and worked as a counselor at a nearby camp.[7]

Jack also served a variety of very small congregations—as every HUC student was expected to do—during the last years he spent at the college. At first the assignments were only for the major holidays. As the students reached their junior and senior years they were transferred to slightly larger congregations that could afford to employ them on a biweekly basis to instruct the children as well as to conduct services. Jack recalled most of those experiences with nostalgia.

> I was either twenty or twenty-one when I had my first holiday job. It was Henderson, Kentucky, and we just got along famously. They loved me and I loved them. They were all older people. There were no young people in the congregation and they treated me sort of like somebody's grandson.[8]

The congregation in Henderson asked for him again the following year. Although in order for the students to gain more varied experience,

---

[7]See note 3 above.

[8]Ibid.

the college usually discouraged such practices, in Jack's case it was permitted. He visited in Henderson after he finished college and maintained contact with one family there throughout his life.

"My third year I went to Jonesboro, Arkansas," he continued. "That was another nice town. I liked it there, too."

He was not so favorably disposed toward the biweekly congregation assigned him in his senior year. It was a harsher community, as distant in temperament as it was in miles from the warm Southern graciousness he had encountered in Kentucky.

> You asked me if I was ever discouraged about becoming a rabbi. Yes. That biweekly almost convinced me not to be a rabbi. . . . I think they were a microcosm of all the evils of the rabbinate . . . a[n] [un]interested congregation who only wanted to make demands on the rabbi. . . . It got so bad that psychologically I would oversleep on the Friday morning I was supposed to get up and catch the train, so that maybe I would miss it. Boy! I remember days when I ran through that brand-new terminal in Cincinnati and just barely made the train![9]

Jack described himself as "sort of lazy" in his studies. Bible was his favorite subject, the Prophets in particular: "It was just what appealed to me. I was not scholarly, not interested in being a Talmudic scholar or anything like that. I was interested in the application of Judaism to the problems of today."[10]

His interests being more practical than scholarly, it may seem odd that, while he liked almost all his teachers at HUC and always delighted in reminiscing about them, he declared the great historian, Dr. Jacob Rader Marcus, the one who most influenced him. To those, however, who know Dr. Marcus, his choice was understandable. Dr. Marcus and his beloved wife Nettie befriended Jack in those early days and when I joined the family generously included me in their affection. I was thus given ample opportunity to see that, in this case, the professor's personality, wit, charm, and attitude carried far more weight with his student than did his subject.

---

[9]Ibid.

[10]Ibid.

One reason why Jack was not as fascinated by Talmud and Jewish law as he was by secular law may have been that these subjects—which required facility in Hebrew—were far more difficult for him than they were for other students, most of whom had come from Orthodox homes where boys were trained in them from earliest childhood. Sidney Berkowitz, who shared Jack's disability in this regard, recalled that the two "sought mutual consolation in the fact that we were both 'Jewishly sterile,' the only two members of our class who had come from Reform homes, had attended Reform Religious Schools, and to the horror of our classmates, had been confirmed and not Bar Mitzvahed."[11]

This paucity of cultural background gave rise to one incident that Jack, supplying the thick German accent of the professor he spoke of, loved to recount. It seems that Jack and another student, one from an Orthodox family, were in a course together, and Jack consistently received higher grades in it than did his obviously more-learned classmate. The classmate bore the indignity as long as he could but finally gave way to resentment and confronted their professor. "How can you do this," he demanded, "when you *know* that I know more Talmud than Rothschild?"

"Silly boy," replied the professor. "I am a teacher, yes? Vat *you* know you knew ven you came here. Vat Rothschild knows, *I* taught him!"

Friends from the college claim that they could always tell that Jack was coming down the hall because his footsteps were so distinctive. "They always seemed purposeful," one friend told me. "As if the person making them knew exactly where he was going."[12] While this assessment does sound somewhat influenced by nostalgia, there must have been something about this "only average" student that augured success. Despite the reputation Jack had acquired as sportsman rather than scholar, and notwithstanding his unrabbinical appearance—a slight, five-foot-eight-inch frame topped with a boyish, fair-skinned face and a mass of curly, strawberry-blond hair that had begun to recede by the time I met him—he was recommended by the college for the best position open that year to the newly ordained rabbis: the congregation in Davenport, Iowa. Before sending Jack off to interview for it, however, HUC President Dr. Julian Morgenstern summoned him to his office to proffer advice. The

---

[11]See note 6 above.

[12]Lillian Waldman Lieberman, conversation with author, ca. 1956.

name Jack sounded somewhat undignified for a rabbi, Dr. Morgernstern believed, so he suggested that Jack change it to "Jacob." Much relieved by the implication that his name was the only impediment to his success in the rabbinate, Jack happily informed Dr. Morgenstern that he would have no difficulty in taking his advice: Jacob had been his Hebrew name all along.

Jack's most vivid recollection of that interview in Davenport, Iowa, was his encounter with the most influential member of the congregation. This wealthy gentleman, upon whom the congregation leaned heavily for support, tested the young rabbi in his own way before giving his stamp of approval. The test concerned not Jack's scholarship but his capacity for Scotch. While Jack only drank at social gatherings, he enjoyed it then and had learned to handle himself when a host or hostess persisted in refilling his glass. The influential elder was just such a host, and Jack weathered it in gentlemanly fashion. "I just wanted to see if you could hold your liquor," the older man later admitted. That being so, they hired him.

Jack enjoyed his time in Davenport. He liked the people there and apparently they liked him. His starting salary—the princely sum of $2,200—was the highest paid to anyone in that class of 1936. At that time it enabled him "to live in the best hotel in town, pay my sister's tuition to college, and pay back my debts that I incurred for graduation."[13]

Before the year was over he had received an offer that he wouldn't have dreamed of refusing—to return to his home congregation of Rodeph Shalom in Pittsburgh as assistant to its senior rabbi, the reknowned scholar and Talmudist, Dr. Solomon B. Freehof. Thrilled with the news he telegraphed his mother and sister: "Am Freehof's assistant. My luck still holds."

Nothing ever diminished that belief that he was fortunate in being able to assist Freehof. If anything, it was further enhanced by the actual experience, for the eminent rabbi and his wife Lillian took Jack under their wing and became his close personal friends. In Freehof's last letter to Jack, written almost forty years later and just before Jack died, he could still evoke the memory of the many happy hours they had spent together, at work and in leisure, during the four years Jack had served as his assistant. "It is a pity we do not see each other more often," the older man

---

[13]See note 3 above.

wrote. "Of all the younger colleagues that helped me, you were by far the most truly my companion." Then he added, "Of course, baseball was a part of it."[14]

Baseball was indeed a large factor in the good times Jack and Dr. Freehof shared, larger even, so far as Jack was concerned, than their mutual enthusiasm for mystery novels—though it was not nearly as significant as Jack's gratitude for the opportunity to learn rabbinical skills from this great teacher. By the time Dr. Freehof and I met, his and Jack's reminiscences dwelt more on the Pittsburgh Pirates than on pulpit and pew, however, so my view of their companionship is necessarily centered around their associations at Forbes Field.

One of their members had generously made available his box for them to use whenever they were free to attend the game. It adjoined one of those used by the players' wives, which in a curious way led to another set of friendships that Jack retained throughout his life. Two attractive young women frequently occupied the adjoining box and often exchanged comments with the rabbis. One day they approached Jack and asked if as a favor to them, he would come with them to the dugout after the game to meet their husbands, Elbie Fletcher and Bob Elliott. Jack was delighted at the opportunity to meet these two popular heroes but couldn't understand how meeting them would constitute a favor to their wives, until the ladies explained. "Our husbands have noticed us talking to you and they won't believe that you're really a rabbi. We thought if they met you, you could convince them."

Jack convinced Bob and Elbie not only that he was in truth a man of the cloth, but also a fairly nice fellow. He succeeded so well in the latter that the day came when they invited him to join in their team poker game, traditional occupation on afternoons when the game got rained out. The occasion almost proved disastrous, however. Bob made the mistake of warning his teammates that as a clergyman would be joining them, they would need to watch their language. The first time one of them forgot and used a four-letter word Bob lashed out at him so angrily that he had no idea of what he himself was saying. It was a stream of expletives, compared to which his offending teammate's comment had been unobjec-

---

[14]Dr. Solomon B. Freehof to JMR, 15 August 1973; Freehof to JOR, 2 January 1974—JMR MSS.

tionable. His *faux pas* broke the ice. As Bob's wife recalled after Jack died, "The fellows . . . were not very religious and were a little bit uneasy around a rabbi at first, but as time went on they decided he was 'Major League' and they took him in."[15]

On at least one other occasion while he was serving in Pittsburgh Jack had difficulty convincing someone he was a rabbi. He brought the problem upon himself, however. Walking past the boys' department at Kauffmann's one day he overheard a clerk tell a customer that there were no more dark blue suits available in the size her son needed. Jack remembered from having worked in the department during his student days that the store always stocked an ample supply of dark blue suits in all sizes, so he went to the stockroom, brought out the suit in the proper size, and with an apology for intervening, asked the startled clerk for his book to write up the sale for him. When the happy customer departed, the grateful employee thanked Jack and meekly inquired if he were the new supervisor on the floor. "No," Jack responded. "I don't even work here. I just couldn't bear to see you lose that sale."

Jack's experience at the Pirates' poker game was typical of the sort of reaction he encountered when strangers learned he was a rabbi. Gregarious as he always was, he soon began to withhold that information until his new-found acquaintance gained firmer ground. Once, during an all-night train ride, his casually met companions in the club car began to discuss their jobs. Noticing that Jack had fallen silent, they asked him what he did for a living. "I'm a salesman," he said noncommittally.

"What do you sell?" they asked. Jack thought for a moment and then said truthfully, "Notions. Out of Cincinnati." That pleased him enormously. He had an irrepressible penchant for puns.

With such stories as these the principal pictures given me of Jack's past in Pittsburgh, I naturally wondered what he had done to serve his congregation there. Once, many years later, I asked him and taped his response. He replied, "The big thing that I did while I was there was create the Junior Congregation. I had to go to the board and fight for it. . . . It's one of the most successful things that ever happened there. It's still active."[16]

---

[15]Mrs. G. Glen Cooley (Skippy Elliot Cooley) to JOR, January 1974, JMR MSS.

[16]See note 3 above.

What else, I wanted to know. Did he begin any of the community involvement that characterized his years in Atlanta? He did. He was one of the founders of the Pittsburgh Round Table of the National Conference of Christians and Jews (NCCJ).

His mother had once shown me a picture of him taken at some sort of Polish festival. I asked him about it. He replied that he didn't remember it but added, "But I do remember one time before we got into the war, when the America Firsters were very powerful and there was an American Nazi League. . . . I spoke in a section of Pittsburgh—I think it was called Yorkville—which was a hotbed of Germans and I had to have a police escort home. The minister of the church who had me talk wouldn't let me go out to my car. They called the police to protect me."[17]

"Were your remarks especially inflammatory?" I asked. "No," he said. "I just told it like it was, like I always do. When they invite me to speak, I'm entitled. I assume they want to hear what I have to say."[18]

As the assistant rabbi his duties included directing the educational program. He prepared the curriculum, hired the teachers, administered the religious school, and supervised the youth group. "In my day I was a good educator," he added wistfully, thinking no doubt of the many years it had been since age and schedule had drained his patience for dealing with young people. In those early days it had been his favorite duty. "I think all of us thought we were going to be saviors of Judaism by bringing it back to the young people, offering them something," he said.[19]

The United States entered World War II in 1941, and Jack immediately volunteered for service in the chaplaincy. When he left his position at Rodeph Shalom in March 1942 to enter basic training at Fort Bragg, North Carolina, his former students in the religious school paid tribute to him by dedicating their forthcoming yearbook to him. Jack responded with a long and thoughtful letter describing his life in the army and pointing out that its difficulties helped build character. But such an obligation to moralize could not suppress his sentiment or urge to tease. He added, "I do miss all of you. I miss seeing you in the halls—even when

---

[17]Ibid.; clipping of picture, "Poles Dance Despite Country Peril," *Pittsburgh Post-Gazette*, 4 Sept. 1939, JMR MSS.

[18]See note 3 above.

[19]Ibid.

you are there when you aren't supposed to be. I miss trying to make you sing. I miss checking up on whether or not you have gone to Detention."[20] The statement about making them sing undoubtedly evoked laughter, since he himself could not carry a tune. His inability to sing became legendary.

His training over, Jack became 2nd Lt. Jacob M. Rothschild and was shipped out of San Francisco with the Americal Division in September 1942. By December his division was in combat, backing up the Marines on Guadalcanal. This turn of events probably made Jack the first Jewish chaplain to see action in World War II. In letters home he made light of the danger. "Tojo didn't put on any sort of show for us," he wrote to his mother. "[It was] the first time since the Marines landed in August that he failed to send a reception committee."[21]

That was the version he gave her. When he returned he gave a more accurate account in an interview for a local newspaper. When asked what it was like to conduct worship services in a battle zone, he told how on Guadalcanal services had to be hurriedly finished before sundown because air raids began as soon as darkness fell. Even in daylight, he recalled, he and his congregants often had to interrupt their prayers to run for the foxholes. On Saturday and Sunday mornings he and his driver would travel to as many of the front positions as they could reach in order to hold services for the men there. They would create makeshift chapels in clearings, using coconut stumps for lecterns and fallen logs for pews. The first time he conducted a service in such a setting someone afterward discovered a dead Japanese soldier lying behind one of the "pews."[22]

Ironically, while Jack was being exposed to the obvious dangers of combat in the Pacific, his closest friend, the childhood companion who had become a gifted physician, was killed in an airplane crash while serving in a peaceful grouping area in the North Atlantic. Jack was devastated. The physician had left a young widow and infant son (whom Jack

---

[20]*The Temple School Shofar* (Yearbook of Rodeph Shalom Congregation religious school) 1942.

[21]JMR to his mother and sister, ca. December 1942. Wartime materials, JMR MSS.

[22]Interviews in *The Sentinel, Jewish Chaplain,* and *Pittsburgh Press,* February-March 1944; NBC, 2 January 1944, clippings in war scrapbook, JMR MSS.

dearly loved) and a sorely grieving friend behind. Jack wrote that he wished he could have been taken in his place.[23]

It was Jack's first tragic encounter with a pain and loneliness undoubtedly shared by all clerics and probably unique to them. For one who is grieving to console others is difficult, but for those to whom we turn as professionals it is infinitely more so. Jack once expressed it—in the guise of a joke—to his congregation in Atlanta. "Remember," he said, "I'm the only one among you who can't take his troubles to the rabbi."

When the American Division was pulled out of Guadalcanal, Chaplain Rothschild playfully told his mother where he had gone by means of a mystery: he wrote her suggesting she call Dr. Freehof and ask him how the ancient Ephraimites would have pronounced the name of the Sabbath that falls between Rosh Hashanah and Yom Kippur.[24] Freehof immediately recalled that the Ephraimites were said to be unable to pronounce the letter *h*, hence the name of the Sabbath—Shabbat Shuvah—would have been pronounced "Sabbat Suvah." He went to his world atlas and scoured the islands of the Pacific until he came to Fiji. He saw that its capital was called Suva and jubilantly telephoned Jack's mother to tell her where her son was.

Jack didn't stay in Fiji long. Within seven months he was hospitalized with malaria. He was sent to Augusta, Georgia, and upon recovery was given a series of public-relations assignments to do for the duration of the war. He went from one enviable locale to another: Washington, D.C.; Atlantic City; Newport News, Virginia; often speaking to civilian groups about his combat experiences. The speeches and articles that he wrote during that time begin to reveal the characteristics that would distinguish his leadership in later years. While his style was still rough and a bit immature, his idealism and sense of social justice, his faith in the American system, his dedication to the cause of brotherhood, and his awareness of current events were apparent.

In an essay entitled "Your Soldier Son," he reported that many were finding strength in their religious faith—they were reaching for it as a source of renewal for the first time in their lives. He noted that many non-

---

[23]JMR to his mother and sister, 29 January 1943, JMR MSS.

[24]Conversations with Lillian Abrams Rothschild, 1946-1962; with JMR, 1946-1973.

Jewish soldiers had attended his worship services on Guadalcanal, and concluded, "Creed and dogma somehow become less important in the face of more pressing need. . . . They rejoice at the opportunity for a quiet hour in which to strengthen their souls. . . . Believe it or not, they wanted to pray!"[25]

Though he considered himself a pessimist, thus training himself to appreciate much by expecting little, his sermons were always optimistic. No matter how disheartening the subject discussed he would conclude with a note of hope or other happy thought. When speaking to the parents of men serving overseas he told them that the horror of their sons' present situation would morally strengthen their sons and make them better people than they had been before.

> Out of cruelty they have learned compassion. From living in hate, they have learned love. From the loss of freedom they have learned the love of freedom. They shall return not only *eager* to create a better world. What is far more important, they shall come back *prepared* to create that world.[26]

Fortunate as he was to be able to practice his oratory on such varied and impersonal congregations, he was less fortunate in effecting a quick return to civilian life when the war ended. As a bachelor with only fifteen months' overseas duty to his credit, he scored too low on the point system to be dismissed early, even though he had served in the army for three years. After serving until he had accumulated the necessary points, he ran up against still another obstacle. Upon enlisting he had falsified his eye examination in order to be accepted into the army. Now that he wanted to get out, he had to convince the authorities that his impaired eyesight was not service-related. He finally succeeded. On 7 April 1946 Captain Jacob M. Rothschild was honorably discharged from active duty.

He followed this momentous step with one that would set the course for his future. Within the month he was offered the pulpit of Atlanta's Hebrew Benevolent Congregation (The Temple). It was available because Rabbi David Marx, The Temple's spiritual leader for more than half a century, was retiring. With two rabbis on its payroll, the congregation of

---

[25]"Your Soldier Son," untitled typescript, World War II materials, n.d., JMR MSS.

[26]Ibid.

only four hundred families could afford to pay no more than $7200 a year for its new leader, but the amount did not matter to Jack. He had no one to support but himself, his needs were few, and he sensed the promise of Atlanta. Nor was he disturbed that the postwar housing shortage precluded his finding an apartment. He was content to make do with a single room at the Atlanta Biltmore Hotel. He accepted the challenge.

Little did he realize that before the year was over he would take still a third giant step, one that would change his life more than either of the others and render both his salary and single room frighteningly inadequate. He moved his books into the spacious study at The Temple and his other belongings into the room at the Biltmore in July 1946. In November he wrote to his friend and former professor, Jake Marcus:

> The other day I took a deep breath and asked someone to marry me. . . . I could go on to describe her in superlatives, but if I didn't feel that way I wouldn't want to marry her, so I presume you will take the missing superlatives for granted. In general, she is tall and dark and very young—22, an Atlantan without a Southern accent. Without a place to live or furniture to put in it or money to buy it, we are planning to be married about the end of December.[27]

He exaggerated. He didn't actually ask me to marry him. Articulate as he normally was, in this instance he was silent and handed me a picture instead. It was a cartoon from the *Saturday Evening Post* depicting a young man on his knees looking up at a young woman primly seated on a sofa. The caption read, "Go ahead, Harry. It's really very simple."

---

[27]JMR to Dr. Jacob Rader Marcus, 6 November 1946, JMR MSS.

CHAPTER • TWO

SINCERELY YOURS

Actually, there was very little that could be considered simple about Jack's first years in Atlanta. He had been there only a month when he wrote to a friend at the Union of American Hebrew Congregations (UAHC):

> The situation here is going to take much longer than I at first suspected. As you know, these people have just not been educated to take an interest in any matters dealing with the College or the Union. They have . . . only a vaguely stirring interest in the much more immediate affairs of their own congregation. . . . Before Atlanta can become a strong supporting link in the national chain of reformed

Jewish life, Atlanta must first become strong in its congregational life.[1]

The correspondent, an older man knowledgeable about the various Jewish communities throughout the United States, assured Jack that Atlanta had a fine community that, if Jack applied enough "sweat and blood," could be molded to "much higher standards and a much more modern outlook." Encouragingly, he added, "I think you can do the job."[2]

At that moment Jack could hardly have shared his confidence in the matter. He was still smarting from his first major collision with his "emeritus," which had occurred when he innocently and amicably broached the subject of plans for his forthcoming installation. "What installation?" snapped Marx. Still maintaining his respectful deference, Jack reminded him that the ceremony had been scheduled for 13 September and that Solomon Freehof had accepted The Temple's invitation to come as installer and guest speaker. The matter at hand was to determine what part in the service Dr. Marx would like to have.

Marx responded by walking over to his desk, opening a drawer and pulling out a paper, which he shook in Jack's face as he declared, "This resolution says I shall be the rabbi of the congregation until my successor has been duly chosen and qualified. Young man, you may have been chosen, but you will *never qualify!*"

This was only one of many incidents that marred Jack's entry into his new job, but once he rebounded from the blow it so appealed to his sense of humor that he often repeated it to his colleagues at the Central Conference of American Rabbis (CCAR). So many of them had similar stories to tell that the subject provided us with an annual bout in one-upmanship. It always seemed to me that Jack won.

Unprepared as he was for the extent of the bitterness he encountered, Jack was neither naive about the facts of aging nor ignorant of his congregation's recent history. It was common knowledge among the rabbis that one of their most amiable and brilliant colleagues had come to Atlanta in 1938, fresh out of HUC, to serve as assistant to David Marx—only to be so devastated by the experience that he not only left Atlanta after one year, he left the congregational rabbinate altogether (to pursue

[1]JMR to Jerome L. Levy, 29 August 1946, JMR MSS.

[2]Jerome L. Levy to JMR, 3 September 1946, JMR MSS.

a distinguished career in academia). Aware of that incident, none of his contemporaries would have considered coming to Atlanta with anything less than a clear-cut offer to serve as *the* rabbi—following the formal retirement of the incumbent. This condition had been fulfilled with great fanfare, sincere affection, and truly deserved tribute prior to Jack's arrival.

The conflict between Jack and Marx grew out of deeply rooted differences that were far more complex than those of personality, generation gap, or any of the other expected and unavoidable frictions normally associated with retirement. It involved their basic concepts of what it meant to be a Jew: diametrically opposed concepts that had been instilled in each from birth and further defined during their years at HUC. Marx had become rabbi of The Temple in 1895, soon after his ordination, and was a product of "Classical" Reform, which espoused universalism, the "Americanizing" of immigrants as soon and thoroughly as possible, the "melting pot" philosophy, and Judaism as a religion and nothing more. A native of New Orleans, he was a privileged Southerner with all the exposure to racial and religious bigotry that the term implied. Jack, on the other hand, came from a family and an area of the country where people were more comfortable with ethnicity. He had been trained by professors of a different generation, some of whom had fled the Nazi Holocaust. Within him, Jewishness and Americanism had been thoroughly integrated.

The congregation welcomed him warmly when he arrived in Atlanta. So many of its four hundred families rushed to extend him dinner invitations that almost immediately his summer calendar was booked solid. The young "elite" scooped him up as a perfect fourth at bridge and tennis, the perfect dinner partner for their unmarried sisters or friends. One family gave him carte blanche at their stables, another the use of a car until such time as he could purchase one of his own. Despite this show of affection very few of them attended services or in any other way indicated interest in the job he had come to perform.

The two of us met when I returned home after summer school in New York in late August. While sunning at the Standard Club pool I saw him playing tennis and asked the friend sunning next to me who he was. When she told me he was the new rabbi I didn't believe her. "That's ridiculous," I said. "Everyone knows Dr. Marx isn't ever going to retire." Besides, all the rabbis I had ever known had been way past their days on a tennis court, even for doubles. Nevertheless, she introduced us.

Actually, I was probably the only person in Atlanta (besides Dr. Marx) who didn't know Marx had already been retired for several months. *I* didn't know it because my parents had so little interest in the affairs of the Jewish community that they had forgotten to tell me. My father, who traveled for a living, had little energy or means to spare for community involvement. My mother, a maverick whom someone later described as "a hippie before we knew what hippies were," gave unsparingly of herself to innumerable causes, almost none of which were Jewish. They belonged to The Temple, enrolled me, their only child, in its religious school (until classes began to interfere with my other activities), and joined the Standard Club when I reached the age of prescribed social necessities.

In those days one didn't have to be rich to belong to the socially elite—at least, not in the South. What one had to be was "connected" (to the "right" families) and that we were. My mother's grandfather, one of the early Reform rabbis in America, had served as minister of this very same congregation in Atlanta in 1877. His wife, my great-grandmother, had close family ties in the community, and although these forebears had remained in the city for only four years, their bonds were still strong when my parents arrived to live there just before I was born, in 1924.

Meeting me complicated Jack's life in several ways. Today's unmarried rabbis, I hope, have an easier time of it, but in 1946 it was no simple matter for a rabbi to "pursue a meaningful relationship" in Atlanta. First of all, he was far too busy—not with meetings as he soon would be, but with the dinner invitations he had accepted weeks before. Then there was the danger of gossip, which being seen together in public more than once or twice would surely induce. With gossip came pressures that could destroy a budding romance, while dating in seclusion could bring pressures of another sort, far more dangerous. Somehow we knew that we had to get through that courtship phase as quickly as possible.

Our "dates" consisted mostly of nightly telephone conversations conducted after Jack had returned from his dinner parties. Our chief activity together was working the *New York Times* crossword puzzle over the telephone during these sessions. Whenever he could take off for an afternoon we met at our friends' stable and went horseback riding. When we announced we were planning to be married, these friends sent us a gold key to the stables as an engagement gift.

We became engaged on 1 November 1946, and were married, with much misguided splendor, at The Temple on Sunday, 29 December. In the interim I managed to complicate Jack's life still further by drawing him into a series of social customs (parties, tidbits in the society pages, "in front of the ribbon" cards for some of the invitations) that my mother and I had been led to believe were de rigueur for weddings in our circle. He resisted as vigorously as any prospective bridegroom would dare to do, but it didn't help. Mother and I went right ahead forging out our fantasies. He succeeded only in confirming Mother's opinion of him as an "unpolished Northerner," and confirming his own view of the South as a backwater of civilization still brackish with superficial courtliness and false values. Both of them got over it in time.

When we returned from our one-week honeymoon in New York we faced an even thornier complication, that of living in close proximity to my parents. We were fortunate that they had a garage apartment we could move into, for the post-war housing shortage had not abated and showed no signs of doing so in the near future. As Jack then wrote in response to someone inquiring about living conditions prior to moving to Atlanta, "I don't like to discourage you but I've been here since July and have finally managed to secure the rear end of a garage—and I had to get married to be eligible for that."[3]

On $7200 a year we could hardly afford a second car, and our house was near neither The Temple nor public transportation. The problem of logistics was far less troublesome than the problem of parental influence, however. In our case the obvious difficulties of a newly wed only child living in her mother's backyard was further complicated by my mother's and my espousal of "Marxist" beliefs (Southern style). We too had been brought up to believe that assimilation was highly desirable, that ritual was an anachronism to be avoided as far as possible, that Zionism implied dual loyalty, and that even a passing acquaintance with Hebrew branded one as slightly déclassé.

Twenty years later, in 1966, we could laugh about it. More than that, the congregation could laugh with us. For its celebration of Jack's twentieth anniversary a member described in song the attitude that had prevailed in those early days in Atlanta. The song began:

---

[3]JMR to Nina Friedman, 7 March 1947, JMR MSS.

(And they said . . .)
"Rothschild! What a lovely name,
And what a lovely family tree.
He's probably a nephew of that charming Baron Guy."
But this Rothschild hit Atlanta like a Jewish General Sherman.
He wasn't related to Baron Guy.
He wasn't even German![4]

Jack knew better than to try to enlighten us all at once, even in regard to his ancestry. Our first shock came when we discovered that he preferred to be addressed as "Rabbi" rather than as "Doctor," a title to which he would have no claim for another fourteen years. We Southerners had simply assumed that "Doctor" was the proper form of address for a Jewish clergyman, regardless of academic qualifications. Ironically, by the time Jack finally succeeded in retraining most of his congregation to call him "Rabbi," his alma mater conferred upon him an honorary doctoral degree, which rendered the effort useless.

He accustomed us to ceremonies one at a time. Most of us had never seen wine used in a wedding ritual until he introduced it at The Temple. Nor had we heard of naming ceremonies for newborn sons of Reform families (in "our crowd" infant boys had always been circumcised by their physicians the day before they left the hospital). In 1946 Jack introduced a ceremony, which he jokingly called a "brisening," similar to the traditional *brit milah* in that it named the child and welcomed him (or *her*) into the Covenant of Israel. Parents could schedule it whenever they found it convenient, for girls as well as for boys, and continue having their boys circumcised at the hospital.

Many members complained of orthodoxy when Jack brought candle lighting and the kiddush into the Friday night service. Little did they realize that the Orthodox would not have tolerated such a practice, nor that those very prayers were contained in the books they themselves had been using for many years. They also complained that he was "making The Temple too Orthodox" by wearing a different style of pulpit attire than they were accustomed to seeing on Dr. Marx, who always wore a dark business suit for services. When Jack first came to Atlanta he still fol-

---

[4]June Reisner Stevens, lyrics for JMR anniversary celebration, ca. April 1966.

lowed the European custom of wearing formal striped trousers and cutaway, as he had been taught to do in Pittsburgh. After a discreet interval of four years he dared to change into an academic robe and drew the same criticism. This time the objections were even funnier than before because the origin of the robe wasn't even Jewish. According to Jack it was a custom borrowed from the Christian clergy.

This instance, too, we could laugh about after twenty years. The song continued:

> He's so Yankee! He's so cranky!
> When we're here—twice a year—hear him fuss!
> He's Reform all right, but to him that means
> Reforming US![5]

My own conversion, of course, took place in most instances just one step ahead of the flock. I usually managed to conceal this situation by staunchly defending whatever Jack said or did whether or not I was yet firmly convinced myself. However, congregation members who had known me all my life didn't hesitate to tell me anything unpleasant that they were too "polite" to tell him, and the ones who had known me longest and best always seemed to be the ones with the most complaints. I found these circumstances very hard to take.

I don't think Jack could have realized fully the extent of my difficulty. He never expected me to be other than myself. I now realize that I took my role as "the rabbi's wife" far too seriously, but it was through no fault of his that I did so.

One thing he could never understand was why I dreaded going to parties in December when, normally, I loved parties. In December someone always managed to corner me with a question about why it was wrong for Jews to celebrate Christmas. All of us had enjoyed Christmas trees in our homes when we were children and never seen the slightest bit of guilt on the part of our parents or grandparents who provided them. Now, in the throes of my newfound Judaism, I was so defensive that I invariably fell into the trap my friends set for me and spent the rest of the evening repeating Jack's latest sermon on the subject. His sermons were all very

---

[5]Ibid.

logical. Intellectually I agreed with every point he made. Emotionally though, it took me several years to stop missing the tinsel. If only I could have seen the situation in the same, humorous light as our friend the song writer, twenty years later. She wrote:

> Why should he object to a Christmas tree?
> When it's such a beautiful sight?
> How mean can he be? Maybe he'll agree
> If we keep the tree—BLUE and WHITE![6]

Had she made that reference to the colors of the Jewish flag at the time the song described we would not have understood what she meant. What most of us knew then about Zionism was that we didn't like it. Dr. Marx, an organizer of the anti-Zionist American Council for Judaism and one of its most effective spokesmen, had opposed it bitterly and taught most of his congregation to do likewise. As a result an enormous rift had developed between the small segment of the Jewish community to which we belonged and the rest of the rapidly growing Jewish population of Atlanta. That one issue alone had prevented many families interested in Reform from joining The Temple and alienated a growing (but still minority) number of those who did belong. Their feelings turned to outrage in the forties, when the desperate, immediate need for a Jewish homeland became so obvious.

Jack never considered himself a Zionist, but neither was he ever an anti-Zionist. A humanitarian with a keen sense of history, he saw the establishment of a Jewish state as necessary and exciting but not as the fulfillment of a personal dream. His enthusiasm for Israel came later, as did his perception of it as a source of Jewish culture that would someday replace and surpass that culture extinguished in the Holocaust. His advocacy of independence for the Jews of Palestine, however, both for their sake and the sake of the thousands still languishing in the displaced-persons camps of Europe, had already begun when he came to Atlanta.

He dared to speak of these matters in his very first Kol Nidre sermon at The Temple. This act could only have exacerbated his problems with his predecessor and driven a number of his original supporters into

_____

[6]Ibid.

what was already being perceived as the enemy camp. It had quite the opposite effect, however, on those members who had long been considered dissidents. After hearing that sermon one of them gratefully wrote to him, praising him for having offered them "the forbidden apple." As the writer expressed it, "Now [that] the dreaded subject has been once openly mentioned from the pulpit all the congregants are more at ease to discuss the matter." He also complimented Jack on his increased use of Hebrew in the prayers.[7]

With both of us caught up in the euphoria of courtship during those months, Jack largely ignored the volcanic rumblings he had begun to hear, and I remained innocently unaware of them. The first great eruption occurred in January 1947, at the annual meeting of the congregation—Jack's first as its rabbi and my first ever. We had returned from our honeymoon just the week before.

The meeting went smoothly until the very end. Under the section designated for "Good and Welfare" one of the old-timers, a character nicknamed "Silent" Sam because of his inability to leave a meeting without making a speech, rose to his feet to make an impassioned statement to the effect that religion should not be mixed with politics. Everything he said, if not the passion with which he said it, sounded reasonable. As Jack told me afterwards, "I was nodding my head in agreement with him until suddenly it fell off into my lap. I had no idea it was *my* throat that was being cut!"

He realized it and I suspected something was amiss when the atmosphere in the room thickened. Apparently we were the only two there who didn't know at the outset of Sam's diatribe that it was directed toward Jack. Sam was referring to Jack's having been listed in the afternoon paper (along with all the leading Christian clergymen of the city) as a sponsor of a rally to be held the following evening in protest of a situation at the state capitol. A battle had arisen when longtime political boss Eugene Talmadge, reelected as governor, died before the beginning of his new term. His son Herman and the newly elected lieutenant governor, M. E. Thompson, each claimed the governorship, and each was backed by an already rival constituency and an arguable constitutional right. The

---

[7]Sermon unknown (Rothschild's early sermons were not preserved); Miriam and Adalbert Freedman to JMR, 6 October 1946, JMR MSS.

impasse took on scandalous proportions when factions of the two men locked themselves in their respective sections of the state capitol and turned the building into something resembling an armed camp. Jack, shocked to behold such a turn of events, agreed unhesitatingly when the Episcopal bishop of Atlanta called to solicit his support for the protest rally. Had it even occurred to him to question whether or not this action was "good for the Jews" he would have concluded instantly that, whatever the risk, *not* to have been included on such a list would have been infinitely worse.

The president of the congregation quickly adjourned the meeting before anyone else could take the floor. He and all the other leaders present immediately surrounded Jack, pelting him with advice. I still didn't know what was happening, but I knew it spelled trouble for us. I was terrified.

Jack told me about it as he drove us home. "Their advice was to say I'm sick, get called out of town, do anything at all so long as I don't show up at the rally tomorrow night."

"What did you tell them?" I asked.

The veins on his neck bulged. Even in the dim light I could see his face redden as he set his jaw defiantly. He replied, "I told them that if I should slip on a banana peel tonight and break my leg, and develop pneumonia in the morning, I'd have myself carried into the meeting on a stretcher, but I'd be there."

That was the first and last night I ever lay awake worrying about his job tenure. By morning I had come to terms with the fact that I had cast my lot with a man who had supreme confidence in following through with whatever he considered right, and that if it ever cost him his pulpit he would find another. The old saw "You're damned if you do and damned if you don't" applied to us, and the only way to live with it was to make certain we could always live with ourselves.

We attended the meeting, of course, and suffered no ill effects for having done so. Furthermore, one of the younger members of the board who had not attended the previous night's Temple meeting heard about the debacle and called the following morning to say that he and his wife would pick us up to go to the rally. He sat on the sponsors' dais along with Jack, which not only strengthened our spirits but gave meaningful support to Jack's iconoclastic attitude in general and to his position on the issue in particular.

Foremost among the ghostly idols he set out to smash was the notion that Jews would be safe only so long as they remained "in the back of the room" and kept silent. This belief had been compulsively fed by Temple members since 1915, when Leo Frank—an upstanding member of their congregation and social group and a leader in Gate City Lodge of B'nai B'rith—was dragged from prison and lynched after being falsely accused and convicted for the rape-murder of Mary Phagan, a young employee. The tragedy of Leo Frank so traumatized the congregation that those members who had lived through it still reacted to events occurring more than thirty years later with it in mind. Jack's outspokenness made them quake in their boots.

On the other hand, there were those who applauded him for having stood his ground. Of the several members who wrote commending him, one, a former refugee from Nazi Germany, praised his courage in standing up for what he believed and said she was deeply grateful that her "religious representative . . . is in the front line in a fight for the fundamental principles of democracy." Another, a fourth-generation Georgian, wrote, "I'm glad you showed the people of Atlanta that you don't subscribe to the theory of Jews voluntarily accepting second-class citizenship." Jack, grateful for these votes of confidence, remained astounded that anyone would question the propriety of his supporting a demand for constitutional government. He saw the issue as so basic to democratic rights that failure to resolve it properly could have brought about "the beginning of the end of any real democracy" in Georgia. Neither he nor anyone else in Atlanta realized at the time that his involvement in that incident marked the beginning of what would be a long and distinguished championship of civil rights.[8]

The next notable event in that arena occurred two-and-one-half years later, in the summer of 1949. An article appearing on the front page of the local newspapers named an employee of the Atlanta Jewish Social Service Agency as a witness for the defense in the trial of an accused Communist. We were out of town at the time. When we returned a few days later the Jewish community was in an uproar, some of its leaders demanding that the social worker be immediately dismissed from her job

[8]Lilo (Mrs. Henry) Meyer to JMR, 24 January 1947; Philip Shulhafer to JMR, 28 January 1947; Sermon, "Keep These Vows," 23 September 1947—JMR MSS.

with the agency. Others, civil libertarians and those sensitive to the threat to freedom constituted in guilt by association, cried "Witch hunt!" and fought back on the grounds of "innocent until proven guilty." They negotiated a stay of execution long enough to enlist direct help from Jack and together they succeeded in blocking the proposed dismissal. The young woman in question soon found employment elsewhere and left Atlanta of her own volition.

Nevertheless, certain members of The Temple who had favored burning her at the stake, so to speak, carried their vendetta well into the following year, tracking her down to her new place of employment and suggesting that she be dismissed from there as well. They kept Jack informed of their progress, which so far as we knew was limited to confirming her association with accused Communists. The incident alarmed him because it exemplified to him one of the great dangers inherent in the tactics of Sen. Joseph McCarthy—who was then in the early throes of his campaign to rid America of Communism. Jack used it in his sermon on the next Day of Atonement, lecturing the congregation against succumbing to the panic ignited by such events. He saw in it a fear beyond that engendered by McCarthyism and spoke of it in the context of the Holyday, as being a sin we needed to atone for.

> As usual, the "bad press" resulting in this instance from a taint of communism affected only individuals—except where a minority group became involved. Soon, the issue grew far beyond the simple fact of an individual's right of freedom of thought and speech.[9]

The following year, 1950, in a sermon entitled "Are You Afraid to be a Liberal?" he cited the recent Hiss-Chambers case as an alarming example of how "both the face and the soul of America" had changed and thus weakened democracy from within as well as from without. In dismay he asked, "What has happened to the American tradition of freedom of thought? Innocent until proved guilty? Loyal until proved disloyal?"[10]

Recognizing the need to tailor his candor to fit the tolerance level of specific audiences, he managed to wait another two and a half years before delivering a similar message to the Kiwanis Club. By that time, June

---

[9]Sermon, "Our Greater Guilt," 2 October 1949, JMR MSS.

[10]Sermon, "Are You Afraid to be a Liberal?" 3 November 1950, JMR MSS.

1953, he had many more examples of McCarthyism to support his point. He told of Congress becoming virtually an investigating body, of everything from the "Voice of America" to public school faculties becoming suspect, and of teachers being forced to defend their patriotism against such accusatory questions as "How long since you attacked the Russians?" and "In your recent monograph on Hopi Indians why didn't you include a glorification of the American way of life?" To this he ruefully added, "Win the war and lose the peace . . . that is the danger that we face."[11]

By 1953 Jack had become so alarmed by the effect of these investigations that he devoted an entire Holyday sermon to the threat they posed to the time-honored safeguards of American freedom. He conceded that communism would destroy democracy if it could, but said that if it did so it would be not by arms, espionage, or infiltration but by our own "spiritual failure of nerve." Instead of worrying about how many Communist teachers there were in our schools, he suggested, we should "dwell with pride" upon the fact that such a small percentage of the teachers had fallen prey to its propaganda. With uncharacteristic pessimism he warned, "Freedom of thought and action have been vitiated. . . . In our great dread of Communist infiltration, we have taken on the protective coloring of Communism's own philosophy and way of life."[12]

Initially, before the onset of McCarthyism, Jack had detected the same type of fear in members of his own congregation, but it was there for a very different reason. More basic even than the continuing influence of the Leo Frank affair was the members' long estrangement from the mainstream of Jewish life. The remedy for the situation was education. He began his treatment with a three-pronged campaign to upgrade the religious school, revive the moribund Temple youth group, and use his Friday-night sermons for such subjects as "What It Means To Be A Jew," "What Is Reform Judaism," "Jewish Customs and Ceremonies," and so forth. Despite the reputation he gained in later years as a one-subject preacher—that subject being civil rights—the record shows that the great preponderance of his sermons throughout his career dealt with

[11]Sermon "Individual Freedom and American Democracy," 5 June 1953, JMR MSS.

[12]Sermon, "The Eternal If," 10 September 1953, JMR MSS.

matters pertaining directly to the faith, heritage, and welfare of the Jewish people.[13]

While such religious subjects were usually uncontroversial, Jack's initial efforts with the youth group did not go quite so smoothly. In order to lure the teenagers to The Temple on alternate Sunday evenings he persuaded one of the parents to contribute a nickelodeon to provide music for dancing, and organized the mothers to prepare a light supper for each meeting. He stumbled on his first hurdle when one of the mothers brought ham sandwiches. "Why not?" she demanded indignantly when he told her she mustn't do it again. "Since when do Reform Jews keep kosher? And how come you didn't complain when I served you baked ham for supper at my house?"

Gently, Jack explained that his own mother served him ham at her house, but that that wasn't the point. The point was not what went into his stomach but what went out from The Temple. While he never succeeded in explaining satisfactorily—even to me—why he drew the line exactly where he did, he banned ham, pork, and sausage from meals served at The Temple and asked me to observe a similar rule at home. Insofar as other equally unkosher foods were concerned, we were free to use our own judgment and were to be guided by our sense of hospitality. If we were expecting guests who would be offended by it, we didn't do it. It was that simple.

While the ham sandwiches posed no real threat to the future of the youth group, another incident following soon after did. One Sunday evening in March 1947, while the young people were dancing to the latest hit on their nickelodeon, police arrived at The Temple. "Blue laws" prohibiting dancing on Sunday in public places were in effect in Georgia at that time, and someone claiming to live in a neighboring apartment building had called to complain that the music was disturbing him.

Fortunately, Jack was still at The Temple when it happened and the music was turned down so low that no one two doors away could have heard it, much less been disturbed by it. The police, chagrined, had to agree. They also agreed with Jack that a Jewish house of worship did not constitute a "public place" in the sense intended by law. They apologized for intruding and left.

---

[13]Sermons 1947, 1948.

Early the next morning Jack received a call from Silent Sam. "I hear the police came to The Temple last night," rasped this zealous defender of the Jewish image. "Don't you know it's against the law in this state to hold dances on Sunday?"

Jack assured him that he knew the law and that the police had agreed with him that it had not been broken at The Temple the night before. His response silenced Sam, but Jack's curiosity was piqued as to who had in fact alerted the police and why. Sam, an elderly widower whose grandchildren did not live in Atlanta, was an unlikely person to have heard the news in casual conversation so soon after the incident occurred. Jack, while trying valiantly not to become paranoid, began to suspect that someone was trying to sabotage his effectiveness at The Temple.

In order to prepare his defense against those board members who openly questioned the propriety of Sunday dancing at The Temple, he wrote to those of his colleagues whose Southeastern congregations were also located in cities subject to blue laws. He asked if they had encountered any objections to the practice with their youth groups. None had. Eventually the storm subsided and the youth group grew.[14]

Other circumstances contributed to Jack's suspicion of sabotage. From the start Dr. Marx had refused to sit on the *bimah** with him during worship service, insisting instead upon sitting in the very last row of the sanctuary. His placement required the other worshipers to choose between greeting him at the end of the service, as they were long accustomed to doing, or greeting Jack where he stood, beside the bimah at the far end of the vast hall.

Marx also refused to perform weddings or funerals with Jack. "If you have him you don't need me," he would tell anyone who approached him on this increasingly delicate subject. Obviously, those families whose life-cycle events he had administered for three generations chose him. Jack was thus blocked from any opportunity to become a meaningful factor in the lives of his congregants. It would be years before any apprecia-

---

[14]JMR to Rabbi Milton A. Grafman, 12 March 1947; JMR to Rabbi Louis Youngerman, 16 March 1947, JMR MSS.

*Platform or pulpit area from which services are led.

ble number of them would begin coming to him for counseling or other personal matters.

Those leaders of the congregation who did continue to champion Jack were extremely anxious for him to become known in the Christian community. Here again, Marx tried to block his way. As the representative of his profession in the Rotary Club of Atlanta it was up to Marx to introduce a younger man as his successor, else the latter would not be eligible for membership. This introduction Marx refused to give, despite prolonged pleas from some of Marx's close friends who belonged to Rotary. Eventually the Rotary members gave up, relinquishing Jack's allegiance to Temple members who belonged to Kiwanis.

Understanding and support for what he was trying to accomplish first surfaced among the women of The Temple Sisterhood. Their support was, quite possibly, the underlying reason for a landmark brouhaha that occurred within the first few years he was in Atlanta. Sisterhood had nominated from the floor a candidate for sisterhood president in opposition to the one already presented by its nominating committee. Sides formed instantly in fairly even numbers. Both candidates came from German-Jewish Reform families who had spent several generations in the South. Both were known as capable, intelligent, dedicated women. What primarily distinguished them—on the surface at least—was that one was a product of Marx's teaching and had close ties to him and his family, while the other had been among those who had most vehemently opposed him for his stand on Zionism during the years before Jack arrived on the scene. Although both Jack and I, and presumably the Marxes as well, assiduously avoided any involvement with the affair, it soon took on the aura of a battle between the forces of Rothschild and the forces of Marx.

In the month that elapsed between nomination and election the issue caught fire and spread throughout the Jewish community. Women who belonged to other congregations but were nominal members of The Temple Sisterhood (having joined during the depression in order to help support it) attended for the very first time simply in order to vote: for Rothschild, Zionism, and a new era of open-mindedness at The Temple. The result was an overwhelming victory for "the forces of Rothschild," and a very unpleasant term of office for the winning candidate.

After that incident the opposition to Jack seemed to subside, though opposition to Zionism began to appear more noticeably. The American

Council for Judaism was waging a campaign to encourage its adherents to leave their fast-changing "old" Reform congregations and form new institutions where they could teach Judaism according to their own beliefs. While Jack greatly doubted that those members of his congregation supporting such ideas had sufficient enthusiasm for any form of Judaism to make such a scheme work in Atlanta, he knew he could not afford to take the chance. If The Temple was to become the strong, viable bedrock of the community that he meant it to be, and that it once had been, it needed another decade of nurturing before it could comfortably survive a split.

He met the situation by invigorating his campaign to educate his members, adults and children, in what it meant to be Jewish. Sometimes he needed help from his sense of humor. One such event was most memorable. It occurred shortly after the magazine *World Over*, published by the Union of American Hebrew Congregations (UAHC) for use in the religious schools of its constituents, had carried in its regular crossword feature a puzzle with the word *Palestine* in the key position across the top. Jack and I were dining out one evening when a member of the congregation came over to our table to complain bitterly about it. "You're teaching Zionism to our children in the Sunday School!" he cried, as we tried to swallow our veal piccata.

Jack solemnly put down his fork, looked up at the man with his most conciliatory smile and said, "Y'know, I'm a crossword fan myself. I work the puzzle in the *Sunday Times* every week, and it never occurred to me that the editors of the *New York Times* were advocating fascism when the key word was *Franco*."

Eventually the Council opinion reached a noise level demanding more serious attention. Jack counterattacked with a major sermon entitled, "What We Teach Your Children." In it he cut through the prevalent canards about Zionism and focused on the underlying cause of the anger vented against it:

> There is always the fear that when we teach Judaism and relate ourselves to the heritage of a people and a past, that we tacitly accept the nationalist interpretation of Jewish life. Then people will believe that for us America is not our homeland—Israel is. Even ardent Zionists do not teach such a belief. America is their home, too, although they may place more emphasis upon the spiritual relationship be-

tween Israel and the Diaspora than do non-Zionists. But to reject our very real connection with a very real past is to vitiate our Judaism to the point of its non-existence. . . . No more can we deny the existence of Israel in the present. . . . Nor can we deny the longings of vast numbers of our fellow Jews for a homeland. We may have other longings—but the hope for and the achievement of a Jewish State belongs in the totality of Jewish life.[15]

The sermon was published and distributed to all members of the congregation. It effectively stemmed the flow of dissent on the issue at The Temple, as similar efforts by other rabbis undoubtedly did elsewhere. One of those rabbis commiserating with Jack on the difficulties of raising funds for Reform Judaism in Israel in light of the Council-sponsored opposition, received in reply this bit of typical Rothschild advice:

I have a suggestion. The American Council for Judaism uses as ammunition for its attacks the fact that there is no Reform Movement in Israel. Here is a project made to order for them. They can make it possible. . . .

I am not even sure I'm kidding. At least it would test their sincerity.[16]

Meanwhile, our personal situation had become both frustrating and fruitful. We were overjoyed by the birth of our daughter Marcia during the first year of our marriage and the birth of our son Bill the next. What was not so happy was that our housing dilemma persisted during most of that time. At first we were told that influence or "key" money (under the table) or both would be the only means of securing a rental. Both scruples and budget ruled out the latter, and although there were several prominent real-estate owners in the congregation none seemed inclined to use his influence on our behalf. This lack of support proved embarrassing when Jack approached non-Jewish realtors with requests for priority consideration. Invariably they would ask why he hadn't gone to "Mr. _____ ," who was a member of the congregation.

My grandparents, who were not wealthy but had no other grandchild to indulge, begged us to let them supply a down payment so we

---

[15]" 'What We Teach Your Children': A Sermon by Rabbi Jacob M. Rothschild from the Pulpit of The Temple," pamphlet, 17 October 1952, JMR MSS.

[16]JMR to Rabbi David Wice, 17 October 1952, JMR MSS.

could buy a small house of our own. At first Jack adamantly refused. It was more than stubborn pride that made him do so. His relationship with the congregation—and especially with those elders who could have ameliorated our housing problem but didn't—caused him to doubt the permanence of his stay in Atlanta. Also, he had an almost pathological fear of debt. Understandable as that fear was in light of his mother's long struggle to repay the cost of his father's illness, neither my family nor I could see how it applied to taking out a mortgage on one's own home. To us that was a way of life. To him it was a debt, the same as any other.

At one point, after about six months of living in my parents' garage, he became desperate enough to go with me to look at houses. Considering our experience with realtors in our own congregation, we felt more comfortable with the owner of one of the leading non-Jewish agencies. As it happened, he showed us a house that we liked well enough to return to for a closer look. Had we not then ruled out the idea of buying it we would have surely have done so the following day: that morning Jack arrived at The Temple to find an anonymous letter on his desk. The writer informed us that we were not wanted on his street.[17]

That was the only time I recall experiencing overt anti-Semitism in Atlanta. While it came as no surprise that there were residential neighborhoods with de facto restrictions against Jews, we were astonished and amazed that a highly reputable realtor would be so careless (or callous?) as to show us a house in one of them. The episode poignantly concluded with a letter Jack received a few days later, this time from the woman who owned the house we had considered buying. In it she apologized for the behavior of her neighbors, saying she found it disgusting and embarrassing. She wrote that she had been deluged with complaints—some of them threats—when the news spread to her neighbors that we had been looking at her house. In conclusion she mentioned that she was a Canadian scheduled soon to receive her American citizenship and that while she previously had been joyously anticipating the event she now was not at all sure she wanted to go through with it.[18]

Shortly after, we were lucky enough to be offered a year's sublet on the upstairs of a duplex owned by friends who lived downstairs. It gave

---

[17]Original note destroyed.

[18]Agnes Partridge to JMR, 27 April 1948, JMR MSS.

us a much-needed break, and we were deeply grateful. We moved in, put our name on the list for a unit in one of the apartment developments being built, and excitedly awaited the birth of our first child (so did members of the congregation, who apparently had been counting the months of our marriage). Marcia was born in mid-October.

Six months later we again found ourselves expecting and in need of a home. Building schedules had fallen so far behind that there was no hope of our obtaining the unit we had spoken for in time to be settled when the new baby arrived. At that point Jack gave in and accepted my grandparents' offer to help us buy a house. We found a tiny, charming New England-style cottage in Haynes Manor, a close-in neighborhood about ten-minutes' drive from The Temple in normal traffic. We moved in during the summer. Bill arrived the following November.

While Jack was certainly not one to "wear his heart on his sleeve," he could hardly have been unaffected by the congregation's failure to show some concern for our personal welfare. The board had voted him a small salary increase when we told them we were expecting our first child, but a year later, with another on the way, the proposal for a further increase was strongly opposed. Those who opposed it said that it would raise Jack's compensation to a higher figure than that of Dr. Marx—who had been retired on his full but hardly munificent salary of nine thousand dollars a year. The impasse was broken by the generosity (and realism) of a member of the board who offered to supply the extra one thousand dollars a year for Dr. Marx out of his own funds if The Temple would raise the pay of its present rabbi to ten thousand dollars.

His help relieved our problem temporarily and we were grateful, but within another year Jack had still another financial responsibility. His mother, long employed as buyer in a downtown Pittsburgh department store, found herself out of work—the store's lease had run out and the building had been sold. At her age she could not find satisfactory employment elsewhere, so her children persuaded her to accept early retirement. In those days the term did not usually imply company benefits as it does today. Jack and his sister Jean provided the necessary supplements to her social security.

As its rabbi Jack was well aware that the congregation itself still struggled to make ends meet—despite the spectacular improvement that had been made since he first arrived and discovered, as he wrote confidentially, "Well fixed members . . . still smarting over the effort made to raise their dues from the $3.00 monthly that they have been paying for the last fifty years." By 1950 he had led his congregants to accept a higher standard of dues and a more efficient system of collection; the membership doubled in his first four years there. On the other hand, there was still a mortgage to be paid and increased expenses caused by the needs of the now eight hundred families, most of whom were young and eager for the development of new activities at The Temple. There were more than three hundred students enrolled in the religious school.[19]

Though he understood and sympathized with the congregation's budgetary problems, Jack often felt their sting as well, and not only upon his personal income. Ever since ordination he had concerned himself actively with the affairs of the Reform movement in America, both through the Union of American Hebrew Congregations (UAHC) and the Central Conference of American Rabbis (CCAR). By the time he came to Atlanta he had been appointed to several committees. The congregation provided him at that time with a modest expense account for travel, sufficient to attend conventions of the two organizations but not enough to attend committee meetings. As he was reluctant to discuss financial problems, even with me, the pressure must have been great that led him in 1951 to write to his close friend, Rabbi Morris Lieberman of Baltimore, then chairman of the CCAR Chaplaincy Committee:

> Dear Morrie,
>
> I really feel guilty about not attending the meeting of the Chaplaincy Committee, but I simply cannot afford to make the trip. I know it doesn't look good only to come when my expenses are paid. However, two children put a dent in one's income. . . .[20]

Although he had no children of his own, Lieberman could sympathize with Jack's position.

Gradually we saw a change, not only in the ability of the congregation to give us more security but in its willingness to do so. After retirement of the mortgage in 1953 the board still felt unable to increase Jack's income by any appreciable amount but as a gesture of good intentions allocated what was available as a travel account for me. That account

---

[19]JMR to Jerome L. Levy, 26 August 1946, JMR MSS.

[20]JMR to Rabbi Morris Lieberman, 19 April 1951, JMR MSS.

added more to our enjoyment of life than many times the amount would have as an increase in salary, for it enabled me to go with him to the major meetings he attended without feeling guilty over the extravagance of the air fare. Up to that time my travel had been restricted to the annual conventions of the CCAR, which took place in late June when we could take the time to go by car and incorporate our vacation in the journey.

Jack was first elected to the executive board of the CCAR in the early 1950s, and to its office of treasurer in 1956. He led in its successful effort to establish equitable guidelines for the placement of rabbis in suitable congregations and helped steer the plan through its acceptance by the UAHC. He also took on the responsibility of soliciting contributions from his colleagues in the Southeast for support of their alma mater, which had recently merged with its counterpart in New York City to become the Hebrew Union College-Jewish Institute of Religion (HUC-JIR). He had become friends with its new president, Dr. Nelson Glueck, while studying in Cincinnati. Now he became Glueck's staunch supporter in the latter's effort to strengthen the newly expanded college.

Another activity that took a great deal of Jack's time and effort was the establishment of a UAHC-sponsored summer camp in the Southeast. He served, as did his colleagues in the area, in organizing and administering the camp in its early stages, when the session lasted only a week and was held at a rented campsite. The earliest sessions that I remember took place in South Florida, in August, a time when I did not regret being unable to go there with him. He seemed to enjoy it, though, in spite of the weather and the lack of air conditioning. He loved the kids and was still a force to be reckoned with on the basketball court and baseball field.

Of all his activities with the national institutions of Reform Judaism the one he enjoyed most was his work with the CCAR Commission on Justice and Peace and its corresponding body, the Social Action Committee of the UAHC. Election to the administrative committee of the former gave him automatic membership in the latter. There he met some of the leading figures in the liberal wing of American politics and by associating with them became more keenly aware of what was happening throughout the country than he could have become otherwise, situated as he was so far from the nerve center of that time.

It seemed—to me, at least—as if he were receiving an unusual amount of honor and responsibility for one so young. Whatever flattery he may have missed in his own congregation was given to him in ample quantity from others who invited him to be guest speaker, and from his colleagues at the CCAR and UAHC. If any of the attention ever threatened to inflate his ego, his sense of humor must have quickly punctured it. A case in point occurred during the early fifties when he was scheduled to appear briefly on the program of an upcoming UAHC biennial convention. The UAHC sent out a news release in which Jack had been given what he considered an unduly elaborate buildup. He returned it to Rabbi Jay Kaufman, who was then assistant to UAHC President Maurice N. Eisendrath, with the following comment:

> Dear Jay,
>   . . . The enclosed arrived yesterday. . . . It is nice to know that I am ". . . regarded as one of the nation's leading authorities on the part which religious groups should play in the resolution of civic matters with ethical implications," but I fail to see how this qualifies me to offer an opening prayer.[21]

Jack was soon recognized by his peers in the Atlanta Christian community despite the impediments that had been placed in his path. The local council of the National Conference of Christians and Jews (NCCJ) learned of his arrival from its affiliate in Pittsburgh and quickly recruited him to represent Judaism on the three-faith panel it sent out on speaking engagements during February, National Brotherhood Month. On Jack's first such assignment, in Columbus, Georgia, the local newspaper devoted the greater part of its coverage of the program to him. It quoted, among other things he said, his statement that "unity can be achieved without uniformity," a phrase we would hear frequently during those early years when his prime concern was teaching Jews to be comfortable as Jews. (A sad commentary on the prevalence of that problem can be seen in the title of a sermon he delivered on 15 March 1947 in Macon, Georgia, and on 8 December of the same year in Nashville, Tennessee. It was entitled, "How to Be Happy Though Jewish.") The Brotherhood Month audiences were mostly Christian, but the maxim applied equally to members of both faiths. So did the phrase Jack often used as parallel to it—"diversity without differentiation." Both reflected his deep faith in the American system and his belief that differences among the peoples

---

[21]JMR to Rabbi Jay Kaufman, 18 January 1955, JMR MSS.

of America were the bedrock of democracy. In later years this belief was
the foundation of his approach to race relations as well.[22]

Although he always cooperated with the NCCJ effort—then largely
because it was "the only game in town" for promoting brotherhood—Jack
was never convinced that the rabbi-minister-priest teams preaching to the
already converted on a once-a-year basis did much to further its purpose.
He longed to see the organization involve itself in "beyond the teacup"
activity, and when the Atlanta Council did he applauded and involved
himself enthusiastically in its projects. Meanwhile he established his own
annual outreach for brotherhood: a day-long Institute for the Christian
Clergy held at The Temple each February and hosted by the congregation, with a noted Jewish scholar brought in as guest speaker. Members
of the sisterhood prepared and served lunch, which often drew more
praise than the speaker, though the latter was always duly appreciated.
After several years I persuaded the sisterhood to pattern its own annual
interfaith program in the same fashion, holding it the following day and
utilizing the same speaker with his message adapted to a lay audience.
This schedule worked well also, albeit with the same measure of attention
resting on the food. (More than once Jack received a thank-you note that
included a request for the ladies' recipe for kugel.)

By joining the Georgia Council of Human Relations and the Southern Regional Council he was able to meet and work with many of those
who would later form the nucleus of organizations effecting social change
in the South. When the Greater Atlanta Council on Human Relations
was formed, nearly a decade later, he was one of the first to be invited to
serve on its executive committee. He became known to others in the area
through invitations to address church and school groups and luncheon
clubs and to offer "devotional" messages on radio (and later on television),
and through an unanticipated shower of publicity that resulted from a
near-tragic fire.

In September 1948, the E. Rivers Elementary School building
burned to the ground—fortunately, when no one was in it. Of the many
institutions immediately offering their facilities for use during the rebuilding, the school board chose three, two of which were Jewish, one of

---

[22] "'Brotherhood' Held Pattern of War Peace," *Columbus* [Georgia] *Inquirer*, 18 February 1947, JMR MSS.

them The Temple. That choice in itself sent ecstasy throughout the im-age-sensitive segments of the congregation and pleased Jack immensely because it brought the building to life during the normally deadly quiet weekdays. As Christmas time approached, however, a new wave of pub-licity titillated these same folk beyond all reason. Jack and the other rabbi whose congregational facility was being used had agreed in the name of hospitality to forgo both their Jewish sensitivities and separation-of-church-and-state scruples, and permit their guests to celebrate the holi-day in their usual fashion. Thus it happened that in 1948 Temple halls were decked with holly and Temple schoolrooms with Christmas trees. This made news.

Pleased as Jack had been to be of service to the community, he was not at all pleased by the almost sycophantic reaction he observed among many congregants. Still disturbed by it as this hospitality began its sec-ond season, he spoke of his objection to it in his Yom Kippur sermon that year. Pointing out that such behavior arises from insecurity, he noted that "no one started a pogrom against actors when Booth assassinated Lin-coln." Then he said, conversely, that while it was natural for us "to feel gratification over the opportunity for public service," a sentiment un-doubtedly shared by church members whose building was also being used by the school, "with us it went further. We looked upon it as a God-given opportunity to cement public relations." In closing, he said that "far more important than filling our school house with strangers is the need for filling our Temple with Jews."[23]

Jack's impact on the Atlanta Jewish community as a whole did much to hasten the changes that characterized those years immediately follow-ing World War II. Doubtlessly, with time, the differences inherent within the community would have healed themselves, for forces set in motion by the war affected every area of American life and would have here as well, but individual leadership set the pace.

Nowhere was the stratification of Jewish society more important than among the loving, old-fashioned black men and women upon whom we still could lean to manage our households in that Jewish quarter of Tennessee Williams's world. Mattie Grier, the picture-book "mammy" who worked for us when our children were infants, probably without re-

---

[23]Sermon, "The Greater Sin," 13 October 1948, JMR MSS.

alizing it gave the most succinct description of the existing culture gap one evening when we told her where she could reach us in case of emergency. We were going to the home of one of Jack's staunchest supporters, a wonderful gentleman with a heart as big as his bank account—and a name that was not listed on Mattie's personal version of the social register. She received the information with a veiled sneer. It was too much for Jack. He pulled up a chair and lectured her on the evils of snobbery, to which she listened appreciatively. When he finished, she nodded her head philosophically and replied, "I guess you'se right, Rabbi. The German Jews, they *has* money. But the Russian Jews, they *spends* theirs."

Her comment said it all. While exceptions did exist, as they always do, she had pinpointed the prevailing situation in the Atlanta Jewish community. Affluent Temple members, scions of old families that had once been the backbone of Jewish philanthropy locally, had become disaffected and disinterested and had finally withdrawn altogether. Leadership had fallen by default to those first- and second-generation American Jews who could still remember being helped by the organizations they now could themselves support. Very few of them belonged to The Temple when Jack arrived.

He set about reversing the trend of leadership affiliation by personal example, taking an active role in many of the secular organizations and thereby inspiring others from The Temple to do likewise. He assisted in the campaigns to build the Jewish Home for the elderly and the Atlanta Jewish Community Center, served on the board and on pertinent committees of the Atlanta Jewish Welfare Federation and of Gate City Lodge B'nai B'rith, and subsequently served as president of both B'nai B'rith in 1950 and the Federation in 1954. His term of office with the Federation coincided with the national observance of the American Jewish tercentenary, which sparked interest in American Jewish history and gave rise to some local events commemorating the occasion, sponsored by the Federation.

In 1950, while heading the local B'nai B'rith, Jack was called upon to co-chair the Atlanta Jewish Welfare Fund campaign with Rabbi Harry H. Epstein of the large Conservative congregation, Ahavath Achim. As preparation for their task the two men were sent to Israel and Europe for three weeks. It was a thrilling, emotional, totally unexpected opportunity for Jack, his first experience abroad other than wartime service in the Pacific, and the impetus for what became a deep personal relationship with

Israel. He returned brimming with enthusiasm for the Jewish state and speaking of it eloquently to audiences throughout the area. He and his colleague steered the campaign to a resounding success.

If it was surprising to hear Atlanta's Reform rabbi publicly lauding Israel, it was even more so to see him and the city's Conservative rabbi enjoying each other's company. When they were overheard addressing each other as "Harry" and "Jack" some thought the millennium was at hand. A new era in Atlanta Jewish community relations had indeed arrived. This collaboration symbolized the turning point.

While Jack got along well with all his fellow rabbis in Atlanta, he held some in especially high regard. He developed a close friendship with one that seemed all the more extraordinary in view of the two men's differences in background and belief. Rabbi Emanuel Feldman came to Atlanta in 1952, freshly ordained from the most traditional wing of American Orthodoxy, in his early twenties and about to be married to a delightful young woman as observant as he. Of course, he and Jack disagreed on matters of Jewish theology. On everything else they seemed to be in perfect accord, including horseback riding.

Whenever possible the two rabbis took afternoons off together in order to go riding. One evening, while seated on a dais waiting for a meeting to begin, they were discussing this mutual pleasure, and their conversation was monitored with growing curiosity by a prominent lay leader, Frank Garson, haplessly seated between them. A noted philanthropist as pithy with his Jewish-accented pronouncements as he was generous with his means, the unwitting eavesdropper listened in silence as long as he could. When he could contain himself no longer he turned to Feldman in mock amazement and asked, "*You* ride horseback?"

"Sure," replied the confident young newcomer. "You think only Reform rabbis can ride horseback?"

The older gentleman took his time to respond. "No," he said thoughtfully after a moment's pause. "But when a Reform rabbi falls off a horse the people ask, 'Did he get hurt?' When an Orthodox rabbi falls off a horse the people ask, 'What was he doing on a horse?' "

Mannie Feldman refuted that stereotype of an Orthodox rabbi just as Jack Rothschild had refuted previous notions of a Reform rabbi. Perhaps it was that quality that attracted them to each other.

As the congregation and the community more fully accepted Jack's leadership, he became more attached to Atlanta. He gave some indication of his feeling as early as 1949, in a sermon for that year's observance of "Civic Sabbath." Insisting that it was "only silly pride" if our sole reason for growth was simply to stay ahead of other cities in the Southeast, he explained that greatness required culture. In order to have that, he declared, we must safeguard our educational system against such dangers as the teachers who had recently been reported defending the Ku Klux Klan in their classrooms. He said they were a "detriment to progress" and warned, "We can't keep ahead in material things and lag behind in the philosophy of living."[24]

By 1953 Jack had clearly identified with Atlanta and the South but, oddly enough, I had not, insofar as our future was concerned. From childhood I had yearned for the advantages of a larger, more cosmopolitan environment, and now that our children were approaching school age I wanted them even more. With finances a continual strain (and Jack's salary still far below that allotted for comparable positions in other parts of the country) I mentally began to pack my bags every time we heard of a suitable pulpit being vacated. Though he did not share my sentiments Jack did on one occasion submit his name for consideration.

That year, Rabbi Roland B. Gittelsohn, our close friend and Jack's college classmate, announced that he was leaving Rockville Center, New York, to serve Temple Israel of Boston. He and Jack so closely paralleled each other's thinking on most vital issues, especially those dealing with civil rights, that Roland felt a "happy marriage" could be consummated between Jack and the congregation in Rockville Center. He wasn't the only rabbi who suggested this to Jack. It seemed to me as if ninety percent of those attending the CCAR in Estes Park, Colorado, that summer also thought Jack should apply. They went beyond suggesting it to him. Many pulled me aside to suggest it to me, in the erroneous belief that it was I, being a native Atlantan, who was reluctant to leave. They also clung to their mistaken image of the South as an unrelieved snakepit filled with race baiters and anti-Semites, and remembered Jack's initial hassles with his emeritus and board. Only one of them voiced a doubt that we would be doing well to leave. Advising Jack to weigh carefully the possibilities of improvement elsewhere, he said with regard to Atlanta, "Remember, they may be bastards, but they're *your* bastards."

---

[24]Sermon, "What Makes a City Great?" 25 February 1949, JMR MSS.

Jack didn't hold quite so negative a view of his congregation. Nevertheless, for my sake and the sake of our children he submitted his name to the Long Island congregation for consideration and went there when summoned for an interview. We never found out whether they liked him or not, because as soon as he returned home and told me about it he notified them he was withdrawing his name. He had no complaint against the people of Rockville Center. It just took one look at another city with the idea of living there, to convince him that he wanted to spend the rest of his life in Atlanta.

Although the days were long past when he had cause to dread each board meeting, he still had no clear sign of board approval. On the one hand gestures had been made to alleviate our budget strain and even to make amends for the earlier neglect in regard to housing. (The suggestion was made that the congregation buy our house from us and maintain it, an idea we quickly put to rest. We had already weathered the worst part of the expense and rather liked the idea of building an equity.) When the children grew older and we needed a more spacious home the board voted to assist us by doubling Jack's housing allowance in order that we might meet the larger mortgage payments. That was in 1955. The congregation was still growing by about 75 to 125 new families each year. We tried to meet them all and welcome them personally by inviting them in small groups to our home after Friday night services, and by inviting the entire congregation to a reception at our home during the High Holyday period each fall. After several years the board also suggested reimbursing us for those expenses. We declined that offer. I had kept costs to a minimum by doing my own catering, and we felt it only right that we reciprocate in some way for all the hospitality we received that Jack had no time for us to acknowledge throughout the year.

On the other hand, Jack had been required to initiate, albeit behind the scenes, any discussion aimed at raising his salary to meet the cost of living; each one, though resolved favorably, was done so well after the fact. As this apparently ambiguous attitude toward him continued into the mid-1950s he concluded that the board intended to observe his tenth anniversary at The Temple, April 1956, with some gesture that would definitely proclaim its endorsement of him. Such celebrations were common practice in other communities.

The winter of 1956 came and went without our hearing anything about a celebration for Jack's anniversary. When he still had heard nothing by mid-March he asked a close friend who served on the board, confidentially, to tell him what had happened. "The subject did come up," the friend told him, "but the board decided it wasn't necessary."

That did it. Jack was so angry that the veins on his neck were still bulging when he told me about it. "So what are you going to do?" I asked, not really expecting an answer.

He took a deep breath and said furiously, "I'm going to have it out with them." "They'll have to make up their minds once and for all whether they want me as their rabbi or they don't. I'm not going to spend the rest of my life going to them periodically, hat-in-hand, begging for a kind word." He paused for a moment and then added, "Even a janitor gets a gold watch after so many years of faithful service."

He told the board exactly that at its next meeting. His words must have had a salubrious effect because it was the last time Jack ever had to bring up the subject of adequate compensation or appreciation of his services. Plans for an anniversary celebration were set in motion immediately. Since it was too late to do a proper job of it in the spring the celebration was scheduled for early fall, just after the High Holydays.

As a final word on the unpleasant subject of salary, it seems only fair to report that future increments appeared at appropriate intervals, sometimes when least expected. Jack did not want a contract because he believed they were useless ("If either party wants out the bond is broken anyway," he always said). Even when the congregation elected him for life, in 1965, he neither wanted nor to my knowledge received any written document attesting to it. The only contract he ever requested was the one providing for his retirement and for my support in the event of his death. He received the draft of it for his approval, to be signed at the next meeting of the board, on the day he died. If I had still harbored any resentment from those first ten years of indifference, it would surely have been dispelled by the immediate and unquestioning action of the board in honoring that unsigned contract.

Jack's delight in anticipating the anniversary celebration caused him to wax sentimental in his Rosh Hashanah sermon that year. He spoke glowingly of the happiness he felt in seeing an increasing number of people using The Temple as a spiritual home, coming there not only to pray but to share other functions of their lives together. He listed changes that had taken place in the service itself, and spoke of the reintroduction of long-discarded traditions and the use of the pulpit for teaching as well as for inspiration and challenge. He stressed that everyone needed to utilize the ideals of Judaism in every aspect of life and that they should not leave the affairs of the community entirely to the rabbi. He even expressed publicly his love for me—something he rarely put into words even privately—and spoke candidly of the personal aspects of a rabbi's service to his congregation. Above all he expressed his attachment to Atlanta.

He concluded with a story about a rabbi who lived in a poor shtetl in Eastern Europe. One day, so the story goes, the impoverished rabbi received a package from a friend who had gone to America and become very rich. It contained many beautiful and much-needed gifts, and also a letter. Upon reading the letter, the rabbi ignored his gifts and ran through the streets excitedly calling to everyone to come and look at his letter. "See?" he exclaimed as each one approached, pointing to the bottom of the page. "See how my friend has signed his letter? He says, 'Sincerely Yours.'" To that story Jack added, "As I wish for each of you a year of happiness and blessing, I would have you know that I am—Sincerely Yours."[25]

The sisterhood members planning his anniversary reception responded by ordering a cake inscribed "Sincerely Ours." It was not the only surprise that greeted him on that auspicious weekend. Without telling him, the congregation had sent his mother an airline ticket to visit from Pittsburgh. The children and I met her at the airport and sequestered her in a back bedroom until time for dinner. The fun was heightened by the presence of both Morrie and Lillian Lieberman. Morrie had been invited as guest speaker and had brought his wife Lillian, who was also an old friend of Jack's since college, with him.

Wonderful as the evening was, the best was yet to come. The board had scheduled a banquet to be held at the Standard Club on Sunday evening, replete with champagne cocktails and squab under glass. When we took our places for dinner, to our great amazement, we were joined at the head table by none other than Jack's eighty-six-year-old former nemesis, Rabbi Emeritus David Marx. It was he who invoked God's blessing on the gathering. Finally, after ten years of bitter opposition he had come to accept another in the place he had once held.

---

[25]Sermon, "Sincerely Yours," 5 September 1956, JMR MSS.

The presence of David Marx at that dinner marked for us the turning point of Jack's rabbinate in Atlanta. From that day on, for the six remaining years of Marx's life, Jack visited him as often as possible and felt a genuine pleasure in doing so. Their reconciliation brought him a tremendous amount of satisfaction. No longer of any consequence to his security of tenure or his ability to serve, it represented a strengthened bond in the chain of leadership, a symbol of continuity that he regarded as significant and even vital to the spiritual health of the congregation. It was this, not salary nor gifts nor accolades, that was for Jack his true measure of success.

CHAPTER • THREE

PREPARATION
FOR CHANGE

It was a bright, frosty morning in 1955 when Jack received another apoplectic telephone call from his self-appointed legal advisor, Silent Sam. "Don't you know that mixed eating is against the law in this state?" rasped Sam with near hysteria.

Jack assured him that he did. He also knew the reason for Sam's call, even before Sam told him. The Temple Sisterhood had just announced its next luncheon-meeting program. It was to be a discussion on "The Moral and Legal Aspects of Desegregation." Attorney Morris B. Abram, who lived in Atlanta then and belonged to The Temple, would speak for the legal side. To present the moral side the sisterhood had invited the distinguished black clergyman-educator, President of Morehouse College Dr. Benjamin E. Mays, who even then had become a legend.

Jack waited patiently while his caller completed his tirade. Then he replied innocently, "You must have been misinformed, Sam. The sisterhood luncheon isn't going to be integrated."

Sam was surprised and asked if Dr. Mays had been "understanding" enough to schedule his arrival for after the meal, just in time for the program. "Not at all," Jack said. "Both Dr. and Mrs. Mays will be with us for lunch, but they're going to be seated at the center of the head table and all us white folks will be segregated around them."

The call was a minor gust in the storm that raged around that sisterhood meeting. The women in charge were bombarded with protests and dire predictions of what would happen should such a meeting be allowed to take place. They stood their ground. The program played to a packed house and the sisterhood received accolades from all segments of the Jewish community. Those members who had trembled with doubt at the outset were only too happy to accept praise in the end.

Bizarre as it may sound today, such action did require an inordinate amount of courage in 1955. Awareness of black personhood had not yet begun to penetrate the consciousness of many whites. Even where it did there was fear that the prejudice would be turned upon any who admitted sympathy or identified in any way with the plight of blacks. Politicians still employed race baiting as their most reliable weapon, promising "segregation forever" and warning that "blood would run in the streets" if the federal government forced Southerners to integrate their schools.

The Georgia legislature at that time was considering a bill that, if passed, would have shut down the entire school system as soon as one unit of it received the order to desegregate. In neighboring Alabama, where determination to keep the status quo was even stronger, it would be one more month before a tired seamstress would refuse to give up her seat on a bus to a white man and would thereby trigger the movement that would change America and lead her pastor, a former student of Dr. Mays, to become a Nobel laureate for Peace.

It required special nerve for Jack even more than for the women. He had not yet received the warm indication of affection and approval that ultimately marked his tenth anniversary at The Temple. Furthermore, he had reason to know that the old fears still lingered. I had told him about a conversation I had had with several of our friends shortly after the Supreme Court had handed down its decision on *Brown vs. Topeka*. When I made a statement to the effect that Jack had advocated compliance with the decision, a woman only a few years older than I turned to me in abject horror and demanded, "What does Jack want to do to us, start the Frank case all over again?"

The main reason he could get by with instigating such daring action as the sisterhood meeting was that he had not waited until the racial issue heated up to begin talking about it. As early as Rosh Hashanah 1947, when he had been in the city just a little more than one year, he had begun mentioning race relations at least once every High Holyday season. At first it was a very mild dose, hardly even enough to recognize today, but he increased it steadily each succeeding year. He also administered doses on at least two other occasions annually, the obviously appropriate one saluting brotherhood each February and a year-end commentary on the most significant events of the past twelve months. By 1954 many Atlantans and all who belonged to The Temple were aware of his stand on the issue. Some even agreed with him.

He did not accomplish these advances by courage alone. He sweetened his earliest pills with appeals to civic pride. On one occasion he relied upon Atlanta's traditional rivalry with Birmingham to compliment his fellow townsmen for accepting a visit of the Freedom Train, a national exhibition that had been banned in Alabama because it defied local segregation laws. With that commendation as his introduction he worked into the sermon a discussion of citizens' rights and equal opportunity for all, and then wryly observed that black Americans were being denied at least one inalienable right: freedom from lynching.[1]

The following year, 1948, he had cause to warn his congregation about the dangers of renewed Klan activity in the area, and also of the emergence of another locally vocal hate group, the Columbians. His warning led to a discussion of the stand on civil rights recently taken by the Democratic party, which he favored, and a reminder that the ideas it espoused were not new ones but tenets written into the United States Constitution at its inception.[2]

---

[1]Sermon, "Have We Missed the Freedom Train?" 2 January 1948, JMR MSS.

[2]Sermon, "The Greater Sin," 13 October 1948, JMR MSS.

Some of the news items he clipped for incorporation into that sermon were so outrageous as to have been incredible even then. Item: A white man had gone, armed, to the home of a black man who had dared to vote, shot him dead, and won acquittal on the murder charge by pleading self-defense. Item: Three black college presidents, summoned to a meeting of all presidents of colleges within the University System of Georgia, were run out of the city where the meeting was being held by Klansmen brandishing a fiery cross. Why? Not because they had broken custom to partake of meals with their peers. On the contrary, they were housed and fed in the homes of local blacks rather than at a college dormitory with the others. The heinous crime for which they were expelled so forcibly was that of sitting at the same *conference* table with their white colleagues! Jack was straightforward and sometimes sarcastic in his condemnation of such incidents. Commenting on them he said:

> . . . living in the South somehow sets us apart from other Americans. When our country tries to implement standards of equal opportunity set forth in the Constitution, the South considers it an infringement of its way of life. When the government wants to insure the safety of all its citizens, the South reacts as though such simple justice were an affront to its moral codes.[3]

He continued, criticizing the press for its sanctimonious reaction to each incident of flagrant bigotry. Editorials in local papers had proclaimed that "every right-minded Southerner" deplored such behavior. Jack ventured to ask "where all these right-minded people might be, and even if the writer of the editorial is one of them."[4]

He also commented on the recent gubernatorial campaign in Georgia, declaring that the candidates had spoken as if "the only issue were having to sit next to Negroes in public places or having them in their homes . . . and marrying their daughters." Charging that only rarely did anyone attempt to disprove the "lying bigots who capitalize on festering hatreds," he decried the "blatant withholding of evidence" in cases where both races were involved and added that "millions of us must know the truth, but we keep silent." In a warning that by our very delay we invite

---

[3]Ibid.

[4]Ibid.

the outside interference that we fear, he pleaded with his large Holyday congregation for honesty in its appraisal of the facts of life in the American South:

> We who take pride in our heritage as Jews, we who bask in the glory of Southern tradition have a greater responsibility for enlightened action. . . . It becomes increasingly obvious that unless decent people take up the burden, the South faces a return to the most primitive kind of bigotry and race hatred.[5]

Jack tempered such candor with discretion, never forgetting that, as he put it, "You can't lead them if you get so far out front that they lose sight of you." When the E. Rivers School PTA invited him to speak on the subject of "democratic living" in 1951, he told his listeners that it was not enough merely to accept academically the principles of democracy. "Dignity is due all people," he said, "not just a chosen few." While he undoubtedly felt more freedom to express himself before that audience than before others—because of the friendship formed when the school used the facilities of The Temple a few years before—he did not limit his treatment of the subject to friends alone. He did, however, decline to speak on civil rights on at least one occasion when he had been specifically asked to do so. The invitation had come from the Lions Club of Cartersville, Georgia, a group that he did not feel was prepared, in April 1951, to receive his opinions constructively. In reply to the man tendering the invitation he wrote, "While I agree that the subject . . . ought to be dealt with in civic groups, I am not at all sure that I as an outsider would do well to come in and speak on so controversial an issue. I would think that leadership in this cause, which is indeed a worthy one, ought to come from members of your own community." As an alternative topic he suggested that the group might be interested in hearing about his recent trip to Israel.[6]

When he addressed black audiences, as he was often invited to do, he had to be cautious in a different way. There he had to avoid making platitudes, statements that appeared to be patronizing, to avoid boring

---

[5]Ibid.

[6]Address to E. Rivers School PTA, Atlanta, "Foundations for Democratic Living," 20 February 1951; JMR to W. C. Henson, 10 April 1951—JMR MSS.

his audience by preaching to the already converted. As Brotherhood Week approached in 1952, Negro homes and churches throughout the South were bombed with increasing frequency and with little if any notice from the white community. In Florida, the director of the NAACP and his wife were killed when their home was bombed, a crime for which no one seemed likely to be brought to justice. In the wake of these events Jack struggled to inject some optimism into his "Brotherhood" address to students at Morehouse College. These obscenities, he observed, might well augur hope by indicating that the hard-core haters were getting desperate.[7]

Jack was well aware that bigotry-related violence was not limited to the South. He included in his denouncements the conditions that nurtured riots then taking place in Cicero, Illinois, the desecration of synagogues in Philadelphia, and above all the wave of McCarthyism that, in his opinion, served to fan the flames of hatred making such acts possible. True to his rule of concluding sermons on a hopeful note, he made the encouraging observation that the year just ended, 1952, was the first in which no lynchings had been reported in America.[8]

He was even more candid with colleagues in the rabbinate. He had been given the assignment of writing the basic draft of the CCAR's statement on brotherhood for 1950. The following year, when asked to critique the basic draft prepared by another rabbi, he commented, "It sounds very much as though we are holding a club over our less benighted white-skinned brethren and saying to them, 'You had better do something about race equality or the non-Caucasian groups will rise up and destroy you.' It seems to me there ought to be more emphasis placed upon the historic Jewish reasons." He added: "P.S. Paragraph three begins as follows: 'It would be redundant to reiterate once again. . . .' Oi! Is he right!"[9]

Jack's most effective weapon was logic. In 1953 he used it in his appeal for brotherhood by pointing out that emergence of the Third World nations gave America an additional reason to purge itself of old prejudices. With bigotry now an international concern, elimination of it from

---

[7]Address at Morehouse College, Atlanta, "Is Brotherhood Just a Dream?" 17 February 1952, JMR MSS.

[8]Sermon, "Year's End Musing," 29 December 1952, JMR MSS.

[9]JMR to Rabbi Roland Gittelsohn, 26 November 1951, JMR MSS.

our own shores, he suggested, might help convince others that our country sought not world domination but freedom "for all people enslaved in body or in spirit." He listed several other practical reasons for practicing brotherhood, not the least of which was pure, unadulterated self-interest.[10]

However unyielding he may have been in attacking oppression, he was always compassionate toward those involuntary oppressors who either had not yet come to understand the error of their ways or who understood but feared the consequences of change. He expressed this feeling tenderly and eloquently in his Yom Kippur sermon of 1954, written in the months following the momentous decision of the United States Supreme Court in May of that year. He approached the subject by acknowledging that as Jews in the South we faced a delicate situation:

> A way of life, a pattern of behavior is being threatened. I firmly believe that no one outside the South can fully appreciate the cataclysmic changes—emotionally and spiritually—that the implementation of the decision will require. . . . Generations of indoctrination must be erased from the heart and mind of man.[11]

Having made that statement he hastened to make clear that the difficulty of the problem in no way absolved us from the duty to face it. He emphasized that it was not specifically a Jewish problem, but one rooted in the moral law of all religions. Responding to the popular cliché "religion and politics don't mix," he cited several notable instances in which they did. He pointed to the Ten Commandments as moral laws that had been eventually enacted into legal statutes, and the antitrust statutes of several decades past as more recent legal measures that predated the people's willingness to abide by them. Regarding the latter he noted with customary logic: "It is a violation of the law to form great trusts that prevent little men from earning a living. Is it not likewise unethical?"[12]

In that sermon Jack attacked those who were advocating the closing of schools as a means of avoiding integration, by asking "What man of

---

[10]Sermon, "Love Thy Neighbor—Democracy's Antidote," 20 February 1953, JMR MSS.

[11]Sermon, "The Challenge of a Dream," 7 October 1954, JMR MSS.

[12]Ibid.

intelligence burns down his house to rid himself of an unwanted guest?" He then commented that it was all the more foolish "when we don't even know if the visitor is welcome or not because we've never really had him in our house—as an equal, that is." Criticizing the "stubborn Southern pride" that insisted upon preserving its "self-perceived superiority" at all costs, he recalled the "indulgent pleasure" with which white parents in the South watch their children at play with the children of their black employees, and asked, "What possible difference would there be if they were allowed to go to school together?"

He was not so naive as to believe that the goal could be reached without a great deal of patience on the part of both communities, black and white. In explaining this point to his congregation he said that integration would not come about all at once. Instead, he suggested, it would develop in small ways, little by little, beginning perhaps with individuals coming together to solve mutual problems:

> a few parents whose hearts make them willing, sitting down together to discuss protection for their children at a dangerous intersection. A handful of people talking over together free clothing for needy children or common problems of health and hygiene. . . . Gradually, a rapport will be built up upon which the idea of common schools will no longer loom so menacing and foreboding.[13]

He followed that statement with a poignant description of the two races as standing on the opposite sides of a raging stream that no one could safely cross. One day, he projected, a log would get caught between the two shores and eventually one brave soul would venture across on it. In time more logs would jam against the first and more people would find the courage to test the crossing. Finally, enough logs and people would have come together so that a sturdy bridge could be built, one on which the most timorous person could walk confidently.

Jack concluded that sermon with a list of practical suggestions for fulfilling the charge he had made earlier to "face up to the nobility of our heritage." Repeating that "customs and mores may prevent us from living up to our ideals but let them not force us to abrogate and deny them," he warned that we should "expect skirmishes along the way." We should therefore be wise enough not to try to "storm the deeply rooted ramparts

---

[13]Ibid.

of tradition in the vanguard of the attack," alone and without adequate preparation, for by setting ourselves up as champions of the cause we could very well destroy it. Instead, he said, we should 1) recognize the issue as a religious one and not leave it to the secular organizations of Jewish life, 2) form study groups to learn what Judaism has to say on the subject and acquaint ourselves with the basic facts of black history, 3) organize a social-action committee within the congregation in order to keep up with developments and provide an authorized voice for public statement, and 4) as individuals join the nonsectarian groups already at work on the issue.[14]

Although the board turned down his request to form a social-action committee it did agree to leave him unhindered in any effort he might make toward accomplishing the purpose of one. He began by motivating The Temple Couples Club to sponsor a Sabbath service at which a dramatic dialogue on the subject would be presented and then discussed in open forum. The next Friday night, he followed that activity with a sermon explaining the purpose and function of a social-action committee. Judaism, he asserted, rejects the idea of "passing on to God all responsibility for our social problems." The committee, he said, was Reform's way of helping us meet those responsibilities.[15]

It was during these months that he persuaded leaders of the sisterhood to plan their controversial luncheon program for the following fall. When the Holydays arrived he caught his "revolving door" members with another lecture on the "revolutionary change in social patterns" facing us in the South, charging that our state government was reacting "with all the heated emotion of secessionary zeal" and accusing its officials of having fed us "large doses of self-delusion and false hope." He urged us to prepare for a realistic future rather than "construct an impossible one out of the words and blind hopes of those who have not yet accepted the inevitable."[16]

Still the board would not approve a social-action committee. It did, however, endorse the establishment of a community-affairs committee. It

---

[14]Ibid.

[15]Sermon, "What Is Social Action?" 13 May 1955, JMR MSS.

[16]Sermon, "Give Meaning to Creation," 17 September 1955, JMR MSS.

was appointed by the president of the congregation and over the years conducted a number of programs designed to educate members in applying religious ideals to problems affecting the total community. Outstanding among them was a series of Sunday morning forums in which the speaker discussed various aspects of the school desegregation problem; a mass meeting of the congregation at which the superintendent of schools, the chief of police, and others addressed the question in the weeks immediately preceding desegregation of Atlanta schools; and a program entitled "Atlanta: Its Successes and Its Failures." It never became involved in passing resolutions or making public statements.

However it might have appeared, our lives were filled with many more concerns than civil rights during those years. When we attended the UAHC Biennial in Los Angeles in 1955, we realized that even among the social-action committees of our Reform movement, civil rights was not the only matter of importance. Of much more heated debate on the West Coast at that time was the issue of statehood for Hawaii.

At home both of us found it challenging to help nurture the newly organized Temple Couples Club, which Jack created as an alternative to a Temple Brotherhood despite pressure periodically applied by the national organization to establish the latter. He maintained that while he was "well aware" of the good work that the brotherhoods did nationally, the organizational life of Atlanta was too complex. There were three Jewish social clubs; besides, many of the potential enthusiasts for a Temple Brotherhood were traveling salesmen who had to be out on the road all week.

The congregation had grown to more than one thousand families by this time, which meant Jack had some four thousand to five thousand individuals to serve completely on his own. We began to feel the pressure every spring even before the dogwood bloomed. By the week after Pesach I found myself wondering if either one of us would last through Shavuot,* when Jack held Confirmation, thus ending the year for religious-school activities. Until central air conditioning became more prevalent Shavuot also marked the cessation of most other congregational and community activities in our part of the country. It meant we could

_____

*Festival commemorating the receiving of the Torah; also a harvest festival.

relax on weekends, which we could never do during the school year, and spend our Sundays at the homes of our friends with swimming pools.

To understand fully the extent of our weariness in those seven weeks between the spring and summer festivals, it is necessary to have some idea of Jack's passion for detail in preparing for his Confirmation service. He had written it himself and always insisted upon conducting the rehearsals himself, even after he had an assistant. When a classmate who also served a large congregation asked his advice on the subject, he sent him the following description:

> My first rehearsal is always held on the Tuesday of Pesach. I give out parts on that day and also give the kids a mimeographed program listing in addition to what's in the regular program the page numbers of the reading assignments. . . . I guess these sessions involve what you'd call "movement rehearsals." This is when we practice getting up and coming to the pulpit and sitting down all at one time and who they follow and how I want them to stand at the pulpit and where, etc. . . . At these rehearsals for the entire class I never have all of the speeches said so that no one is bored by having to listen to sixty or seventy talks.
>
> The kids rehearse their individual parts by meeting with me individually after school on days other than the class rehearsal. . . . I have them come back as many times as they need to until both they and I are satisfied. . . . Then . . . I have all of them come back individually one more time just before Confirmation to make sure that they're still saying their parts well.
>
> Along about the fourth week of the class rehearsals I have the organist come in so that we can then practise with the music.[17]

Add to that program the many telephone calls and other aggravations inherent in dealing with sixty to seventy-five teenagers, and it should come as no surprise that Jack was not easy to live with during those last few weeks of spring.

Clearly he no longer found time for bridge, tennis, or spontaneous excursions on horseback. His expertise at bridge had long since atrophied from disuse (he enjoyed blaming it on my lack of card sense, but actually he had no regularly free evenings for practice). When he realized the dan-

---

[17]JMR to Rabbi Robert I. Kahn, 11 June 1965, JMR MSS.

ger he was courting by not taking time off for relaxation and exercise he resorted to the sport he had formerly derided as "the old man's game": golf. Thereafter, he took a cue from his friends in the medical profession and declared two afternoons a week "sacrosanct" in order to spend them on the golf course.

Perhaps it was divine retribution for his having so long spurned the game, but for whatever reason, golf became his only athletic endeavor at which he was unsuccessful. His difficulty galled him. Much as he complained, however, and threatened regularly to give up the game, he continued to struggle on. His swing was a horror to behold, so bad, in fact, that to this day his surviving golf partners still joke about it. He responded to jibes about his "unorthodox" swing by punning, "What else would you expect from a *Reform* rabbi?"

Jack's affection for animals was well known. When we moved into our first house, just before Bill was born, our pediatrician, who was a good friend and a member of the congregation, came by one day with a cocker spaniel puppy "for the baby," he said. "This one'll be a boy and every boy should have a dog." We knew he was really bringing it for the baby's father.

Both Bill and Marcia enjoyed the puppy, as did I, but the puppy himself loved Jack so much that he literally pined away for him during the three weeks Jack was in Israel. After moping about for most of that time he disappeared—two days before "the master" returned. Another cocker spaniel, this one older, strayed filthy and half-starved onto The Temple lawn the following day. Jack fed him, brought him home via the vet's, and after watching the lost-and-found column for several days with no results, considered him ours.

This cocker spaniel was still very much with us when we moved into our larger home five years later and still another canine joined the family—an oversized black standard poodle, the gift of a member of the congregation who bred them. We named him Lafayette, "Laffy" for short, and taught him some spectacular tricks such as putting out a match with his paw, and "playing" the piano on command. He loved to show off. Once when a newspaper photographer came to the house to take a picture of our family lighting the menorah for a story on Hannukah, Laffy upstaged us and so impressed the visitor that the next day's newspaper sported not a picture of us but one of him—standing on his hind legs at the piano.

Such antics served us well in helping to relieve tension, but the time came when we needed more relaxation than a romp with the dogs. We had tried driving to Florida for a week in winter as guests of members of the congregation who had a house there. Unfortunately, such a trip wasn't really relaxing—certainly not for me because, while the men were out fishing or cruising on someone's yacht they left me to be entertained by their wives, whose greatest joy seemed to be getting decked out in their finest at ten o'clock in the morning and going to an elegant brunch at the Eden Roc. All I wanted was to be left alone in the sun.

Later we tried making a getaway with the children during their December holiday, but that strategy didn't work either. With a congregation as large as ours was by that time, someone always wanted to be married during the holidays, thereby delaying our departure, and someone usually died, which necessitated calling us back. The most disturbing aspect of it, to me, was that even when Jack was home with us we could see that he was not really with us. In theory we understood that his greatest need was to be left alone. In practice, though, a young wife and children do not always understand.

Occasionally, Jack would be invited to speak in New York or elsewhere in the vicinity or be called to a meeting there at a time when he could take an extra few days and make it worthwhile for me to go with him. Such instances were always a great treat for me. Once, when he spoke at New York's Central Synagogue, we were able to read the report of his sermon in the early edition of the Saturday *New York Times*, which we picked up on our way back to the hotel. It made us feel like celebrities.[18]

What Jack had said that especially interested the *Times* reviewer was, in effect, that the current attempts to muzzle dissent in the South reminded him of the situation in a totalitarian state. He was saying nothing in New York that he had not already said to his congregation in Atlanta (nor did he ever make statements away from home that he had not already made there), but such frankness from a rabbi serving in the South seemed so daring to Northern editors that several papers less conservative than the *Times* sensationalized the story with bold-face captions referring to the statement. Later, in an interview, a reporter from one of the

---

[18]Address at Central Synagogue, New York City, "Fires of Fear—Flame of Faith," 4 January 1957; "Rabbi Finds Curbs on Liberty in South," *New York Times*, 5 Jan. 1957, clipping in scrapbook—JMR MSS.

Jewish weeklies asked Jack how his congregation felt about his making such statements and if his board had ever tried to stop him. Jack told him that the board had not, but that the members "might not be so happy about getting all this national publicity." The board never did take him to task for it.[19]

In Birmingham, at a meeting of the southeast region of the UAHC in January 1956, Jack could see the enormous gap between what he had been able to accomplish with his congregation in Atlanta and what his colleagues in other Southern congregations had done to prepare their members for the inevitable changes about to occur. Roland Gittelsohn had given a keynote address on civil rights that Jack admiringly described as "a powerful and uncompromising" statement. It so infuriated the delegates that they were still unable to settle down for a peaceful plenary session the following morning. They turned it instead into a vituperative debate in which they used such expressions as "evisceration," "hooded monsters," and that old standby, "blood will run in the streets." When the resolutions committee brought before them what Jack called an innocuous statement, similar to those passed by every other major religious group in the South, the delegates turned it down. He then asked them what sort of resolution they would endorse and the answer was "none." One of the rabbis emphasized the point by commenting that he wouldn't risk "one hair on the head of one of my members for the life of every *shvartzeh* in this state."

Jack told me about these events without criticizing them, for he was not one to condemn his colleagues even in the privacy of his home. It was obvious that he was deeply shocked, though, as he was upon realizing the extent of insecurity paralyzing Southern Jews. He did comment on this paralysis in a forthcoming sermon.

It was inconceivable to him that the very people who should have been the most secure—scions of old, established families well settled in the South for generations—were the ones who ran for cover first. It was they who claimed to be completely accepted by the Gentiles in their communities and they who insisted that for them Judaism was a religion only. That they should become terror-stricken "at the first point where they can

---

[19]"Atlanta Rabbi Hits Bias Reign of Fear," *New York Post*, 11 Jan. 1957; Norman Shavin, "Jewish Editor Confirms Rabbi's Sermon on Threats," *National Jewish Post*, 11 January 1957—clippings in JMR MSS.

show themselves as guided by the principles of their faith" was incom-
prehensible. Jack said he did not know if what we needed was greater understanding of Judaism, greater faith in our government, or greater faith
in the decency of people, but he did know that "if our very physical well-
being is so tenuously preserved—then America has failed—and we,
somehow, have failed America."[20]

Shortly after that time he wrote an article on the subject for publication in the *CCAR Journal*. In it he said:

> One must understand that hysteria prevails, that there has been
> an abdication not alone of reasonableness, but of reason itself. . . .
> There is no freedom of thought or speech; government is rapidly be-
> coming government not by law but by men. . . .
>
> If white Christians are fearful, the Jew is panic-stricken. . . . He
> prefers to take on the protective coloration of his environment, to hide
> his head in the cotton patch in the dual hope that he won't be noticed
> and the problem will go away.[21]

One had only to read the daily newspapers to know how unreason-
able some Southerners had become. A White Citizens' Council in Alabama advocated that all music written or played by or in the idiom of
blacks be banned. A telephone company in Mississippi was ordered to
segregate all its party lines. In our own state of Georgia the attorney general recommended that it be made a crime *punishable by death* to aid a
federal officer in enforcing any law tending to break down segregation in
the South. And the president emeritus of the Georgia State College for
Women, a highly respected educator, was stripped of his title and told his
pension might be revoked because, as chairman of the Georgia Interracial
Committee—a group of equally respected and respectable persons—he
had appeared before civic clubs saying we needed "moderation and discussion" of compliance with the Supreme Court decision.[22]

The idea that Jack's outspokenness might bring harm to any of us
in Atlanta simply did not occur to me in those days, and if it occurred to

---

[20]Sermon, "Southern Reform Speaks," 26 January 1956, JMR MSS.

[21]Rothschild, "The Southern Rabbi Faces Desegregation," *CCAR Journal* (June
1956), copy in JMR MSS.

[22]Ibid.

him he never mentioned it to me. I was not so confident about his safety elsewhere in the South, however. When he was invited by the B'nai B'rith in Jackson, Mississippi, to speak there I begged him not to accept. I even cut out an article from the newspaper to show him. It reported that Mrs. Nat King Cole had persuaded her husband to cancel a concert commitment in that state because of fear for his safety. Jack's response? "I'm neither famous nor black, so forget it."

Not only did he go to Mississippi, he spoke there with the same frankness he exhibited elsewhere. He told his brothers in the Magnolia State:

> Injustice, inequity, inequality, the failure to achieve human rights anywhere challenge the basic principles of Judaism. . . . And we cannot evade or escape what it says. Even when we live in the South and are faced with a decision that has distressed and outraged large numbers of our fellow Southerners. . . .
>
> Unless we are willing to admit our status as second class citizens—a fact which I, for one, deny—then we have the need, the right, and the responsibility to state what our religion says about the problem. . . . There is no uniquely Jewish point of view. But there is a religious point of view . . . and we look to similarly motivated men of all religions by whose side we can stand.[23]

Fortunately, he returned to Georgia without tar or feathers.

The dam broke in late August 1957. At Central High School in Little Rock, Arkansas, the first Deep South city ordered by the Court to desegregate its public schools, United States soldiers stood guard to protect the right of six black teenagers to study there. Violence ensued, and national television delivered it to our living rooms. It happened as Jack was putting the finishing touches on his sermons for the High Holydays—and became the first in a sad series of similar events relating to the opening of the school season, thereby coinciding with the Jewish Holydays, the Days of Awe. Although hardly a redeeming feature, it must have served other rabbis as well as Jack with superb material for their sermons on the Sabbath of Repentance and the Day of Atonement, and it

---

[23]Address to B'nai B'rith, Jackson, Mississippi, "Judaism—A Living Faith," 29 April 1956, JMR MSS.

gave all of us cause to appreciate the wisdom of our ancestors in having ordained an annual time for reflection.

Jack had long deplored the inaction of President Dwight D. Eisenhower in regard to the trouble brewing in Southern cities. He believed that strong words delivered in time from Washington could avert the confrontation that loomed ahead. Once it occurred, however, and federal law had been flouted by a local government, the federal government would be compelled to use any means available to enforce the law. Therefore, though he was horrified by the broadcasts of American troops policing an area of one of our own cities while grown men and women threw rocks at children, he applauded the president for using government muscle when he did.

He began his Shabbat Shuvah sermon that year by observing that the times demanded such self-appraisal as had never been needed before. We were faced with a course of events, he said, so dangerous that it threatened the very foundations of American life—events constituting an issue deeper even than that of integration:

> It has become a question of law or force as the controlling power of authority in America. . . . Unless there is an abrupt about-face on the part of both leadership and followers here in our South we are going to have to live through a period of violence and riots fostered by a surly, stubborn, deeply rooted opposition to change in our racial structure.

The struggle in Little Rock, he added, was "but a foretaste of the struggle everywhere if we do nothing to halt its spread."[24]

On Yom Kippur he opened his sermon with a discussion of two international abrogations of human rights, far distant in concept and emotional impact from that of school integration at home. They were the nuclear arms race and the Dharan Agreement, a recently signed treaty between the United States and Saudi Arabia in which the Saudis permitted the United States to maintain an air base in their country as long as army chaplains did not wear their insignia in public or hold public worship services, and as long as Jewish personnel were banned. Jack saw the

---

[24]Sermon, "The Shame of Little Rock," 27 September 1957, JMR MSS.

agreement as a short-sighted, morally indefensible, and "unbelievable act of disloyalty to the traditions of American democracy."[25]

Often he had referred to the popular slogan "states' rights" as "a specious cry," because the doctrine of interposition it espoused had long been ruled unconstitutional. Now he mentioned the phrase again, in connection with another righteous-sounding cliché recently used even by the president: "You can't legislate the hearts of men." Jack admitted that the latter sounded plausible on the surface but declared it to be "as specious a statement as ever beguiled the soul" because, "every moral advance in the history of the human race was made possible because enlightened men saw the vision of a nobler law. Laws do not wait for general acceptance. They stimulate and coerce."[26]

In conclusion, he said he could not believe that persons, even in the South, could hold their customs dearer than the unity of the nation and that he still was convinced of the good in most people. He then drew a heart-wrenching picture of the enormous burden being borne by the valiant young boys and girls who stood in the front line of the battle:

> It amazes me that America—which so readily takes to its heart the courageous and the brave—has so little appreciation of these children. . . . You have little ones of your own. Could you find it in your hearts to ask them to do what these Negro citizens have required of their children? Even if you demanded it of them, could they have found the inner strength to do it? Just think of it: tots of six years, scrubbed to a shining brightness, off to school for the first time in their lives. This is the day to which they—as every child—have looked forward with gleeful joy. But to attend that school, they must run the gauntlet of adults—not of children, of adults—seething with fury. They must walk sedately through the mob, deaf to jibes, blind to brandished fists, enter the school, take their seats in class. Once there, open hostility waits for them. Children do not hate—but they quickly learn to imitate their elders. And children can be cruel. The pointed finger of scorn, the suppressed giggle, the deliberate snub, the outright blow—all these must be endured. Until at last the day is ended; the menacing lines of grown-up hoodlums are crossed; they are home and safe at last. But only for a passing moment. Another

---

[25]Sermon, "The Challenges of Adversity," 5 October 1957, JMR MSS.

[26]Ibid.

day dawns. School bells ring. And off they go again. Less eager now, hurt, bewildered and fearful, but no less bravely, they walk the familiar gauntlet and take their places in that alien classroom. How much of human dignity can we witness without a show of sympathy? How much human courage can we see without a strengthening of our own will, without a tightened resolve to offer comfort and hope? "To make Thy name known to Thine adversaries"—this is the challenge of man. We have been privileged to watch Isaiah's words brought to life, brought to life by children, Negro children. God grant that we have the strength and the wisdom to join the fight.[27]

The travail of Little Rock did impel some progress in Atlanta. Within weeks, eighty members of the Atlanta Christian Council found the courage to sign a statement setting forth the Christian position on the issue of race relations. In it they specified six points upon which Christianity had spoken indisputably. These points were: freedom of speech, obedience to the law, preservation of public schools, racial "amity" as exemplified in the golden rule, maintenance of communication between the races, and the guidance of prayer. The list was preceded by a carefully worded disclaimer in which the ministers declared that they spoke for themselves and not for any church or other group. Still, only eighty out of many hundreds of ministers who belonged to the association dared to sign it— telling evidence of how potentially inflammatory it seemed at the time.[28]

Jack, although he had long advocated that such a statement be issued and had even helped formulate it, was not among the eighty who signed. His reason is obvious when one reads the text. He knew, as did they, that in order for the text to be effective it had to be couched in the most Christological of terms, language that would make it impossible for a self-respecting Jew to embrace the statement. The ministers offered to tone it down to a point that Jack could accept, but he preferred that they keep it as it was, a strong appeal to the broadest Christian following. He

---

[27]Ibid.

[28]"Text of Ministers' Racial Statement," *Atlanta Journal and Constitution*, 3 Nov. 1957, copy in JMR MSS.

honored them that week in a sermon entitled "The Eighty Who Dared."[29]

The statement came to be known as the Ministers' Manifesto, and it made the first crack in the wall of silence that surrounded those Atlantans hoping for progress. The first such opinion to be publicly voiced by any major group in the city, it is generally regarded as the turning point in what became the victorious, twentieth-century Battle of Atlanta.

The Atlanta newspapers, after publishing the manifesto, ran a feature series in which various clergymen were invited to proffer their views as guest columnists. The one Jack wrote received a banner caption, running the width of the page in bold print. "Moses, Prophets, Jesus Fought to Erase Inequality." It somehow found its way to the desk of Congressman Abraham J. Multer, Democrat of New York, and thence into the *Congressional Record.*[30]

The winter of 1958 came and went with no lessening of frustration for those seeking social justice. President Eisenhower suffered a stroke, which fortunately did not leave him seriously impaired. Jack, while wishing sincerely for the president's good health, noted that his absence from the Oval Office had not visibly changed the quality of leadership coming from Washington, which he viewed as lacking in much-needed forcefulness.

In February of that year Jack doubled his normal dose of "Brotherhood," occupying two Friday evening sermons rather than the usual one with the subject of good will. Noting bitterly that the very word itself had come to imply a subversive doctrine, he warned that the present intransigent attitude posed a greater threat even than the threat of closed schools or economic disaster. Its danger, he said, was in "what it is doing to us, to our hearts and minds, our ideals and goals." Again he admonished us not to debase Judaism by expecting it to support our "lesser aims and more comfortable beliefs."[31]

---

[29]Sermon, "Eighty Who Dared—A Salute to My Christian Colleagues," 8 November 1957, JMR MSS.

[30]"Rabbi Rothschild Speaks. Moses, Prophets, Jesus Fought to Erase Inequality," *Atlanta Journal and Constitution,* 17 Nov. 1957, copy in JMR MSS.

[31]Sermon, "Indians on the Warpath Again," 7 February 1958; Sermon, "Good Will Toward Whom?" 13 February 1958—JMR MSS.

By the end of May he had become so discouraged that he preached a sermon entitled "Can This Be America?" In it he referred to the recent wave of terrorism that had resulted in the desecration of synagogues and Jewish community centers in Miami, Charlotte, Nashville, and Jacksonville, pointing out that there was no pattern of cause connecting the attacks with each other. They had occurred in some cases in cities where no Jewish person had spoken out, yet in Nashville, where one of the rabbis had done so, it was not his synagogue but another that was bombed. From these facts he concluded, "hate is hate—and violence is directed against all minorities when it becomes possible and fashionable to use it."[32]

He bitterly criticized United States Attorney General William P. Rogers for upholding the contention of FBI Director J. Edgar Hoover that no federal jurisdiction had been violated in the bombings (therefore the FBI could not be involved), and urged support of the bill then pending in Congress that would make it a federal offense to transport dynamite from one state to another or to possess it for illegal purpose. He also repeated his reminder that the problem was not a specifically Jewish one.

> We are the immediate victims—but no one is safe. . . . Maybe these events will shock some sense into both our leaders and the rank and file of Southerners. . . . They have demonstrated a growing concern wherever bombs have exploded. We pray that they may also see their own guilt in setting off the explosions.[33]

Earlier in the sermon Jack had observed that most people chose to ignore the subject of race relations, presumably believing that "if we talk about it we'll be bombed, too." In the conclusion he asked, "What of our own city?" and said, "I am encouraged to think that our mayor and law enforcement officers will never be themselves a party to creating the atmosphere that makes possible such acts. . . . We must resolve not to surrender to violence. Or submit to intimidation."[34]

A few nights before he delivered that sermon something happened that might have been a warning of things to come. A man carrying an

---

[32]Sermon, "Can This Be America?" 9 May 1958, JMR MSS.

[33]Ibid.

[34]Ibid.

anti-Semitic placard picketed the First Baptist Church on Peachtree
Street at Fifth when Jack was scheduled to speak there. Church officials,
noticing the man walking back and forth on the Peachtree side and unable
to make him leave, quickly stationed themselves in the parking lot in order to meet Jack as soon as he arrived and whisk him in by a side door so
he wouldn't see what was going on in front. They told him about it afterward because the same man came into the church and heckled during
the question-and-answer session following the talk. Deeply embarrassed,
they apologized profusely for the usher's having admitted him to the
church, and assured Jack that he was not a member of their congregation.
They had no idea who he was.

It didn't seem very important at the time. When Jack came home
he told me about it and we had a good laugh over his being important
enough to inspire picketing.

Earlier that spring Jack had received a letter from another rabbi in
the South, a dear friend for whom he had great admiration and affection.
The other rabbi criticized statements coming from what he called "the
nice, safe Union headquarters in New York." He said, too, that he hated
to see a colleague "martyrizing himself" because, as he expressed it,
"dammit all, I am involved—his congregation is involved. All Jews in the
South are involved." He continued with a plea to Jack, "as a bright and
intelligent young leader of the colleagues . . . to lead the red-hot boys to
be a little more prudent and cautious."[35]

Jack liked this man very much. Furthermore, he realized that many
of his colleagues in the South were in positions far different from his, in
cities and in congregations where actions such as he took in Atlanta would
have been not only dangerous, but foolhardy and useless, perhaps even
counterproductive. He did not expect them to do as he did, but neither
could he let them stop him. He answered his friend with patience, care,
and compassion, but not without the underlying anger and frustration he
felt in reaction to all Jews in the South who shared his friend's view.

In his reply Jack acknowledged the special risk imposed by anti-
Semitism, but noted that we Jews had come to expect others to risk their
lives for us simply because it was right, and asked how, therefore, we
could expect any less of ourselves:

---

[35]Rabbi Norman Goldburg to JMR, March 1958, JMR MSS.

How can we condemn the millions who stood by under Hitler or honor those few who chose to live by their ideals . . . when we refuse to make a similar choice now that the dilemma is our own? That attitude . . . smacks almost of being indecent. . . . When you—and many others in the South—seek to silence those who would speak out, then you really do more than just remove yourselves from the battle. You also seek to deny the right of those who want to act with courage to do so.[36]

He then told his friend that, in his opinion, the concerted silence of every Jew, North or South, would have not the slightest effect upon the security of Jews in the South because "the lunatic fringe doesn't really care who it bombs." If we did not do something about the situation soon, he said, it would lead to the collapse of our constitutional government.[37]

Finally, on a personal note, he wrote his friend that he thought he had been circumspect in his treatment of the matter, but that, in any case, he would not desist from his present course. He continued, "If this is dangerous, then I shall have to live dangerously. Because, I firmly believe, that this is my responsibility as a rabbi. And even if I weren't a rabbi, it would be my responsibility as a human being. . . . Don't think that I like endangering the security of our institutions—and even my family—God forbid. But I'm here, and life requires it—and so be it."[38]

The summer passed without incident, and the school season opened without any major debacle to demand comment from rabbis in the course of their High Holyday sermons. At The Temple in Atlanta there were more pressing matters to be brought before the congregation as it greeted the Jewish New Year. A building campaign was about to begin. Consequently, Jack saw as his prime responsibility the need to instill his members with enthusiasm for the future of their institution.

To relieve its long over-crowded schoolrooms and other facilities, the board had taken action to purchase adjacent property for a parking lot and expand the existing building over the present parking area. Such expansion would require much money. In order to raise the needed funds,

---

[36]JMR to Rabbi Norman Goldburg, 27 March 1958, JMR MSS.

[37]Ibid.

[38]Ibid.

professionals had been engaged and were expected to arrive in Atlanta to begin their work immediately after the Holydays.

During that Holyday period Jack channeled all his powers of persuasion into convincing his listeners of how important The Temple was to them in their everyday lives. He mentioned civil rights only once, briefly, with fewer than 600 words out of a sermon that totalled more than 3,600. Little as that was, there would always be some who believed it had been too much.[39]

---

[39]Sermon, "Our Gift to the World," 24 September 1958, JMR MSS.

CHAPTER FOUR

THE BOMB
THAT HEALED

We were awakened by the jangle of the telephone on that Sunday morning, 12 October 1958. It was not quite 7:30 A.M. Jack had been sleeping soundly, exhausted after returning the night before from a speaking engagement in St. Paul. Always able to shake off sleep more quickly than I, however, he scurried around to my side of the bed to answer.

I heard him groan, a long, horrified "Oh, no!" Then, in fast staccato, "I'll be right there. You'd better call Mrs. Shurgin." With that, he hung up and told me. "The Temple's been bombed."

It had been Robert Benton, longtime custodian, weeping as he spoke. He had discovered the damage when he arrived to open the building and ready it for religious school. Apparently an explosive had been placed against the rear door on the north side of the building, detonating inward. Everything in its path had been blown to bits, upstairs as well as downstairs. He had already called Eloise Shurgin, The Temple administrator, before he called us.

Jack was dressing as he spoke. I was sitting straight up in the bed, no longer groggy from sleep but disoriented from what I was hearing. I watched as he grabbed a slightly used sport shirt from a hook in the closet and heard myself say, "Wear a coat and tie. There may be reporters."

It was completely irrational, for I had never told him what to wear and doubted that he would have listened if I had. Actually, I had been thinking about how fortunate we were that, if it had to happen, it happened when it did, when no one was in the building. A little later there would have been hundreds of people inside—most of them children—including our two children and Jack.

"Don't be ridiculous!" I heard him shout as he dashed into the bathroom and turned on his electric shaver. "This is an emergency, not a fashion show!" I said no more, but when he came back into the room he threw off the sport shirt and put on a dress shirt and tie.

As he dashed down the hall, jacket in hand, I followed him asking what I could do to help. He told me to stay home and answer the telephone. It would be useful to have a message center away from the hubbub of The Temple itself. At the moment it was vital to call quickly as many families as possible to tell them not to bring their children to religious school. After that he wanted me to notify a friend of ours who was scheduled to be married in his study later that morning. "Tell her I'll call her myself as soon as I arrange some other place to hold the ceremony."

I came back into the house and began making the calls. Marcia and Bill, awakened by our shouting, came out to see what all the noise was about. Since I seemed to be preoccupied with telephone calls, they fixed their own breakfast and ate it, gleaning the news from my conversations with others. Once I realized they were there I could see they were becoming upset and needed some attention. I tried to reassure them, explaining that no one had been hurt. Then, remembering that work is the best antidote for fear, I suggested that they help me by bicycling, each in a different direction, to tell Temple families who lived in our neighborhood. That job satisfied them and also amused some of our friends who could enjoy the sight in spite of the situation. One of them told me she had answered her doorbell at about 8:30 that morning, looked down, "And there was Paul Revere—on his bicycle!"

Even with Jack's sense of humor there would be no laughter in what he and the others saw when they arrived at The Temple that day. He described it for us:

> A gaping hole, sixteen feet wide, where once a columned entrance had stood. Crumbled walls, broken pillars, shattered glass everywhere. A jagged piece of wood ripped from somewhere and imbedded in a solid wall by the force of the explosion, a sagging stairway, a hanging ceiling—the whole made colorful by shiny bits of brilliantly colored glass that had once been the beautiful stained-glass windows of the sanctuary. And over all, tons of water from a broken main in which swam the sodden remains of bright blue choir robes that children wore—and books that children read. Crushed and broken menorahs—symbols of yet another age in which a Temple had been rededicated.[1]

It was typical of him that even then he thought not of the parallel to the *destruction* of the Temple in the time of the Maccabees, but of their *rededication* of it.

The sanctuary sustained only slight damage: broken windows and splintering around the door near where the blast had occurred. A heavy steel vault in the closet of the anteroom to Jack's study had shielded the vast hall as well as the study and the anteroom, which served as an office for Eloise. She and her husband, Abe Shurgin, were already there when Jack arrived. So was another member of The Temple, Capt. Fred Beerman, assistant chief of police.

It wasn't long before a small crowd gathered, leaders of the congregation, reporters and cameramen, police, assorted friends and sympathizers. Police hastened to block off the area and keep curious onlookers at a distance. Not even Jack, recalling the emotion of that moment, could express it adequately. He wrote, "A consummate artist might be able to describe what we felt, sketching in a few sharp lines the fear, the deep concern, the growing unbelief mirrored in the drawn faces, the slumped

---

[1]Address, "Violence and Its Aftermath" (first delivered in Cleveland, Ohio, 11 January 1959), JMR MSS.

shoulders, the bowed heads of men and women face to face with the reality of so unreal and incredible an act. . . . For a bombing is something to read about. It happens somewhere else." Even when it happens to you, it seems as if it has happened somewhere else.[2]

The police estimated the damage at two hundred thousand dollars and the amount of dynamite used at forty sticks. They also said that headquarters had received a call at 3:37 A.M. that day from someone in the vicinity of The Temple reporting a "loud explosion." Others later reported having windows broken and even being knocked out of bed by the force of the blast. Headquarters had dispatched a patrol to investigate but after driving up and down that area of Peachtree Street the patrol officers reported that they found nothing amiss. Because The Temple is situated on a high knoll and the blast occurred toward its rear, no damage was visible from the street. Apparently, the police did not drive around to the back of any of the buildings.

The news spread quickly. Mayor William B. Hartsfield heard it on his radio while he was en route to church and redirected his driver to take him to The Temple. His instant, impromptu reaction to what he saw there, broadcast and quoted widely by the media, set the tone for what was to be an unprecedented, overwhelming show of support from all segments of the general community. Outraged that such a thing could happen in *his* city, Hartsfield said, "Whether they like it or not, every political rabble-rouser is the godfather of these cross-burners and dynamiters who sneak about in the dark and give a bad name to the South. It is high time the decent people of the South rise up and take charge if governmental chaos is to be avoided."[3]

This off-the-cuff fury injected spiritual penicillin into a soul-stricken citizenry. Equally important, it reassured those Jews who had experienced the horror of the Leo Frank case and the events it triggered that this incident would not cause another such wave of anti-Semitism. It was clear that in 1958 it would not be necessary, as it had been in 1915, for Jewish merchants to board up their storefronts or send their wives and

---

[2]Ibid.

[3]Hartsfield quoted in "Jewish Temple on Peachtree Rocked by Blast," *Atlanta Constitution*, 13 Oct. 1958; and in "Rabble Rousers Share the Blame," *Atlanta Constitution*, 13 Oct. 1958. Copies in JMR MSS.

children to visit out-of-town relatives. This time we were regarded not as pariahs, but as heroes.

That morning, in churches throughout the city, preachers angrily denounced the crime and railed against those who had contributed to it. Politicians hastened to be seen and heard making similar pronouncements. Reporters and editors ran to their typewriters to do likewise. The *Atlanta Constitution* published two particularly powerful pieces on the subject, one of them a poignant description by Editor Eugene Patterson, who had spoken at The Temple the preceding Friday night when Jack was in Minnesota. And Publisher Ralph McGill, whose daily column appeared on the paper's front page, won a Pulitzer Prize for what he wrote that day. To Bible Belt Southerners, finally cognizant that such an act had occurred, the desecration of a house of worship was an abomination. That its members were Jewish made no difference. That they were well known and white probably did.[4]

Offers of help came from all sides. Contributions began to pour in despite repeated announcements that the damage was fully covered by insurance. Temple officials broadcast their appreciation and suggested that the money be designated instead for the reward fund that Mayor Hartsfield had initiated on behalf of the city, to be given to anyone helping apprehend and convict the guilty parties. His initial pledge of one thousand dollars grew to more than eight thousand dollars before the end of the day, and exceeded twenty thousand dollars by the time the suspects were indicted five days later.

The bombing became national news when President Eisenhower, arriving to address a largely Jewish gathering in New York City, learned of it later in the morning. He expressed his shock and sympathy, and personally directed J. Edgar Hoover to engage the FBI in helping the Atlanta police. By mid-afternoon the news was being broadcast overseas.[5]

At home, our telephone began ringing in mid-morning and didn't stop all day. No sooner had I hung up from one conversation than it would ring again. I couldn't leave it even long enough to pour a cup of coffee.

---

[4]Editorial, *Atlanta Constitution*, 13 Oct. 1958; Ralph McGill, "A Church, A School," *Atlanta Constitution*, 13 Oct. 1958, p. 1A—copies in JMR MSS.

[5]Statement by Pres. Dwight D. Eisenhower, *Atlanta Constitution*, *Atlanta Journal*, 13 Oct. 1958. Copies in JMR MSS.

One of the calls came from a friend who said she would pick up Bill to spend the day with her son. Another was from Julie Weiss, whose husband, Bud, was then president of the Atlanta Jewish Community Council and a vice-president of The Temple. He was with Jack and undoubtedly would remain so for the rest of the day. She said she would come with her seven-year-old son Mike to spend the day with me, keeping me company and helping with the telephone calls. Marcia, having reached her grandmother's house earlier on her bicycle mission, had decided to stay there for the morning and was scheduled to attend a class at the Jewish Community Center that afternoon. It never occurred to me not to take her there.

Jack's primary concern was to prevent hysteria. He and William B. Schwartz, Jr., president of the congregation, too busy to be aware yet of the huge outpouring of support they were receiving, quickly composed a public statement designed as much to calm as to inform. It said, in part:

> We are shocked and sick at heart at the wanton damage to our House of Worship. We thank God that the explosion took place before our children and teachers arrived for Sunday School this morning.
>   . . . We feel certain that the entire community joins us in the condemnation of this despicable and outrageous act which damaged our Temple, but is in fact directed against the total community. We are confident that the law enforcement officials of our city are doing and will continue to do all in their power to apprehend those responsible for this criminal attack upon the religious and democratic foundations of our country.[6]

Schools, churches, and a host of other institutions offered the use of their buildings while ours was being repaired. Most appropriately, the congregation chose to accept the offer of E. Rivers Elementary School, which had used The Temple during its own rebuilding ten years before, and hold religious school there on Sundays. All other activities, as well as administrative offices, were transferred to the Jewish Community Center, conveniently located just a block away. Worship services continued to be held in the sanctuary without interruption. In order to assure everyone that services would be held, Jack decided on the title for his forthcoming

---

[6]Statement, William B. Schwartz, Jr., and JMR, 12 October 1958, JMR MSS.

sermon that very afternoon and had it placed on the bulletin board at the foot of the hill in time for passersby to see it on their way to work Monday morning. His title: "And None Shall Make Them Afraid."[7]

By mid-afternoon Eloise, with the help of Shimon Gottschalk, our newly engaged educational director, and a number of devoted volunteers from the sisterhood, was able to set up her temporary office in the Jewish Community Center, salvaging as much as possible and making do without the rest. Among the papers irretrievably lost were all the carefully prepared records pertaining to the building campaign. The professional fund raisers, having arrived in Atlanta just the day before, had been given temporary office space in precisely the area where the bomb had been set. They were later heard to quip that it was the first time in their professional careers that a campaign had started off with such a bang.

Still in shock, most of us functioned automatically. Both Jack and I, unaware of how the other was responding, reacted with compulsive attention to small details—in my case, unnecessary ones. Not only did I take time out to drive Marcia to her class at the Center (without going the extra block to visit The Temple, because Jack had told me not to). I also tracked down two people with whom I had appointments the following day to tell them I'd have to cancel—and assured one of them that sandwiches I had offered to bring to a reception that night were in our carport freezer if someone else wanted to pick them up. In retrospect it did seem absurd.

Toward evening Julie and I grew hungry. With me still on the telephone, she found some leftover spaghetti in the refrigerator and heated it up, handing me a plate where I sat and arranging herself and the two children at the table a few feet away. Except for driving Marcia to the Center I had not left that corner of our porchlike family room all day. By that time I was tired and numb, hardly aware of what I was saying to the friends and strangers who kept calling from all parts of the country to offer sympathy. When a call came in that was different from the rest I heard myself say "Thank you very much," the same as I had been saying to others. I must have looked stunned, though, for Julie asked me what the caller had said and I, still in a trance, told her word for word, in front of the children, "He said he was one of 'them' that bombed our church,

---

[7]Sermon, "And None Shall Make Them Afraid," 17 October 1958, JMR MSS.

and he was calling to tell me there's a bomb under our house now and it's lit. He said we have five minutes to get out and save our lives."

When I came to my senses I was standing in the doorway, purse and car keys in hand, irrationally wondering whether or not to go back inside to save some priceless heirloom, and, if so, which one. Julie, five months pregnant, had scaled the retaining wall behind our garden and was standing in the woods beyond, holding onto the two children and yelling at me to get out of the house. The dogs were there too, barking in accompaniment to her pleas.

I joined them and went with them to our next-door neighbor's house, which was situated at the top of the hill far behind ours. We notified Jack and Bud, and the police, and then tried to settle down and regain our equanimity. It wasn't easy. Our neighbor, who had been drinking heavily, yelled that he wasn't going "to let those sons-of-bitches run you out of your house" and strode toward our house, permitting his own young son to accompany him. That was the straw that broke the camel's back for Marcia, and she began to cry hysterically. I called my mother to come over, hoping she could take both children to her house until the crisis was over. I also called the friend at whose house Bill had been spending the day and asked her to keep him overnight and not to let him hear the news on television or read the morning paper. I preferred to tell him about it myself when I picked him up for school.

Jack, Bud, the police, and FBI agents arrived shortly. Bill Schwartz came, too, but stayed only a moment because his own home had just received the same type of call. All of us realized the calls were probably hoaxes, but we were shaken nonetheless. And tired. Very, very tired.

While one team of agents checked the premises for a bomb, another questioned me about the call. I repeated what I had heard, describing the caller's voice as male, not very well educated, probably from middle Georgia. When my questioner seemed puzzled at my ability to give such detail, Jack explained that I was a theater buff, having studied drama in college, and that I enjoyed trying to identify regional accents. The officer seemed even more startled at his explanation but continued with his investigation. When it was finally determined that we were safe, the crew departed, leaving two officers in a patrol car in our driveway to guard us through the night.

Then we realized how hungry we were. Jack and Bud had not eaten all day. Mother suggested that she take Marcia and Mike to her house so the four of us could go out for a quiet supper alone. The problem was, as it had been since she arrived, that Marcia refused to go. Still crying hysterically, she was afraid to let us out of her sight.

Jack tried to reassure her. "It's all right," he said. "Nothing's going to happen to us. We'll be right back as soon as we get something to eat."

No deal. She kept right on crying.

I tried next. "Honey," I said, "we want you to go to Granny's so you'll get some sleep tonight. You have school in the morning."

Still no deal. This time I crouched down to meet her eyeball to eyeball, and in my very best, most expressive "childrenese" began to stress the likelihood that the telephone would keep us awake all night. "People from all over the country are concerned about what happened to us. Why, President Eisenhower even interrupted his speech today to say what a terrible thing it was."

That got her attention. The weeping stopped as she looked up and said matter-of-factly, "If he had interrupted his golf game, it really would have been something."

We laughed so hard that even she had to join in. Then she agreed to go—not to my mother's but to our next-door neighbor's—to spend the night where she could keep an eye on our house, just in case.

It was almost ten o'clock when we left the house, but our favorite hamburger place was still open and crowded. I remember looking around at the people sitting at the other tables as we waited for our food, wondering if any one of them had been the person who had called, or who had bombed The Temple, or if any of them hated us enough to contemplate such actions. I realized that I was being melodramatic in even entertaining such thoughts, but they persisted. Jack and the Weisses were so quiet that I suspected that they were having similar thoughts.

The day was not over for us when we returned home. We had telegrams to accept, calls to return, and Jack's mother in Pittsburgh to reassure that we were safe and well—in case she had seen the television coverage concerning the bomb threat to our house. We sat at the telephone in the family room, where I had spent most of the day, opposite the jalousied door that led out onto our driveway. Later that evening we looked up to see a frightening apparition at the glass door: a stranger in jeans and a plaid shirt, carrying a rifle, standing there staring at us.

The man quickly realized our distress and introduced himself. He was a police officer who, because of his expertise, had been called back from his vacation especially to protect us. He had come directly from hunting camp in the North Georgia woods, without taking time to go home and change into uniform.

We relaxed, offered him a cup of coffee, and continued making our calls. It was well past midnight when we finished, but we still needed to unwind. That was the only time I ever remember Jack taking a drink for other than a purely social purpose. He poured a Scotch for himself, a bourbon for me, and we sipped them quietly as we tried to put our minds in order.

The whiskey had helped but we were still left with a long, unwelcome stretch of time in which to think before we slept. I lay there wondering if we would ever wake again, if someone would bomb us while we slept, if soldiers in a battle zone had similar thoughts each night as they tried to sleep, if Jack had had such thoughts when he served on Guadalcanal. . . . I didn't ask him, of course. I hoped he was comfortably asleep.

The telephone jarred us awake an hour later. I grabbed it, hoping to keep it from disturbing him. The call was from New York. It was a reporter asking to speak to the rabbi. I whispered that the rabbi had just fallen asleep and I preferred not to wake him. That was too polite. The caller insisted.

I held my ground, still whispering. I explained that the rabbi had had a very trying day and needed his sleep. It did no good. My adversary claimed that his paper was holding its presses for him. He had to get a story for the early edition.

By that time Jack realized he would do well to get it over with as soon as possible. Reaching across me for the receiver, he said, "This is Rabbi Rothschild. What can I do for you?"

From the other end of the line came the question, "Was that Mrs. Rothschild I was talking to?" Now thoroughly alert and appalled, Jack replied, "If it wasn't Mrs. Rothschild, do you really think I'd tell *you?*"

We slept soundly for a few hours, then started early on our separate Monday duties. I picked up Bill, delivered both children to school, and left word with each of their teachers where I could be reached in case either of them needed me during the day. Our housekeeper, Johnnie Mae Beaseley, was off on Mondays; there would be no one at home to answer the telephone while I was at the sisterhood meeting being held later in the morning. There had been no question of canceling either the board meeting or the luncheon program that was to follow, so determined was

Jack to continue with everything as planned. Only the place of meeting was changed—to the Jewish Community Center.

The sisterhood drew a far larger crowd than usual, due at least in part to interest in the scheduled speaker and in the subject he planned to discuss. He was Nahum Astar, consul of Israel for the Southeastern United States. As it happened, he had served as a demolition expert for the army long before he entered the foreign service. He had been one of the first to arrive at The Temple when he heard about the bombing, and had correctly assessed the size of the explosive well in advance of the police. By Monday noon he was so wrapped up in our situation in Atlanta that he almost forgot to talk about Israel.

Jack managed to free himself from other duties long enough to come to the sisterhood meeting, greet everyone, and give us an update on plans for the rest of the week. The children's choir and recently instituted Hebrew classes would meet as usual the following afternoon—at the Center. People were asked to stay away from The Temple itself because it was considered unsafe, although several of the women came each day to help salvage as much as possible from the waterlogged rubble of the social hall and sisterhood gift shop, the latter newly stocked with gifts for Hanukkah. After the meeting friends came home with me, hoping to help, actually to commiserate, which also helped. Between the phone calls and the neighbors coming to offer their support, we managed to enjoy some humorous anecdotes of the day before.

Reporters, photographers, police and FBI agents, and other officials continued to distract Jack from the ever-mounting business of the congregation and his personal correspondence. During one of the many interviews he granted, a reporter asked him how old his children were, causing Jack suddenly to remember that the day was 13 October: Marcia's birthday. He had forgotten to congratulate her. (So had I, although we had celebrated the event with a party the previous Saturday.) The reporter wrote of Jack's remorse in the evening paper, which resulted in our eleven-year-old daughter receiving good wishes and even flowers from total strangers. It was very exciting but did little to relieve the trauma of the previous day.

Jack continued to treat his own pressures by making jokes. When friends who had seen the television coverage of the previous evening's events called to offer sympathy, and asked, "Is Janice upset?" he told them, "She sure is. She's upset with me because she's been telling me all

summer that the downspouts on the front of our house needed painting
and I neglected to have it done. Now, she says, the whole world can see
how bad they look."

The next day, when someone reported that the temple in Peoria, Illinois, had been bombed and asked Jack if he had any message for his colleague there, his first reaction was to say, "Welcome to the club!"
Fortunately, he caught himself in time to plead, "Don't print that!" and
compose a more fitting statement for publication.

We had another laugh when we received a clipping from one of the
New York area papers—one with a heavily Orthodox Jewish readership.
It was a picture that had become familiar from frequent use—the image
of Jack with Hartsfield crouching to examine the debris of the bombing
on Sunday morning. In that paper the caption read, "Mayor Hartsfield
and the Hatless Rabbi." I couldn't resist reminding him that if it hadn't
been for my "ridiculous" fashion advice, the rabbi would have really
looked disreputable, not only hatless but coatless and tieless as well.[8]

In all the excitement we hadn't stopped to consider that Johnnie Mae
Beaseley, the young country girl who lived in and worked for us during
the week but went back to her parents on her days off, might be afraid to
return to work on Tuesday after all the publicity we had received. She
showed up, but not without an argument from her parents and a subsequent promise to them that she wouldn't stay alone in our house at night
with the children for the time being. Her promise to them meant that
either Jack or I would have to change our plans for the following evening.
Jack had a crucial meeting of the building-fund committee and both of
us served on our children's PTA board, which was meeting the same
night. Normally, attending a PTA meeting would not have been vitally
important to either of us, but in this case it was because of Jack's determination to carry on as usual. He transferred the building-fund committee meeting to our house so he could stay home and let me represent us
at the PTA.

We began to hear stories about Jewish children, some even in other
cities, who were having nightmares about the bombing. Unnerved, I went

---

[8]Photograph, with cutline, "Above, Atlanta Mayor William Hartsfield and hatless
Rabbi Rothschild," a Long Island newspaper, ca. 20, 21 Oct. 1958. Photograph accom-
panies news story: Bernie Bookbinder, "The South: A New Marketplace for Hatemongers." Copy in JMR MSS.

to speak with a child psychiatrist whom we knew socially and who knew our children, to ask for guidance in handling our own problem. After listening patiently to my account, complete with anecdotes and quips, he assured me that we were on the right track, except for one major point. The round-the-clock police patrol that had been stationed in our driveway since Sunday night had to go, and as soon as possible. "But won't the children be in danger?" I asked.

"That I can't tell you," he said. "I'm not in a position to judge what might happen to them physically if you dismiss the guard, but I can sure tell you what will happen to them emotionally if you don't."

I notified Jack right away and he agreed to tell the police we wouldn't need them anymore, except for two nights the following week (and then only from 9:30 until daybreak, so Marcia and Bill wouldn't see them) when he was scheduled to be out of town. As it happened, that day Bill rode his bicycle to school and stopped by a friend's house on the way home without calling to tell me where he was. I was frantic. When he was only a few minutes late I was certain it had been an hour or more. I even dispatched the police guard, who had not yet received word to leave, to search the neighborhood and find him. Fortunately, Bill arrived, from the opposite direction, just as the patrolman returned to tell me he couldn't find him. My not-quite-ten-year-old son could not understand why I was so upset. He also didn't understand how we could be so "cruel" as to send away the police patrol. Having been spared all the fear and hysteria of Sunday night, he was thoroughly enjoying its consequences. He was delighted with the envy of his peers who wished that they, too, could have their own personal police officers stationed in their driveways.

The Temple office had to hire extra help to handle the mountain of mail that arrived each day. Hundreds of letters poured in, from all over the world, from people in all walks of life. Many contained contributions. They ranged in amount from large checks—the governor-elect of Georgia sent his for $250—to wadded, dirty one-dollar bills, stuffed into envelopes addressed in pencil, anonymously, in a barely legible childlike handwriting or print. School groups and churches, lodges and synagogues, some from as far away as California, took up collections for The Temple knowing that the money wasn't needed, simply in order to show their support. One such contribution came from a most unlikely source, the White Citizens' Council of Dallas County, Alabama. Jack, uncertain about the propriety of accepting something from that organization, passed it on to Mayor Hartsfield with the suggestion that he use it for the reward fund and thank the donors accordingly.

The many opinions and attitudes contained in the letters so fascinated Jack that later·in the year he based one of his sermons on the subject. His notes for the sermon had such subheadings as "pessimism," "latent and unsuspected prejudice," and "freethinkers." Some writers offered to help in practical ways. A stained-glass artist, for example, suggested that he would like to replace the windows, and a retired secretary—Gentile—volunteered her services for as long as they were needed. Hers was one offer the congregation accepted.[9]

Some of the most interesting letters that came to The Temple, especially when one read between the lines, were those from members of the black community. Without exception they were sympathetic, and some contained contributions, but they also reminded us bitterly that no such attention had been accorded black victims of such acts—and there had been hundreds throughout the South within the past few years. One of the letters, written not to Jack but to Ralph McGill, who forwarded it to Jack, came from the daughter of the slain NAACP director in Florida. She and her sister had been in the house when their parents were killed by a bomb thrown from a passing car.[10]

We were especially grateful for those personal friends sensitive enough to empathize with the stress we were under. One of Jack's rabbinical colleagues wrote that he and his wife "just keep thinking about the way this dreadful thing has disrupted your private life" and added that they felt "a gnawing indignation over what has been done to you and Janice and the kids." Another such friend, a woman whom Jack had seen in Cincinnati the preceding spring, misinterpreted the situation. She wrote, "I was thinking about your telling me when you were here last year that Atlanta is an oasis in the South. I suppose that you now feel the oasis isn't so green anymore." Unwavering in his love for the city, Jack replied, "Atlanta is still an oasis. . . . If you had any idea of the response which this violent act has elicited, you would agree with me in my estimate of last spring, which is still the correct one."[11]

---

[9]Sermon, "Letters That Cross My Desk," 23 January 1959, JMR MSS.

[10]Annie Moore to Ralph McGill, c.c. to The Temple, 14 October 1958, JMR MSS.

[11]Rabbi Samuel Silver to JMR, 14 October 1958; Janet Solinger to JMR, 13 October 1958; JMR to Janet Solinger, 27 October 1958—JMR MSS.

More than one correspondent referred to the well-known tendency of the Anti-Defamation League (ADL) to capitalize on situations such as ours. A most distinguished elder statesman among the rabbis wrote Jack that he hoped we were not "too much annoyed by the fact that national organizations will be using your pain for their publicity." We had no doubt at all as to which organization he meant. Another rabbi wrote more bluntly, naming the organization and asking if it were true, as its representatives were claiming, that the FBI and police would not have been able to apprehend the suspected bombers without its assistance. Jack did not save a copy of his response to that letter but I am reasonably sure that he would have confirmed the truth of the claim while deploring the context in which it was made, for however annoyed he was with the tactics of the ADL he always respected its results. He agreed with the older rabbi who had written farther down the page, "Their cause is good and you constitute an opportunity for them."[12]

At that time, however, Jack was very angry with the organization, especially with its regional office, and his anger was shared by many others in the Atlanta Jewish community. The Community Relations Committee, of which the regional director was a member, in order to avoid conflict and confusion had voted unanimously to channel all inquiries through The Temple rather than let individuals deal with them. But the regional director had instead appeared on television and permitted himself to be quoted frequently in the newspapers in regard to the bombing. Jack felt that he and his organization had been "completely merciless in their exploiting of the situation." For his own part, Jack avoided any act that might have been exploitative, even refusing the many tempting invitations to speak on the subject until months after the excitement had subsided.[13]

---

[12]Dr. Solomon B. Freehof to JMR, 14 November 1958; Rabbi Bernard D. Rosenberg to JMR, 6 November 1958; Freehof to JMR, 14 November 1958—JMR MSS.

[13]Pat Watters, "Blast at Atlanta Temple Blew Lid Off Brew of Hate," *Atlanta Journal,* 19 Oct. 1958; Pat Watters, "How to be a Hate Fanatic," *Atlanta Journal,* 21 Oct. 1958; Bernie Bookbinder, "The South: A New Marketplace for Hatemongers." Unidentified clipping, ca. 20, 21 Oct. 1958. See note 8 above; Pat Watters, "Who Are These of Unholy Rage Against a Faith," *Atlanta Journal,* 23 Oct. 1958; Pat Watters, "Temple Incident, Though Bad, Blew Some Good," *Atlanta Journal,* 27 Oct. 1958; John Pennington, "Bombers Now Play for Keeps, Levin Believes," *Atlanta Journal,* 14 Oct. 1958; Minutes, Atlanta Jewish Community Council, Community Relations Committee, 12 October 1958, p. 1, 26 October 1958, pp. 3-4—JMR MSS.

By midweek the police had made some arrests in the case. By the time Shabbat began on Friday five suspects had been indicted, to be held without bond and with the promise of an early trial. Jack had dictated replies, many of them individual, to the hundreds of letters he had received, he had prepared to leave town on Sunday for a meeting in New York, and had written one of the most powerful sermons of his career.

Even though all of us realized there would be extra protection for us at The Temple that Friday night we could not stamp out a tiny ember of fear that some further act of terror would take place. In spite of that fear, a huge crowd filled the sanctuary, gathering as a family might in time of trouble, each member giving strength and gaining it. Jack and I were amazed and thrilled to see so many people sitting in that damaged hall, with panes still missing from its windows and doors still askew on broken hinges.

He began his sermon by reciting the "Sh'hechianu," an unusual choice of prayer because it is customarily spoken in times of rejoicing, offering, as it does, thanks to the Almighty for "having sustained us and brought us to this time." Jack explained that it was appropriate because "truths that we and so many of our fellow Southerners had been reluctant or afraid to face" had now been brought into the open.[14]

He praised his listeners for having come out in such large numbers, especially in the face of danger. He said that blame for the bombing should not be laid entirely on those who had planned it, nor even on those whose "irresponsible pronouncements" might have encouraged the action. Blame, he said, belonged equally to those "good and decent people who choose to remain silent in such a time." Whereas the fear of violence had served to silence persons, this act of violence had "freed their tongues and loosed their hands for the work of righteousness." The "curtain of fear" had been lifted and decent people were at last convinced that there could be "no retreat from their ideals."[15]

The countless messages of support he had received, Jack said, were proof that the dynamiters "do not represent America." He called them "a cancer that should be cut out of the body politic and left to die." Then he reviewed the various factors that might have contributed to the bombing,

---

[14]Sermon, "And None Shall Make Them Afraid," 17 October 1958, JMR MSS.

[15]Ibid.

not neglecting his own outspokenness, which he knew many considered
the principal cause. He conceded,

> I would not—could not—have done otherwise. And I do not
> seek to exculpate myself when I tell you that I firmly believe that I
> cannot justly accept the blame—or the credit, as you will. Unhappily,
> ours is not the only Jewish House of Worship that has been damaged
> by the blast of dynamite. And there is neither rhyme nor reason to
> the site selected for destruction.[16]

He said that although our building had been the latest target for the
small, poisonous nest of neo-Nazis in Atlanta, they also hated blacks and
had simply taken advantage of the growing acceptance of lawlessness and
"aura of hatred" in the South to carry out a personal vendetta. They
failed, he declared, not only in their attack upon us, but by arousing the
conscience of the whole nation.[17]

Powerfully and prophetically, he concluded:

> Tonight, our shattered building stands as mute witness to the
> evil that lurks in the hearts of men ruled by hatred and dedicated to
> the destruction of our noblest dreams. Our answer to them speaks
> louder even than that monstrous blast that shook the silence of a
> peaceful night. The symbols of that answer stand untouched and
> strong in every house of God—as they are visible in this sanctuary
> which bears the scars of man's sad failure as a child of God.
>
> There is the Eternal Light. It shines forth once more and speaks
> its message of reassurance and of hope. God lives. He dwells in every
> human heart. If only man will seek to find Him there. And God lives
> eternally—even as this light is everlasting. So must our faith be eter-
> nal—it cannot be extinguished or dimmed—nor put to rout by the
> threats of witless men.
>
> In our Temple, that light hangs from the Great Seal of America.
> The ideals of democracy upon which our freedom rests have not been
> shaken by this blast any more than the walls of the building have been
> weakened by it. . . .
>
> And here, in the Ark of the Covenant, are the scrolls containing
> the moral law. . . . Proudly they bear witness to the law of God, to

---

[16]Ibid.

[17]Ibid.

the ideals towards which man is urged ceaselessly to strive—and which will yet become the pattern of his life on earth. . . .

This law still lives in our hearts, still guides our steps, still lifts us up to the vision of a world of brotherhood and peace. . . . It has reached the hearts of men everywhere and roused the conscience of a whole community.

We are grateful for their support and sustained by their devotion. With God's help we shall rebuild in pride and gratitude—and create a stronger Home of the Spirit where He may dwell in our midst. Together with an aroused humanity we shall rear from the rubble of devastation a city and a land in which all men are truly brothers—and *none shall make them afraid.*[18]

---

[18]Ibid.

CHAPTER • FIVE

ORDEAL
BY TRIAL

L ife returned to normal after that weekend. At least we thought so. Jack left for his meeting in New York, and I began studying the script of a play to open in January, soon to be cast at Theatre Atlanta—the community drama organization to which I belonged. The following Friday night Jack welcomed new members at a Sabbath reserved annually for that purpose, and promised that he would not spend the rest of the year talking about "the event." Except for his sermon on Hanukkah, which constituted too close a parallel to resist, he didn't mention it again.[1]

---

[1]Sermon, "The Flame of Courage," 5 December 1958, JMR MSS.

While Jack was out of town the FBI telephoned me to request that I come to headquarters and listen to some tapes. They had made transcripts of all the threatening calls that had been reported—such calls had been made to the Atlanta newspapers and other institutions as well as to the Schwartzes and us.

Each of the indicted men was asked to identify himself and then read the transcripts. Remembering the detail with which I had described the caller's voice, the investigators hoped that I would be able to identify it when I heard the tapes.

I knew nothing about legal procedures, but it seemed to me that such an identification made ten days after the event would not hold up very well in court. I said so. The agents assured me that I was right and that they did not intend for it to be used in the trial. What they wanted was information that would help them get a confession from the man who had telephoned me, whom they were convinced was one of those being held. They were equally sure that these five men were responsible for the bombing.

It was exciting being called by FBI agents and taken to their office to help in an investigation. Aware of my tendency to romanticize, however, I could not trust my opinion when one of the voices did sound like the one I remembered from the night of the bombing. To further my suspicion—of both the voice and my romanticism—that particular man had been the only one to stumble in his reading of the transcript. After identifying himself and stating that he was reading a prepared script at the request of the FBI, as each of the others had done, Chester Griffin paused and said something like, "Gee, somebody might really think I did this." Then he continued reading, but not without some hesitation during the part relating to his alleged conversation with me.

I told myself to stop playing amateur psychiatrist, but still felt obligated to tell the agents that I did think Chester Griffin's voice sounded familiar. They thanked me, assured me that I would not be called upon to testify to it in court, and escorted me home.

Two weeks later I received a subpoena to testify on behalf of the state as did Jack, Eloise, Robert, and his assistant custodian. I was still nervous about testifying, although it seemed reasonable to assume that I wouldn't be asked about the tape—the first defendant slated for trial was George Bright, not Chester Griffin. When I mentioned my apprehension to a friend, one of the leading attorneys in town, he told me to relax, that even if I was asked about the tape it was highly unlikely that defense would make it difficult for me. He explained that it was considered counterproductive "to badger a lady—especially if she's a preacher's wife."

The trial opened 1 December 1958. Waiting outside the courtroom to be called to testify, Jack and I couldn't help being revolted by the faces of the friends of the accused. They were faces the likes of which I had seen only in movies and newsreels. They would have looked appropriate in a Roman amphitheater cheering the lions, or on the streets of Paris grinning while tumbrels rolled toward the guillotine, or outside a courthouse in Atlanta forty-five years earlier.

Jack was called to the stand before I was; thus, I did not hear his testimony. He did hear mine however, as we were permitted to remain inside the courtroom after being dismissed. He reported having been asked some ridiculously prejudiced questions such as, "You don't think very much of Adolph Hitler, do you?" We weren't surprised—the chief attorney for the defense was James R. Venable, long recognized as an anti-Semite. (His family owned Stone Mountain, traditional rallying ground of the Klan.) Not ruffled by persons such as Mr. Venable, Jack fielded his remarks with disdain. Responding to the query about liking Hitler, he replied, "I didn't think any civilized person did."

Questions to me were routine, simple and ostensibly friendly, designed, as were those put to Jack and the other Temple staff members, to establish that the defendant and his group had planned a campaign of intimidation against the Jewish community. I was questioned about the call but not about the tape and treated, as our friend had predicted, with great courtesy. My first experience in the witness box ended with no ill effects. We learned in the course of the morning's session that the man who had picketed the First Baptist Church when Jack had spoken there the preceding May had been the defendant, George Bright.

Both Jack and I had other obligations to attend to that week, so we had given little thought to indulging ourselves by hanging around the courthouse. Besides, when Temple members had asked him if they should attend the trial he had discouraged them because he wanted to avoid giving the impression that it was we the congregation, rather than the state of Georgia, bringing suit against the indicted men. Midway through the week he received word from the prosecuting attorney's office asking him to reverse his advice to the congregation. Friends of the accused, he was told, had so "polluted" the courtroom atmosphere that it

was necessary to "neutralize" it by bringing in some less hostile spectators. Members of the Jewish community were only too happy to oblige.

The two of us returned on Friday to hear the closing arguments and
again after services on Saturday. By that time Bright was in the throes of
his own statement to the jury, which ultimately lasted for eight hours, and
we didn't care to stay to hear the end of that. Venable had already demonstrated such flagrant anti-Semitism that it seemed certain to hurt
rather than help his client, and Bright seemed to be following in his footsteps. Midway through his statement we left and went home to await the
outcome.

Late that evening someone called to tell us that the jury had finally
been retired. The following week, after eighty-four hours of deliberation,
it despaired of reaching agreement and requested Judge Durwood T. Pye
to declare a mistrial. The three dissenting jurors, it was reported, had
withheld their decision of "guilty" only because such a verdict carried
with it a possible death sentence. With only circumstantial evidence having been presented, they could not thus vote for conviction.

Again Jack and I returned to the business at hand. The building-
fund campaign was winding to a close—with spectacular success. Such
a result was predictable under the circumstances, but it elicited rumors
from hate groups that we had arranged the bombing ourselves in order
to gain sympathy and donations. Actually, we were so amazed at the enthusiasm of some of the contributors that we had to pinch ourselves to
remember that the rumors were false. While Jack met with architects,
accountants, and those planning the victory dinner, I wrote and directed
a musical parody on the campaign for the evening's entertainment and
began rehearsals at Theatre Atlanta for its upcoming play, scheduled to
open 12 January. Little did we dream, when I read for the role, that there
would be a second trial of George Bright also scheduled to open on that
date or that I would be in any way hurt by my involvement in it.

The second trial of George Bright differed from the first in several
ways. The charge was different, so no death penalty was involved. The
presiding magistrate was different; instead of the stern, unpredictable
Judge Durwood T. Pye, Judge Jephtha Tanksley, mild-mannered and conciliatory, now occupied the bench. Radically different, however, was the
change in counsel for the defense. Instead of the anti-Semitic Mr. Venable
who came near to killing his client with his own prejudice, the accused
would be represented by Reuben Garland, a flamboyant, crafty show-

man, well known for his tactics of success-by-any-means in criminal cases. Well versed in the law, he was equally understanding of psychology and theatrics, and displayed far more respect for the latter subjects than for the court.

What we didn't know at the time, learning it quite by accident five years later, was that my identification of Chester Griffin had been correct and had elicited from him the hoped-for confession. He had subsequently retracted it. Because what he said to me was self-incriminatory, the conviction of all five codefendants might have been obtained by that confession. Without it, the state had to prove the validity of my identification.

Reuben Garland did not intend to let that validation take place, and the state solicitor was no match for him. The latter began his case in much the same manner as before, calling to the stand Jack and the others from The Temple staff. Garland, in cross-examining them, didn't give them any trouble, but he used a technicality in excusing them that excluded them from the court after they had testified; they were thus unable to hear any of the ensuing testimony. Because I had come in my own car and didn't need transportation, and was no longer fearful after testifying in the first trial, Jack saw no reason to remain at the courthouse. It was Wednesday, his golf afternoon. If he hurried he could make it to the club by tee-off time.

Predictably, Garland objected when the state began to question me about the tapes. His objection was overruled. He fought unsuccessfully to keep out my testimony identifying the caller, then tried to discredit it on cross-examination. He first pelted me with lengthy questions fraught with false statements, misleading implications, and deprecating asides. I was determined that he would not trap me and that I would show no doubt about the identity of the voice I had heard. (By this time I was convinced that the FBI had properly identified the guilty parties. I refused to give the opposition any help in defending them.) One question Garland asked me during that period, or at least, the preamble to it, may serve as an example. He began, "Now Mrs. Rothschild, when you got in your Cadillac at your estate on Arden Road and went downtown to listen to those tapes . . ." I waited patiently until he was finished and then said, "Mr. Garland, you made so many false premises in the course of that question that I really don't know how to answer it. I don't drive a Cadillac.

I drive a Ford. And my home is not on an estate as yours is." (He was known to have purchased one of the city's most famous mansions.)[2]

The spectators tittered. Judge Tanksley rapped for order and told Garland to restate his question. He did, but with his next question he committed the same offense.

Eventually he gave up trying to make me look like an evil capitalist. Turning instead to what he apparently hoped would reflect on my moral character, he peppered his questions with references to my "career" on the stage. Again I gritted my teeth and managed to rebuff him. For every snide suggestion that I was "an actress" (spoken with meaningful inflection) I answered with some mitigating information, stating that "theater arts was my major at the *University of Georgia,*" or that I "considered it important to help establish good community theatre" in Atlanta. When he saw he could not maneuver me into the corner he had in mind, he blurted out angrily, "But you do consider yourself an actress, do you not?" (I did, but I wasn't going to give him the satisfaction of saying so.) I smiled demurely and replied, "Why, Mr. Garland! That's not for me to say!"[3]

Again an appreciative titter rippled across the courtroom, and again Judge Tanksley called for order. Garland then turned his talents toward making me look foolish. He grilled me at length about the exact wording of the telephone call, always including some reference to my alleged ability to recognize regional accents. Finally he got to the point he had been leading up to: a request that I imitate the accent I had heard. I didn't want to accede to his request for two reasons, one of which was that I had never been very good at imitating accents. Judge Tanksley came to my rescue and instructed me that I wasn't required to do so. I said that I preferred not to.[4]

-----

[2]"Rabbi's Wife Ties Griffin to Threat," *Atlanta Journal,* 14 Jan. 1959; "Rabbi's Wife Tells of Threat," *Atlanta Constitution,* 15 Jan. 1959; "Night Sessions in Bright Trial," *Atlanta Journal,* 15 Jan. 1959. Copies in JMR MSS; *The State of Georgia vs. George Bright et al.,* docket no. 76657, filed 17 October 1958, Fulton County Courthouse, Atlanta, Georgia. Because there were no appeals on either case (one was declared a mistrial and the other was an acquittal) no transcripts were made and the court reporter's notes were not preserved.

[3]Ibid.

[4]Ibid.

It was what Garland had been waiting for. Smiling in anticipation of the kill, he asked softly, "Why not?"

"Because it isn't dignified," I replied.

Now he really had me where he wanted me. Puffing up with feigned surprise, he drew out his first words, "Oh . . ? You put your dignity above the life of my poor, innocent client?"

Again the right words came into my mouth. A divine hand must have been holding the cue cards, for I could never have consciously thought of them. I said very meekly, "No, Mr. Garland. I was thinking of the dignity of the court."[5]

This time it was not a ripple but a tidal wave of laughter that swept the courtroom. Judge Tanksley threatened to order it cleared if he heard any more. Garland resumed his badgering and I continued to hold my own without giving an inch.

After ninety minutes of questioning me Garland accomplished at least a part of his purpose. He had wound me to the breaking point and knew exactly which string to pull. With a seemingly innocuous question that caused me to think of the way the threatening call had affected our children, tears began to roll down my cheeks and I choked with emotion. Judge Tanksley excused me and asked his clerk to take me to chambers to recuperate.

As we passed the reporters in the hall outside, one told me that Jack had left—which did little toward helping me regain my composure. As soon as I could get to a telephone without being overheard I called the club, caught him before he left the locker room, and delivered such a hysterical tirade that he was dressed and back at the courthouse by the time I regained my composure and came downstairs. He had no idea what had happened, of course, and I was too angry to tell him. I got into my car and went home. He had one of the reporters fill him in and then followed me home to make amends.

The afternoon paper carried a front-page story captioned "Rabbi's Wife Ties Griffin To Threat" and reported that I had left the witness stand in tears. When my mother saw it she spilled a pot of freshly brewed coffee on her arm and spent a painful evening applying baking soda to it. She didn't tell us about the incident until the next day, though, because

---

[5]Ibid.

she knew that both of us had to leave home early in the evening. Jack had to give an invocation at a dinner meeting and I had to perform in the play at Theatre Atlanta.[6]

I knew something was wrong when the director caught me after the third-act curtain to say, "Wait for me before you go out to your car. Jack called and asked me to follow you home." It had been a long day for me, and my imagination had had all the encouragement it needed to make me fear the worst. Afterwards, I realized that the theater director was more frightened than I. What had happened, which Jack had asked him not to tell me, was that another anonymous call had come to our house, this one received by Johnnie Mae while we were out. The caller had said, "You tell Mrs. Rothschild that she identified the wrong man—and she'll pay for it!" With all the conversation in court about my performing in the play, there was no secret about where my car would be during the evening if anyone wanted to tamper with it.

Fortunately, Johnnie Mae had the presence of mind not to respond to the caller or to react in front of Marcia and Bill. After they were safely in bed she tracked down Jack and told him what had happened. He came home at once to be there in case the children needed protection and called the theater to arrange protection for me. Neither he nor the director, of course, would have known how to avert foul play, but he believed—accurately, as it was later found—that the call was only a hoax, just as the earlier one had been. Besides, who could expect logic at a time like that?

The trial was still in progress at week's end. On Saturday morning I took Marcia to the theater for children's auditions and while there received a summons to return to court—immediately. Headquarters sent a car to pick me up, and I arranged a ride home for Marcia. The police assured me that I would be back at Theatre Atlanta in time for our matinee at two o'clock.

I wasn't. I spent the next few hours waiting in an anteroom along with the men whom I was told comprised the entire Southeastern staff of the FBI and the detective squad of the Atlanta Police Department. They said that they had been "interned" there all week; rarely was one called to the stand. They believed that Garland was keeping all of them on call merely to harass them and that at that moment he was doing the same to

me. Apparently, he was. At 2:15, he suddenly realized he didn't need me
as a witness that day. Since we had no way of knowing when or if I'd be
free to leave the courthouse, and my role was not a major one, there was
no point in trying to hold the curtain for me. Consequently, after a hair-
raising top-speed drive through downtown Atlanta in a patrol car (a new
one, not yet equipped with markings or siren) I arrived at the theater only
to find that my "big scene" had been satisfactorily performed without me.
I couldn't tell which hurt most that afternoon, my nerves or my ego.

The following Thursday evening I was summoned again to reappear
in court, this time for the prosecution. Again Garland fought to keep my
testimony out of the record. Again he was overruled. As I took the stand
he made some unchivalrous remarks about me, loud enough for everyone
to hear. Judge Tanksley sternly reprimanded him for it; Garland responded by shouting, "I'm going to try to make this as obnoxious as I
can."[7]

Tanksley then asked the jury to leave so he could scold the attorney.
It did little good. The jury returned and Garland began questioning me,
interspersing the questions with requests for adjournment. The stolid,
even-tempered judge refused. Garland continued to ask. Finally, when all
else failed, the florid-faced white-haired attorney went into an act worthy
of a Barrymore (someone in the audience was heard to say that there was
some doubt as to where the best show in town was playing—at Theatre
Atlanta or in the courtroom). He clutched his throat, tore open his already loosened collar and tie, and gagged several times, giving—for all
its melodrama—such a convincing imitation of a person having a heart
attack that Judge Tanksley evidently felt he couldn't risk ignoring it. He
recessed court until nine o'clock the next morning whereupon Garland,
having thus recovered his good health, proclaimed that he didn't believe
a word of my testimony and intended to keep me on the stand all day long
the following day to prove it.[8]

Jack had remained on hand for moral support this time, though he
was still prevented from entering the courtroom. He returned with me
on Friday morning, both of us expecting the worst. While Garland kept

---

[7]James Sheppard, "FBI Agent Takes Stand to Clear Undercover Man," *Atlanta Constitution*, 23 Jan. 1959. Copy in JMR MSS.

[8]Ibid.

his word about making it tough on me, he only kept me on the stand for forty minutes. He questioned me primarily about the wording of the call. In one of the previous sessions he had asked me to write down the message as I remembered it. That morning he claimed to have misplaced the paper and asked me, therefore, to write it down again. After I did so he "miraculously" discovered the original paper (in his shirt pocket) and compared the two. I had changed one of the words, out of a total of thirty-one.[9]

Savoring his victory, he began questioning me in detail about what I had done on the day of the bombing. Finally, his voice dripping with sarcasm, he asked why I hadn't been curious enough about the bombing to go to The Temple myself. The question reminded me again of the children, causing the lump once more to rise in my throat and the tears to well in my eyes. Before I broke down, however, thoroughly infuriated, I managed to spit out, "Because I considered it more important to keep people from bringing their children there for Sunday School than it was to satisfy my curiosity!"[10]

After that I was finally dismissed, though not without having once more supplied the *Atlanta Journal* with material for a front-page story. That afternoon's caption announced, "Tearful Rabbi's Wife Winds Up Testimony." This time I warned my mother about it before she saw her newspaper.[11]

The trial ended that evening, after two full weeks of acrimonious debate. To supplement what we read in the newspapers and our own limited view of it, we received a most discriminating report from a friend who attended the trial every day. In her opinion the state had made a strenuous effort to gain a conviction and, with one exception (that being its failure to instruct me or to make proper use of my testimony) had organized and presented its case very well. Unfortunately, it had very little evidence that actually placed the accused at the scene of the crime, notwithstanding a substantial amount of it that indicated his intention to commit such a crime. The only witness for the prosecution with testi-

---

[9]Ibid.

[10]Ibid.

[11]John Pennington, "Tearful Rabbi's Wife Winds Up Testimony," *Atlanta Journal,* 23 Jan. 1959. Copy in JMR MSS.

mony to the effect that Bright actually took part in the bombing was his cell mate in jail, an unsavory character whose word was easily discredited. Incredibly, the witness who corroborated Bright's alibi as to his whereabouts that night was a woman currently committed to the state institution for the insane, a reputed nymphomaniac who claimed that Bright had been with her all night. A poised, intelligent, witty person, physically attractive and well groomed, she was able to qualify as a witness by proving she was at that time in a lucid interval, and succeeded in convincing the jury despite its knowledge of her condition.[12]

Jack predicted that the accused would go free and his attorney be sent to jail. After only two hours of deliberation the jury returned its verdict and that was exactly what happened. George Bright was declared innocent of having bombed The Temple and acquitted, along with the four codefendants (against whom the state had even less evidence than it had on Bright), and Reuben Garland was cited with a forty-day sentence for contempt of court. He appealed it, succeeded initially in having it overturned, but finally had to serve a part of it one year later.

As a footnote to the trial, believable only if one understands Garland's colossal chutzpa, I received a call from him while he was serving his time in prison. He was campaigning for the position of state solicitor and sought my help in dispelling the rumors that he was anti-Semitic. "You know, Mrs. Rothschild," he said, dripping with honey and feigned innocence, "I don't have anything at all against the Jewish people. I was just trying to save the life of my poor, innocent client, and I'd appreciate it if you'd tell your folks at The Temple so they'd vote for me."

I was so flabbergasted I could only say, "Mr. Garland, your lack of respect for the American system of jurisprudence is so appalling that whether or not you are anti-Semitic is totally irrelevant." Then I hung up. Jack, who overheard my side of the conversation, told me I should have said, "Mr. Garland, I wouldn't vote for you even if you were Jewish."

Actually I, Jack, and the friend who attended the trial believed that Garland was not anti-Semitic himself but attempted by innuendo to draw out such feelings as might have been latent in some of the jurors. Most witnesses for the defense, however, were violently anti-Semitic, members of the neo-Nazi National States' Rights Party, of which the accused were

---

[12]Comments on trial, Phoebe Franklin, ca. February 1959, JMR MSS.

also members. Although it was apparent that all of the defense witnesses had been carefully coached and told not to evince any anti-Semitism, some did anyway.

Jack and I of course were disappointed at Bright's acquittal, particularly with the speed at which the jury arrived at the "not guilty" verdict, but we were neither surprised nor dismayed by it. We had every confidence that the law-enforcement agencies would keep an eye on the group to prevent further mischief, and that the five had been intimidated enough that they would probably leave the Atlanta area and keep out of sight.

Many members of the Jewish community failed to share our equanimity. Jack tried to explain how difficult it had been for the state to build its case. Most criminal prosecutions, he pointed out, are made possible by virtue of deductive reasoning, whereas this one had to be proved by evidence gathered from inductive reasoning. The explanation made for interesting conversation but did little to allay fears. Jack sensed a "disturbing and disquieting mood" in the community.

In a moving sermon called "Ordeal by Trial," he told his congregation that, regrettably, the "drama of the courtroom" had not engendered "the same magnificent courage, the same deeply rooted faith in the soundness of our fellow-citizens" as had the experience of the bombing. He analyzed what had occurred, reminding his listeners that what we had witnessed had been an honest display of the democratic process. It differed from the Frank case, he pointed out, in that whatever threats had been made had come "not from a citizenry roused to mob violence" but from "a bigoted few who themselves drew the wrath and scorn of the community." While the result of the trial may have left us dissatisfied, he asserted, "the process was sound, and it is in the process that our freedom and security rest."[13]

Jack acknowledged that many non-Jews harbor a latent anti-Semitism, but said he believed that for the first time, many of these otherwise decent people had seen where their prejudices would lead them and had been horrified. He understood that the real root of fear within the Jewish community was the lack of confidence its members had in their own sta-

---

[13]Sermon, "Ordeal by Trial," 6 February 1959, JMR MSS.

tus as citizens, and he tried to attack the problem by forcing his listeners to face it.[14]

Reemphasizing his belief that the acquittal indicated not indifference on the part of the jurors but "an absence of sufficient proof to make a case for conviction—nothing more" he stressed that the general community was as distressed as we were. Persons were distressed, he said, "not because justice was not done. That is not for us to say. But because a stronger case could not have been made."[15]

In conclusion he admitted that the experience of the bombing, traumatic as it was, had led us to hope for a conviction. Nevertheless, he said, we must not be misled by the acquittal. He declared:

> We are not a weak, despised minority. This was not *The Temple vs. George Bright et al.* It was *The State vs. George Bright et al.* There is a vast difference.
>
> America is a land of cultural and religious pluralism. Let us uphold the truths of our own faith, be strong in our own heritage, find security in the challenge of our own tradition. Then will we add our strength to the strength of America, discover a real security for ourselves and bring to fruition the challenge of the prophet's words: "Justice, Justice shall ye pursue."[16]

His sermon ended the saga of The Temple Bombing as far as we were concerned. We returned to our normal pursuits. Construction and repairs to the building progressed. In commemoration of the support offered by the hundreds of non-Jews who sent sympathy and unsolicited contributions—approximately fifteen thousand dollars in all—the congregation named its new auditorium Friendship Hall and placed a plaque appropriately inscribed on the wall near its entrance.

Jack had refused all out-of-town invitations to speak about the bombing until after the building-fund campaign was finished. In midwinter he began to accept them, traveling to many different cities and congregations where the members sought to understand what had happened in Atlanta. I went with him when I could. On one such occasion

---

[14]Ibid.

[15]Ibid.

[16]Ibid.

a woman came up to me after Jack had spoken and introduced herself as the sister of a man who belonged to our congregation in Atlanta. In a manner clearly intended to be complimentary, effusive even, she told me that she had been visiting her brother on the High Holydays just prior to the bombing, and had gone to The Temple with him for the Yom Kippur service. This was the service in which Jack had made his annual prime-time pitch for civil rights, although it should be remembered that this was also one in which only six hundred words were devoted to the topic. As the climax of her accolade she told me that she had enjoyed the Yom Kippur sermon so very much and added: "My brother said he should have kept his mouth shut, but *I* thought it was *wonderful!*" We enjoyed that very much.

Wherever Jack went he always spoke of his faith in the people of Atlanta, especially in its leaders. In the years that followed both we and they would know that this faith had been justified in full. The experience of the bombing and its aftermath, in spite of everything, had enabled us to see the goodness in our fellow citizens. It had brought us together, closer in spirit than we had ever been in modern times. Far from having plunged us into another era of darkness and fear, this potential disaster of our own day had actually brightened the future for Jews and non-Jews alike and restored confidence to the hearts of those who still trembled with the memory of Leo Frank.

CHAPTER SIX

BATTLE
OF ATLANTA

The bombing closed one period of our lives and opened another. It seemed to us that it did the same for Atlanta. Certainly it marked a turning point in the struggle for racial justice. The boil had been lanced and healing could begin. It would be a long, slow process, but it did begin.

In early November, just three weeks after The Temple was bombed, another "ministers' manifesto" was issued, this one stronger than the first and signed by 312 clergymen, including all the local rabbis. In addition to reemphasizing the points made in the previous document, it called for organized, open discussion of the school situation and asked that the governor appoint a citizens' commission to hold hearings throughout the state to ascertain the true feelings of most Georgians in the matter. Eventually, this committee was established and a highly respected Atlantan, John Sibley, appointed chairman.[1]

Jack did not meet with instant success in this request for a citizens' commission nor in the one he made for a discussion on the national level. In his letter thanking President Eisenhower for his prompt, "forthright" response to the bombing, he had said:

> Our people are at last united in their determination that violence and anarchy shall not be the measure of life in America. Under your determined leadership, the United States will once again be restored to a land ruled by law and not by men.
>
> May I urge that you convoke a White House Conference on law and order so that the roots of this evil that grows in our land may be destroyed by the counsel and the wisdom of those who best represent the noblest ideals of American life.[2]

The president replied that such a conference was being given "careful consideration."[3]

In Atlanta the siege had been broken and the battle for open schools begun. When it was over, some three years later, a colleague at UAHC headquarters asked Jack to write an article about it for the magazine *American Judaism*, and added flatteringly, "I am sure that you had your quiet but firm hand in it."[4]

Jack replied, "Thanks for the compliment, but whatever part I played in the Atlanta story was an extremely minor one—unless it can be said that over a period of years I changed some people's minds and made the final result more possible." He accepted the challenge to write the article but added, "I would suggest that you wait to read it until you de-

---

[1]Pamphlet, " 'Out of Conviction': A Second Statement on the South's Racial Crisis," 22 November 1958, signed by 312 ministers of Greater Atlanta (Atlanta: Georgia Council of Churches, 1958); see sermon by JMR, "Light for the Lamp of Learning," 19 December 1958—JMR MSS.

[2]JMR to Pres. Dwight D. Eisenhower, 24 October 1958, JMR MSS.

[3]Pres. Dwight D. Eisenhower to JMR, 30 October 1958, JMR MSS.

[4]Rabbi Balfour Brickner to JMR, 5 October 1961, JMR MSS.

cide. It might be that you won't want anybody to see it and then you won't
have to apologize for not distributing it!"[5]

The article did appear in *American Judaism*. In it Jack continued to
downplay his own involvement. As he described it, "The real story behind the happy headlines is a story of little people, of parents—largely
women—who dared to fight for open schools, of courageous and dedicated ministers who dared the wrath of their custom-encrusted congregations, of ordinary citizens without money or influence who created the
climate in which the final victory could be won."[6]

As the new phase began Jack and I had our own, more personal aspect of it to deal with. Neither of our children seemed to be achieving his
or her potential in public school. The school they attended was so
crowded that the children were not permitted to speak while they were
eating lunch. We were especially concerned with Bill's behavior and the
school's less-than-satisfactory method of dealing with it. The previous
year, when he was in the fourth grade, I had been called in to speak with
his teacher about his inability to abide by that rule. I restrained myself
from telling her that I considered the policy both barbaric and unrealistic.
Having been taught that rules are rules, however barbaric and unrealistic,
I agreed with her that Bill would benefit from learning to abide by them
and asked her how she had disciplined him for his offense. Proudly,
clearly expecting to be lauded for her wisdom, the lady replied, "I told
him if he was going to behave like the colored people he'd have to go out
in the kitchen and eat with them."

Well! I bit my tongue even harder than before and tried to decide
what to do. Bill was obviously in enough trouble already. With seven
more months of the school year yet to go he didn't need his mother to
give his teacher a lecture on bigotry.

I smiled wanly, thanked the teacher, told her Bill's father and I would
cooperate in any way we could, and departed feeling like a first-class trai-
tor. I didn't feel any better after I stopped at The Temple for the sisterhood's annual luncheon program on public affairs. The speaker was

---

[5]JMR to Rabbi Balfour Brickner, 12 October 1961, JMR MSS.

[6]Rothschild, "The Atlanta Story," *American Judaism* 12, no. 1 (Fall 1962). Original
and printed copy in JMR MSS.

Rabbi Eugene Lipman, then of the UAHC staff. He gave an inspiring lecture on racial justice.

I began to think seriously about the possibility of sending our children to private school. My grandmother had been pleading with us all along to do so and assuring us that she would pay for it if we did. At first I had refused out of hand, not even mentioning the suggestion to Jack. I agreed with him that in theory public education provided the best preparation for life in a democratic society. He looked upon all private schools "as a potential danger to the system of public education which undergirds our democratic system" because, he said, "they tend to fragmentize and create divisiveness in the total society."

Because we both still believed in pluralism in education, we did not favor Jewish day schools, although in the next few years Jack would soften his approach with regard to the newly organized Atlanta Hebrew Academy. At that later time he spoke of our responsibility to preserve our Jewish heritage, saying that "to the extent that the Hebrew Academy achieves these transcendent needs for positive Jewish life it deserves the support of all of us." Even then, however, he would have been loathe to send his own children there, and I would have been equally so. Today both of us might feel differently.[7]

The only private school I had in mind for Marcia and Bill at the time was Westminster, in which were taught grades 1-12. It had an excellent rating academically and was generally considered to be the best college-preparatory school in our part of the country. Although it advertised itself frankly as "A Christian Preparatory School," the many Jewish families we knew who had sent their children there praised the experience and education it had given their children. On the rare occasions when a parent had called Jack to complain of some particular incident of Christian indoctrination at Westminster, he invariably would reply that the school had every right to do so. From what he could observe (throughout our own experience there) Westminster placed no more emphasis on the teaching of religion than, as he stated it, "already exists illegally in the public schools here." He added that "there, at least I am assured that religion is being taught by people who know something about it and come to it with the proper perspective." Far from tending to wean the Jewish

---

[7]JMR, undated notes re Atlanta Hebrew Academy, ca. 1962, JMR MSS.

young people away from their heritage, it served in many cases to strengthen their interest in Jewish studies and enhance their appreciation of all religion.[8]

As 1958 came to a close Georgians with school-age children were bracing themselves for what appeared to be inevitable: a decision on the discrimination suit brought against the Atlanta public schools, and passage of a bill then pending in the state legislature that would close all schools in the state if the court ruled in favor of the plaintiff, which it was sure to do. All parents who could afford it, it seemed, were rushing to enroll their children in private schools, some in order to escape integration should it come, but most in order to assure their children's continued education.

I was especially concerned because of the problems we were having with Bill. I might be able to teach Marcia at home, but I could not imagine how I would manage her brother. (Another of Nurse Mattie's sage observations when Bill and Marcia were infants had been, "I don't care whether they're white, black, Jew, or Gentile, the preacher's son is always the worstest child on the block." We were trying to keep Bill from exemplifying that saying, but I knew we would need outside help to do so.)

Perhaps my unpleasant experience in the second trial of George Bright had made me edgier than usual. Or perhaps we were just beginning to feel the shock of the bombing. Whatever the cause, during the winter of 1959 I became obsessed with the idea of entering our children in Westminster for the following fall. When Jack continued to resist I became adamant. People were still complimenting me for avoiding hysteria during the bombing ordeal. I couldn't see that my behavior merited having a medal struck in gold, but I did see in it a few usable "brownie points" and proceeded to use them. Accordingly, I confronted Jack, saying, "I didn't get hysterical then, but *now* I'm going to get hysterical. I want you to speak to Dr. Pressley—*tomorrow!*" Dr. William Pressley was headmaster of Westminster Schools, and the competition for places was such that one needed priority consideration regardless of how well one's children scored on the tests.

This method of persuasion was so out of character for me that Jack, thoroughly shocked, responded equally uncharacteristically and did as I

---

[8]JMR to Rabbi Sidney Lefkowitz, 22 March 1966, JMR MSS.

had "asked." Both children tested well, but there were no places open in the seventh grade: Marcia could not be admitted until the following year, when she would enter the Girls' Preparatory School. An extra section was being added to the sixth grade of the Boys' Lower School that autumn, so Bill could be admitted without delay. I was tremendously relieved to have enrolled him there and believe to this day that had we not done so he would not have received the superior education that has set the direction for his life as an adult. So much for our idealistic adherence to public education.

My zealous insistence upon what was good for our children in this instance was not good for Jack's reputation. People were furious when the news got around—which it did quickly. Those who knew us well enough to tell us directly let us know that they resented our having used the prestige of Jack's position to obtain something for our children that they could not obtain for theirs. I wondered if they were also resentful that their children had not received the threatening telephone calls or experienced the other pressures that were part of our children's birthright. Jack and I were not terribly disturbed at the "sink or swim with the rest of us" attitude, for we had expected it. We also knew that those who favored Jewish day schools and resented our lack of enthusiasm for the Hebrew Academy would criticize us for choosing Westminster. That there was as yet no Hebrew High School in Atlanta and that both Marcia and Bill were close to high-school age seemed immaterial to those who thought a rabbi should send his children to the Hebrew Academy.

The criticism that disturbed me—I should have expected it but didn't—was the accusation that we were sending our children to private school in order to avoid integration. It was an idea so patently foreign to our thinking, and Jack's personality was so lacking in hypocrisy, that I deeply resented anyone's so impugning our motives and felt guilty at having brought so unfair a criticism upon him. Admittedly, it did not occur to either of us to look for an integrated private school in the Atlanta area in 1959. We did, however, take every opportunity to urge the authorities at Westminster to change the school's policy. (It eventually did, but not while Marcia and Bill were students there.) On one occasion, in order to demonstrate his disagreement with the school's segregationist policy, Jack refused to contribute to its building-fund campaign. He wrote Dr. Pressley an explanation, praising the quality of education that Marcia and

Bill were receiving, and assuring him that neither they nor we had been disturbed by its emphasis on Christian theology, but adding:

> However, as a rabbi and even more important as a religious person I find it impossible to accept—precisely because Westminster is a school which prides itself upon being Christian—its unwillingness to educate qualified children of any race. To allow private schools which are under religious sponsorship to become the last bastion of segregated education seems to me to be contradictory, untenable and indefensible.[9]

Not even church-sponsored private schools, it would seem, could move more rapidly than the feelings of those who supported them.

Meanwhile, there was a movement afoot to change public opinion about segregation, and Jack was one of the first to be recruited to serve on its guiding body. During that winter, 1959, he and two Protestant ministers joined the executive board of an organization called HOPE, an acronym for Help Our Public Education. It was not an organization of the elite. As he described it in an article for *American Judaism*:

> It had no members from the "power structure" or the politicians (except one or two) or the so-called civic leaders. All the more important people were "playing it cozy." But H.O.P.E. persisted and grew in numbers. By the time the Sibley Committee . . . held its meetings, it was possible for more than half of those who appeared before it to avow publicly their desire to keep the schools open.[10]

It would be more than a year before the Sibley Committee would focus its attention upon Atlanta. By that time persons would have become accustomed to seeing bumper stickers distributed by HOPE reading "We Want Public Schools" and to hearing the same sentiment caroled by a growing chorus of liberal voices, among them those of the faculties of Emory University and Agnes Scott College, the Church Women of Atlanta, and the city PTA. One could detect a gradual ground swell of agreement reflected in the newspapers, especially in the letters to the editor. Writers expressing the liberal point of view were permitting their

---

[9]JMR to Dr. William Pressley, 20 April 1964, JMR MSS.

[10]Rothschild, "The Atlanta Story."

names to be published with their letters. The pleas were not for justice, for equality of opportunity, or any other moral aspect of integration. They were for public education, nothing more. They targeted the lowest common denominator—self-interest—as the surest, if not the most commendable, means of gaining influence, pointing out the economic and cultural losses Atlanta and Georgia would suffer should the schools close.

Jack hated to use such reasoning, but he understood that expediency was at that stage most important. Accordingly, he exercised patience in demanding, or even hoping for, an acknowledgment of the moral issue involved. It was only after many years of waiting that he became frustrated with the public's failure to see the problem as one involving human decency.

As the theme of the liberals grew louder so did its counterpoint. The segregationists fought back with a barrage of name calling, accusing those who spoke out for open schools of being quislings, lawbreakers, carpetbaggers, Communists, anarchists, and a host of other things. Jack warned his congregation not to be misled by those names. The real anarchists, he declared, were those who would undermine the law by refusing to obey laws they disliked. He reminded his listeners that democratic government functions by relying upon the people to make a proper decision about an issue when they have had the opportunity to understand it. It was for this reason, he said, that those "who would destroy our school system to preserve the power structure that keeps them in office" were trying so hard to prevent people from discussing the present issue. If these thwarters of discussion were allowed to succeed, he predicted, there would be dire consequences for "untold generations to come."[11]

While Jack did not indulge in name calling, at least one of the segregationists feared he might. Attorney Charles J. Bloch of Macon, as courtly, cultured, and highly respected a Southern gentleman as ever stood before the Georgia bar, had been the principal author of a bill aimed at closing the schools should they be forced to institute token integration. He was also Jewish, which rankled many Jewish liberals unable to understand how such an educated, intelligent member of "the tribe" could be so perverse in his thinking.

---

[11]Sermon, "Little by Little," 3 October 1959, JMR MSS.

Jack was scheduled to speak in Nashville, Tennessee, in May 1959 at a congregation of which one of Bloch's daughters was a member. Apparently, some others who had been invited to address this audience had berated Bloch in the course of their presentations. Realizing how embarrassing these remonstrances were for his daughter and assuming that Jack would do the same, Bloch wrote to him to ask him to refrain. He also used the opportunity to argue for states' rights. The ensuing correspondence eloquently testifies to the convoluted reasoning employed at the time by otherwise intelligent men and women.[12]

Amazed at receiving such a letter, Jack first told Bloch that to refer in his presentation to Bloch or to his position had "never crossed my mind." Then he picked up the gauntlet and replied:

> Since you were kind enough to enclose a copy of one of your own speeches, permit me to comment on one of the marked passages. You say: "We are faced with the question of whether we shall sit idly by and let our rights to live under the law be whittled away— one by one." Is not this precisely the question that is now being asked by minority groups in this country as they see their right to vote, to serve on juries, to attend public schools, to enjoy recreational facilities withheld from them? Is it not true that under our American system of government all citizens are entitled to the same rights and that as you say, no one should sit idly by and let their rights to live under the law be "whittled away?" It would seem to me that this is the crux of the matter and, although I am not one skilled in the law, I cannot see how, if such a position is accepted, anyone can deny that it is true for all citizens, regardless of creed or color. To make such distinctions would be to deny the basic principles of American democracy— equality under the law.[13]

Bloch rebutted:

> . . . I respectfully suggest that you consider this: The Fourteenth Amendment to the Constitution of the United States was adopted in 1868. For almost ninety years it was consistently and unanimously held that despite its provisions, one of the liberties reserved to the states and to the people of the states was their right to operate their

---

[12]Charles J. Bloch to JMR, 28 April 1959, JMR MSS.

[13]JMR to Charles J. Bloch, 8 May 1959, JMR MSS.

public schools, segregating the races therein. Suddenly, after almost ninety years, this liberty has been wiped out by judicial edict. If the liberty of the states—the people—to operate their schools is that insecure, are not your and my right to worship as we please equally insecure?

After receiving that missive Jack must have realized the futility of debate on the subject. His next correspondence with Bloch is dated many years later, concerns a different subject, and is not at all contentious.[14]

That summer we went to Europe on our first "Grand Tour," a trip we had been planning, along with Bud and Julie Weiss, for the past two years. Although we looked upon it as a "dream vacation," we had built it around our attendance at the conference of the World Union for Progressive Judaism being held that year in London. Both Europe and the World Union became addictive for us.

So too did travel in general, but it took us some time before we could unwind enough to enjoy it thoroughly. Once we did, we discovered, or rediscovered, facets of each other's personality that had so long been hidden beneath the turmoil of our daily lives that we had forgotten they ever existed. The one area of mutual fascination we shared from the start was that of meeting people. From the seven-foot-tall British peer who chaired the conference banquet (opening his remarks with the question "What makes this [k]night different from all other [k]nights?) to strangers on a train in northern Italy (with whom we could communicate only by signs and those few words I remembered from Italian opera arias), we found our greatest delight in making friends with strangers. Jack especially enjoyed the challenge of making himself understood to waiters in French, which he recalled slightly from high school and the practice he'd had in the Pacific during the war. His greatest triumphs were finding that he could obtain ice in his lemonade by asking for it *"avec de la glace"* and get eggs the way he wanted them when he said *"oeufs sur le plat."*

Disagreements centered around my overzealous desire to sightsee and his insistence that we take time to rest (an idea with which I agreed, but in theory only). I had such a long list of masterpieces I wanted to see that I had spent the previous two years boning up on where they were—

[14]Charles J. Bloch to JMR, 11 May 1959; Charles J. Bloch to JMR, 7 November 1966—JMR MSS.

even to the exact room in the museum, when such information was available—and disdained guided tours in favor of allotting my limited time to viewing only those paintings and sculptures that were most important to me. Jack usually found a comfortable place to sit in the first or second gallery we passed through and told us we'd find him there when we got ready to leave. He kept my enthusiasm for Gothic cathedrals in check by insisting that for every cathedral he visited with me I would have to find a synagogue to visit with him. Julie and Bud managed to remain friends with us by means of an understanding previously arrived at that we should amiably go our separate ways whenever the situation called for it. It frequently did.

Actually, both Jack and I became more appreciative of each other's interests during that summer of travel. He was so enchanted by the haunting beauty of La Sainte Chapelle that on subsequent trips to Paris we had to visit it "just to say hello." He even found something to enjoy in museums—in addition to his game of giving funny titles to voluptuous masterpieces. He was so fascinated by the social commentary and wit of Hieronymus Bosch that he made several return trips to the gallery of the Prado Museum containing those works.

We also went to see a film in Paris that we were sure would be banned in America, not because it was pornographic: it contained nothing more salacious than a shot of young people skinny-dipping. Our reason for wanting to see it and expecting it to be banned at home was that it showed the racial situation in America in a radically anti-American propagandistic light, and Jack wanted to see for himself just how bad it could be.[15]

It was awful, such a travesty of the truth that we were devastated to believe that vast numbers of persons all over the world would see it as a valid interpretation of life in America. Years later we noticed an advertisement for it displayed in X-rated movie houses in the United States. Curious as we might have been to know how it had been changed from one kind of filth to another, we hardly cared enough to sit through it again.

One of the most moving and memorable moments of the trip occurred during our visit to the Roman Forum. Standing on the hill beside

---

[15]*J'ai Cracher Sur Vos Tombes* (English: *I Spit On Your Graves*), French release 1959.

the Arch of Titus, looking down on the rubble that was once the nerve center of the Western world, we could not help reflecting upon the reason why the arch was erected: *Judea Capta*, the "final" defeat. Defying the custom that says we Jews must not walk through the arch because of its original significance, Jack and I did and were amply rewarded. Inside someone had taken a rock and scratched the Hebrew words *Y'chi Yisrael*—Israel Lives. In that setting the two words made up a sermon in themselves.

Jack was already beginning to think of his sermons for the coming Holydays, and he made use of the Arch of Titus incident in one of them. Insofar as his admonitions on civil rights were concerned, he was beginning to find it difficult to avoid repeating himself. For Rosh Hashanah he used the text of Isaiah 28:13, "little by little," to warn that we should guard ourselves against hopelessness and expectations of instant success, that there would be "no gigantic earth-shattering victory." Instead, he predicted, it would be an "imperceptible pattern of bright threads." One of those threads, he pointed out, was the growing awareness of the dangers inherent in the current trend of events. The segregationists were relying ever more heavily upon McCarthy-like tactics to stifle open discussion. Even in their actions, however, Jack saw a ray of hope because those tactics appeared to be "the last, desperate gamble of players who know they hold a losing hand."[16]

That fall, morality was further assaulted. It was discovered that a popular television quiz show, "The $64,000 Question," had been routinely rigged. For Jack the situation raised the question of public morality, or rather, the widespread public immorality being witnessed at that time in America. In a sermon on the subject he said sarcastically, " 'if it is legal it is moral' is the newest commandment." He then connected that scandal to the "legal manoeuvering of Southern state governments to avoid compliance with the Supreme Court ruling." Asking "Whom are we fooling?" he concluded that with such lack of self-discipline among adults it was no wonder that we Americans had a problem with juvenile delinquency.[17]

Invited to address the UAHC biennial convention in November, Jack spoke on "the Personal Demands of Social Justice," codifying some of his

---

[16]Sermon, "Little by Little."

[17]Sermon, "A Question Worth $64,000," 6 November 1959, JMR MSS.

previous statements. In order to translate religion from abstract concept to positive action, he said, one must 1) be willing to accept religion as a guide in all aspects of life, 2) apply religion's ideals to the problems of society, 3) display personal courage, 4) be sincere, and 5) be patient but persistent. He told the Northerners present that they should question their own sincerity before speaking scornfully of Southerners who refused to sit next to blacks in restaurants and schoolrooms. "What is your reaction," he asked them, "when a Negro moves onto your street?"[18]

In January 1960, Jack again spoke out against the suppression of free speech in Georgia. The chairman of the state board of education had written to its members that their job was to educate all the children of the state and to keep the schools open. Roy Harris, a powerful and demagogic politician who sat on the board, declared that the chairman did not share the views of his committee and should therefore resign. Jack, still able to be optimistic about such matters, commented, "as more voices are raised for open schools . . . the more desperate becomes the effort to preserve the silence of the fearful." Reemphasizing the need to safeguard our right to disagree, he said that it was a question of totalitarianism vs. democracy, and that the real challenge was not "going to school with Negroes, but the right to oppose the majority and the right to convince them that they are wrong."[19]

Unusual as it was for him to attack anyone by name, he did so in his "Brotherhood" sermon that year, naming Roy Harris as one of the leaders who "fan the flames of hatred by their own violent and uncompromising speech." He said "Brotherhood" must become more than "the bathos of a suddenly turned-on shower of good will." The world would always have its share of psychopaths ready to commit violence, he said, but the decent people must see to it that they have no environment in which to be "encouraged into activity."[20]

Whether or not he was retaliating for these remarks we will never know, but at about that time Roy Harris unleashed a wave of "Harris-

---

[18]Address at the UAHC Biennial, Miami, "The Personal Demands of Social Justice," 17 November 1959, JMR MSS.

[19]Sermon, "No Room for Dissent," 29 January 1960, JMR MSS.

[20]Ibid.; sermon, "Symbols of Hate and the Heart of America," 21 February 1960—JMR MSS.

ment" against us. Since he had openly advocated using such tactics against all persons who spoke out for open schools, we confidently believed that others were being "honored" in the same way. In what seemed to be a very well-organized campaign, someone would call our house at some hour of the day or night and continue to call without speaking, hanging up as soon as we answered. This was often done for hours on end. It happened at times when we could see no provocation, but without fail it would happen whenever Jack appeared on television or was mentioned in the newspaper. Once, when he had been interviewed on television about a subject unrelated to civil rights or schools, the telephone began to ring even before the program was finished.

Annoying as these tactics were, they did not cause us great distress—indigestion sometimes, for the calls often began with the evening news and continued through dinner—but not serious distress. The two o'clock in the morning calls that continued until daybreak did bother us, though, because we needed our sleep and we couldn't leave our phone off the hook for fear one of our mothers would need to reach us in an emergency. I begged Jack to change to an unlisted number but he refused. He believed a rabbi had a duty to be directly available to his congregants at all times.

He did solve the problem of the late-night calls, however. The next time we were awakened by one of them at three o'clock in the morning he answered, put down the receiver, picked it up, and called the number of the Roy Harris home. When a sleepy male voice answered, Jack cheerily announced, "Your boys are on the job, Roy. Just thought you'd be happy to know." We didn't receive any more late-night annoyance of that sort.

The Sibley Committee began its hearings in 1960, with plans to reach Atlanta in the early spring. Under PTA sponsorship, parents of children enrolled in public schools were polled to determine their feelings on the matter. The three questions were 1) Do you favor local option on integrating public schools? 2) Do you favor controlled integration rather than closing public schools? 3) Are you opposed to any form of integration in the public schools? The answers at the school Marcia attended were heavily "yes" on the first two and "no" on the third. To my knowledge they were never announced. I knew only because, as a member of the PTA board at that school, I was allowed to assist in counting the votes.

During that time Jack was involved in the question of whether or not to permit the use of Jewish communal buildings for substitute schools should the public schools be closed. A matter of extreme delicacy in public relations, it required both tact and integrity on the part of the Jewish community. As a guiding influence on the Community Relations Committee of the Atlanta Jewish Community Council, Jack helped formulate the policy it would follow in the anticipated emergency. It was 1) to deny occupancy of the buildings to those who would use them to circumvent the Court order, 2) to make them available in cases where "the only purpose is to meet the needs of children locked out of public schools," 3) to insure that classes held under the latter conditions would be private and nonsectarian and would not be considered an adequate or permanent substitute for public schools, and 4) to make no public statement implying the availability of the buildings prior to the closing of the public schools.[21]

The rabbis prepared a statement of their own, which Jack was asked to read before the Sibley Committee along with the other statement. I went with him to the high school where the hearings were being held. We had no idea what to expect as we parked and walked up to the auditorium that warm spring afternoon. That it was crowded was unsurprising, of course, but the general tone of those who attended was suprising. Subconsciously, perhaps, we had assumed it would be similar to that prevailing at the first trial of George Bright. It was not. On the contrary, if there were any "rabble" in the crowd they were so outnumbered by the "decent folk" that we could not detect their presence. Not that we naively believed that everyone there agreed with our point of view. Far from it. The opposition, however, no longer stood out as red-necked and violence-prone.

Gradually, almost imperceptibly, the mood of intransigence and despair shifted to one of acceptance and optimism. As Jack described it:

> The politicians began to feel the groundswell of changing attitudes. The State legislature backed away from the final irrevocable confrontation of State vs. Federal law. It was possible to allow "token integration" without destroying completely the public school system.

---

[21]"Guide to the Use of Jewish Communal Buildings If Public Schools are Closed," confidential notice to members of Atlanta Jewish Community Council, Community Relations Committee, unsigned and undated, JMR MSS.

Atlanta—which faced the first court-ordered admission of Negro students—breathed a little easier.[22]

When a Temple youth conclave met in Atlanta that summer, Jack addressed the young people on the same matters that he had been stressing to their elders throughout recent years. He told them that the struggle for civil rights was no longer an academic one, that white supremacy was dead "here in our own country" as well as in the emerging nations of the Third World, and that they would do well to see the problem in its total setting. He also read them a statement in which students at the predominantly black Atlanta University Center had listed the goals sought by members of their race in their effort to obtain human rights. Noting that the governor of Georgia had condemned the statement as "communist" and "subversive," he pointed out that on the contrary, it was actually "the realistic application of the very ideals which we profess as citizens of the greatest democracy in the world." He mentioned, too, the direct-action technique then coming to the fore under the leadership of Martin Luther King, Jr., and others, telling the Jewish teenagers that it was not unlike the personal commitment demanded by their own religious faith.[23]

The High Holydays of 1960 called for more than one reference to civil rights. On Rosh Hashanah Eve, Jack gave a mild "nudge" with a mention, within the context of world peace, of Atlanta's progress:

> Another city in the South—gracelessly and reluctantly, but nonetheless definitely—chose to maintain its public schools. . . . Not the millennium, to be sure, not the dreams of a day of peace and brotherhood stemming from the heart of man. Only a little progress—enough to get us through one more day in hope.[24]

The following morning Jack developed his subject in more detail and with more despair. He spoke of a new school building in Georgia that remained empty and unused in spite of dire facility shortages because, as he said, "it had the misfortune to be built in the wrong place for children with the wrong color of skin." Recalling the incidents at Little Rock, New

---

[22]Rothschild, "The Atlanta Story."

[23]Address to Youth Conclave, Human Rights Day, ca. August 1960, JMR MSS.

[24]Sermon, "Day by Day," 21 September 1960, JMR MSS.

Orleans, and other places where the school-integration order had been defied, he asked if we, too, would "choose the path of ignorance, the blind alley of stunted growth," and commented sadly that the outlook for courage and wisdom was not very bright. Even in Atlanta, he noted, the wise and the powerful "refuse to speak wisely or lead bravely."[25]

His sermons on Rosh Hashanah that year were merely a warmup for what he was to say on Yom Kippur. Somewhat sheepishly he began, "I suppose you are tired of hearing the problem discussed. I confess that I, too, wish there were a way of forgetting it. I cannot—and neither can you." Then he said that the immorality of segregation was no longer an issue and that public education was only the immediate question, not the basic one. What was basic was human dignity and equal rights for all.[26]

Comparing the current public reaction to that of Jonah, who fled in panic when God challenged him, Jack accused us of taking refuge behind whatever shelter we could find in the hope that we could conceal from ourselves our abject surrender, adding, "As we flee from the moral commitment, we pretend that our use of the law makes us law-abiding citizens, facing up to our great decision. But in our hearts we know that we use the law as a legal means of evading what is right."[27]

He ended that sermon with a reference to the high school in Tennessee that had been the first victim of violence caused by the Court order to integrate. The principal of that school had recently been quoted in his reaction to parents who had withdrawn their children to avoid integration and who had later returned, complaining that their children were unmanageable. The educator had commented that his former students had been overtaken by hatred brewed within them by their parents. Jack added, "You see, like Jonah we raise a storm that threatens to engulf us all. We brutalize ourselves—and all mankind."[28]

That autumn was an exciting one in the Rothschild household. Jack received two honors, one of which was not wholly unexpected, the other, one which he had grave misgivings about accepting.

---

[25]Sermon, "Old Values for a New Year," 22 September 1960, JMR MSS.

[26]Sermon, "Man Calls—God Answers," 1 October 1960, JMR MSS.

[27]Ibid.

[28]Ibid.

In recent years it had become customary for the Hebrew Union College-Jewish Institute of Religion (HUC-JIR) to confer honorary doctorate
degrees upon its alumni after they had served twenty-five years in the
rabbinate. In Jack's case the college added the distinguishing features of
presenting it to him in the calendar year prior to his twenty-fifth anniversary of ordination, and also by inviting him to give the address at the
ceremony, which he shared with two other recipients. I went with him to
Cincinnati for the weekend. Mother Rothschild and Sister Jean met us
there. It was a very happy time.

Jack had hesitated to accept the second honor—it was an invitation
from the German government to be its guest for a month-long tour of
Germany. Still unwilling to buy major products made in Germany because of the ever-present memory of the Nazi Holocaust, he believed it
would be hypocritical to accept the hospitality of its government. Upon
mentioning his dilemma to his colleagues, however, he learned that other
rabbis whom he respected had already been on similar tours. They advised him to do the same as a means of learning whether or not there was
a sincere attempt to stamp out anti-Semitism there. "Your congregation
will benefit from your first-hand report," they told him, "and besides,
with the generous per diem the government gives its guests, you can salve
your conscience by not spending any U.S. dollars while you're there." He
went, and even managed to bring home some lovely gifts for the children
and me without breaking his self-imposed rule about American currency.
Members of the congregation who were stationed in Germany with the
U.S. Army took him to their post exchange to do his shopping.

The month in Germany provided Jack with significant insights into
the conditions prevailing among the remnants of Jewish communities
there, and provided him with several memorable experiences. Through a
mutual friend he met the U.S. ambassador and his wife, who in turn invited the American correspondents stationed in Bonn to a party to meet
him. In Freiburg he met a wonderful couple who had saved the life of a
Jewish friend by hiding her in their attic. When we went to Europe for
another World Union meeting in 1964—this one held in Paris—Jack took
me across the border to Freiburg just long enough to meet them. We've
remained family friends ever since.

Jack met many officials, of course, who claimed that they had not
sympathized with the Nazi program. He also met one honest enough to
tell him, confidentially, that not only were all of them Nazis, himself in-

cluded, but that he enjoyed needling his former colleagues by teasing them about it. Jack was thoroughly satisfied, however, of the sincerity of the German government in its claim of vigilance in outlawing anti-Sem-itism. So vigilant was it, he noted, that officials tended to turn their eyes away from the illegal and borderline practices of some Jews in businesses such as import-export and prostitution. From what he was told by Jewish leaders there, this "hands-off" tendency on the part of the law had en-couraged disreputable Jewish entrepreneurs from other countries to take up residence in West Germany.

Of all the fascinating insights he gained on that trip, none intrigued him more than a parallel he began to note as he traveled through the southern state of Bavaria. He enjoyed his stay in Munich, its capital, more than anywhere else because, as he described it, his hosts there were re-laxed, "utterly charming and hospitable," and completely opposite "from the stereotype of the rigid, unbending German that we think about."

> The people here are . . . so much like United States Southerners that it is frightening. They are charming and friendly and even have a dialect all their own that is softer than the language in other parts of the country. . . . They are the only State that refused to sign the federal constitution under the Adenauer government and haven't signed it to this day. They go our Southerners one better. The South seceded from the Union. . . . Here they never even joined it. . . . I wonder whether Hitler didn't find it easy to begin here because here he could best appeal to the super-patriotism of the people. I can just hear him saying that these outsiders are defiling our Southern tra-ditions and we have got to restore them to their rightful place. I think no other section of Germany would have responded with rebel yells to the extent that Bavaria did. . . . And yet, with it all, these people are by far the nicest Germans that we have met.[29]

He expressed the hope that someone would one day write a treatise on the relationship between superpatriotism and the willingness to support extremist movements like Hitler's—which began in Munich—and like the present-day organizations' advocacy of violence over school integra-tion—which was taking place in the American South. So far as I know he

---

[29]Report on visit to Germany, untitled, ca. December 1960, JMR MSS.

never found one, nor did he find the time or the inclination to do the study himself.[30]

Before accepting the invitation to go to Germany, Jack had stipulated that he would not be bound by obligation to report only his favorable reactions. Accordingly, when he returned he had one set of circumstances to report favorably and another, one dealing with the Jewish communities themselves, unfavorably. He divided them into sermons for two successive Friday nights. As luck would have it, the German consul who had extended the invitation came with his party to hear only the second of the two—the unfavorable one. He remained a friend in spite of it, however, and eight years later, even endorsed his successor's invitation to Jack for a return trip.

Jack came home as Atlantans began to shift into the final stage of the school crisis and start the first stage of the struggle to desegregate public facilities. As he described it in *American Judaism*:

> Now it became a battle to create a climate of opinion in which desegregation could be carried out in peace and dignity without harming the image of Atlanta as a modern and progressive city. This was no easy task. Atlanta has its share of racists and trouble-makers. . . . Segregationists of both the rabble rousing and the aroused rabble variety are present in significant numbers. In addition, every outside racist gravitated to the city to defend that "sacred way of life" that seems to draw defenders of an ilk that somehow make "sacredness" a questionable virtue, to say the least.[31]

He began by instituting another series of programs at The Temple, this one designed to allay fears persons might have in dealing with school integration. He showed a film produced for such purposes by the UAHC, and encouraged his community-affairs committee to sponsor a series of Sunday-morning discussions. Sisterhood, having continued to address the issues at hand in at least one luncheon program each year, now presented a program in which actors gave brief, impromptu enactments of crisis situations likely to arise in families as a result of school desegregation. Each scene was halted at the peak of tension and followed immediately by a

---

[30]Conversations with JMR, December 1960.

[31]Rothschild, "The Atlanta Story."

professionally led group discussion. The actors, whom I had recruited from Theatre Atlanta, also gave such improvisations for other groups throughout the city during that period.

In his traditional year-end sermon Jack wryly observed that the new year, 1961, read the same upside down but would be no different from the past year if we didn't do something about turning prevailing conditions upside down. He reminded his listeners of what he himself could never forget, the scenes of white mothers in New Orleans spitting on black children as they walked the path to their newly integrated school. He said he had learned recently that what on television had appeared to be a mob had in reality been estimated at only 100 to 150 people, a fact that led him to believe that the "decent" people had simply abandoned the conflict. He begged Atlantans not to do so, repeating his warning that it was no longer a matter of what was happening to the blacks, but of what the white majority was doing to itself.[32]

He also commented on some incredible testimony given by the president of the University of Georgia in the recent trial challenging segregation there. This official had declared that there had never been a law against admitting blacks to the university and that no discrimination had been practiced in processing applications. Jack sarcastically called that "the long arm of coincidence."[33]

He always enjoyed the challenge of speaking to college groups, but that winter he was especially delighted with his assignment as one of the ministers-in-residence for the "Religion in Life" week at the University of Georgia. The "Be Kind to God" week, as some of the students irreverently named it, began soon after the start of winter quarter, at which time two highly qualified black students were admitted to this previously all-white institution.

From all reports, Charlayne Hunter and Hamilton Holmes had encountered no resistance from school authorities when they registered for classes, but they met with highly publicized resistance on the part of the student body. At least, so it seemed, judging from reports in the newspapers and live television coverage of the riots that ensued when the two

---

[32]Semon, "The Great Events of 1960," 6 January 1961.

[33]Ibid.

took up residence on campus. We saw students shaking their fists in defiance. We even saw one waving a Negro puppet in front of the camera.[34]

Jack had received advance information about his assignment at the university indicating substantial student interest in the religious-emphasis program. When he and the others were briefed upon arrival they were given the same encouraging outlook and also told that they would have no trouble dealing with the subject of religion as it related to the crisis of integration. "No matter how you begin the discussions," the school authorities said, "they will inevitably be turned to integration, the recent riot and its implications."[35]

Such was not the case. According to Jack the students made a concerted effort to avoid the subject, told him that the recognized religious organizations on campus (Wesley Foundation, Canterbury House, and Hillel) attracted only "an infinitesimal minority" of the student body, and that another organization—one made up of fundamentalists—was "going strong and trying to undermine the others." Had his success in reaching any appreciable number of young listeners been his measure of worth in spending a week on campus he would have been disappointed indeed. It wasn't, of course. He spent his time not speaking but listening, questioning rather than being questioned.

The picture gleaned from conversations with reporters, school officials, and some students indicated a story far different from what had been shown on television. Informants made Jack promise not to mention them by name and then proceeded to speak freely, each corroborating stories told by another. They said that nothing had occurred when Holmes and Hunter first arrived. The crowd that had gathered was merely curious, not hostile—until a newsman suggested that they shake their fists so he could get a good picture. Jack learned also that the student who had been photographed waving the puppet had not been the one who had brought it. A photographer had asked that student to wave it and he had refused, whereupon the photographer asked for a volunteer and got one. The authorities learned of it when the photographer pleaded with them not to take action against the student in the picture.

---

[34]Sermon, "Behind the Headlines at the University of Georgia," 10 February 1961.
[35]Ibid.

Great pressure had been brought to bear upon the administration to reinstate the students suspended for these actions, but authorities were determined not to give in. Apparently, someone had assured the students of protection in the event that they were caught. No one had been able to ascertain who that someone was, however. All the students would admit was that "they" had said "they" would take care of them if anything happened. Jack had no doubt that the university had been sabotaged by the state on the night of the riot. "All precautions had been taken to prevent it," he told me, "and they knew it was coming."

As for the brave young man and woman who dared to be the first, he reported, "Charlayne Hunter cooks her own breakfast in her room and has her other meals with Hamilton Holmes in a Negro restaurant." So far as Jack could discover, neither of them had been seen in the library or any other student haunt. "They go to classes with the others and that's all," he concluded sadly. "The University may have been integrated but the student body has not."[36]

Jack remained optimistic about Atlanta's ultimate response to the school crisis once the initial hurdle of keeping the schools open had been passed. Mayor Hartsfield ordered the parks and transportation system desegregated in the spring of 1961, quietly, without fanfare and without attracting protest demonstrations. Department stores promised to desegregate all facilities including lunch counters after the schools opened in the late fall. While there had been some well-publicized demonstrations in that regard, it remained peaceful and the goal was achieved. Furthermore, the police force, under the direction of Chief Herbert Jenkins, could be depended upon to do its job with fair-minded restraint.[37]

We had no doubt at all that members of the news media, print and electronic, would do everything in their power to help effect a peaceful transition. They had done so throughout the years and no doubt would continue to do so. Above all, our friend Ralph McGill would continue to write his prizewinning column that appeared each day on the front page of the *Constitution*, telling the public what it needed to hear regardless of how unpopular an opinion it was.

---

[36]Ibid.

[37]Rothschild, "The Atlanta Story."

Jack found it absolutely uncanny the way Ralph would continually express in his columns ideas that he himself had been dealing with, intending to use in a sermon. Many a morning I would be awakened by Jack, who never ate breakfast, ensconced in the morning paper, exclaiming, "Damn! He did it again!"

I finally stopped asking "Who did what?" I knew Jack meant that Ralph in his column that morning had scooped the sermon he was preparing to preach on Friday night.

As Jack himself would later write, "almost without exception the Jews of Atlanta stood up for and out as champions of the liberal cause." Many had been leaders in HOPE. Now they came to the front of a new coalition called OASIS, Organizations Assisting Schools in September. This coalition was based on a much wider foundation than HOPE and included such establishment groups as the Atlanta Chamber of Commerce, churches individually and collectively under the banner of the Atlanta Council of Churches, all of the city's synagogues, the Catholic Church, many civic groups, the Jewish Community Council with all its constituent members, and many others including HOPE itself. OASIS formed subcommittees to give special attention to youth-serving agencies, to supply speakers and trained discussion leaders, to work individually with civic groups, neighborhood groups, church groups, and so forth. A religious committee prepared material for clerics of all denominations and sponsored a citywide observance of "Law and Order Sabbath" on the weekend just prior to the opening of schools. A "Layman's Letter to His Child" appeared in the paper that Sunday, over the signatures of nearly one thousand persons of all faiths. Leading citizens taped spot announcements for radio and television use in the days preceding the start of the school year. A public-relations committee, headed by a very capable woman belonging to The Temple, made detailed arrangements for the care and comfort of the visiting press, a move as much designed to help avoid some of the excesses that had been observed elsewhere as it was to extend our traditional Southern hospitality.[38]

Grateful as he was for the work of the coalition and what it was able to accomplish, Jack and his fellow members of the Atlanta Council on Human Relations—as well as other individuals, no doubt—deeply regretted

[38]Ibid.

and felt uncomfortable that OASIS by its very nature was required to speak only in terms of civic pride, economic necessity, law and order. As he described it:

> Business men bombarded the city . . . with reams of statistics proving that our economic future was at stake. Ministers pleaded that we act like good Christians. What was strongly implied—and often openly said—was that even if the court decision was wrong . . . we must act correctly superficially because that is what is expected of good Christians.
>
> So we still have the more basic and difficult challenge. . . . We still haven't fought on the only battlefield where a real victory can be won—in the hearts of men.[39]

Atlanta swarmed with reporters as D-Day, 31 August 1961, approached. Through the meticulous sifting of two hundred Negro applications for transfer to previously all-white high schools, nine students had been selected and assigned to four different schools. One of them was Northside High School, which was located across the street from my mother's home. When the names of the students assigned there were announced, Mother called each of the families and invited them to bring their young people to visit her before the crucial day, so they would be acquainted with someone in the neighborhood in case they should "need a friend."

Elaborate precautions had been taken to insure the safety of the students, and every known troublemaker had been followed for weeks, but the streets adjacent to the selected schools were not closed off. Only the grounds of the schools themselves were off limits to the press and public. By inviting ourselves to Mother's for breakfast that day we were able to witness whatever might happen from the nearest vantage point. Quite accidentally her house also became "field headquarters" for a reporter from out of town and for the news director of one of the local television stations.

At about 8:30 A.M. we walked down Mother's driveway to stand at the foot of it, directly across from the entrance to the school driveway, while the cars carrying the students arrived. I wondered if Jack felt the same cramp at the pit of his stomach that I felt in mine. Even the freshness of the early morning sunshine couldn't dispel the strange mixture of

---

[39]Ibid.

apprehension and confidence, awareness of the past and faith in the present that gnawed at us as we waited there. Whatever happened, or didn't happen, we knew we were witnessing firsthand a milestone in our city's history.

Jack described it in the sermon he was preparing for Rosh Hashanah, two weeks later. He led up to it with reference to the Akeda story, the sacrifice of Isaac, which is read each year during that service. Reminding us that we, like Abraham, "trudge wearily up the mountain of life, holding the hand of the child who is all of our tomorrows," he asked if we would choose to save him for a better life than our own or bind him "upon the altar of ignorance and shame."[40]

He praised the fact that "in our own city, the children's bonds were loosened," but deplored that the victory had been one of expediency only and that we had yet to face the moral issue. In reference to the moral issue he reminded us that it could not have been an easy matter for Abraham to "forsake the tried and comfortable practices which had served man for untold centuries" but added that he must have been overjoyed when he finally had the courage to heed God's command—even as we were at that proud moment of our own history. "So it has been with us," he declared. "Now we can feign deafness no longer."[41]

He concluded by telling the congregation what he had seen and felt as he watched from my mother's driveway two weeks before.

> I stood . . . in the midst of a little group of newsmen and observers. . . . Suddenly the three Negro children drove up to the driveway of the school. They got out of the car and walked—oh so slowly to the door. A lump rose up in my throat too big for me to swallow. I almost wept. And there were those who did cry. Why? Because these, too, were Abraham's child. Because another human sacrifice had been broken down. Because they dramatized another victory of the human spirit. Most of all, because they too had arms and legs and hearts and souls. Because—despite the color of their skin they were just three more children of the living God. And I began to wonder what all the preparation had been for, all the dedicated labor of so many dedicated people, all the careful planning, all the logistics of a

---

[40]Sermon, "Isaac Unbound," 11 September 1961, JMR MSS.

[41]Ibid.

battle. It was so simple, after all. Three children went to school. All they really needed was for our hearts to go with them.[42]

---

[42]Ibid.

CHAPTER SEVEN

TIME
FOR DINNER

One afternoon a year or so before the school crisis peaked my mother telephoned me excitedly to say she had just met "that nice young man who led the Montgomery bus boycott." She wanted to know when Jack and I would be free to come to a dinner party she planned to give for him and his wife, who had only recently taken up residence in Atlanta. "His wife is a musician," Mother added, especially pleased because music was her own field as well.

Jack had already met Martin Luther King, Jr., at a session of "the dinner group," a nonorganization, which never even gave itself a name but had already begun to have a deep impact on our lives. He described its beginnings in this way:

One of the transcending problems in the field of Negro-white
relationships is that of communication—or the absence of it. . . . A
few of us determined to do something about developing contacts and
deepening friendships along interracial lines. We organized a dinner
group which meets every other week. It has no officers and no program and no agenda for its meetings. But it numbers among its participants such members of the Negro community as Benjamin Mays,
President of Morehouse College, Rufus Clement, President of Atlanta University, Albert Manley, President of Spelman College, Martin Luther King, and several leaders of Atlanta's outstanding
churches. From time to time, we invite—successfully—members of
the power structure to meet with us.[1]

From time to time, also, they invited us wives to meet with them. In that
way I became acquainted with some of the men whom Jack knew through
his years of work on the Atlanta Council of Human Relations, the Southern Regional Council, the Urban League, and so forth. Also Jack and I
had the opportunity to meet their wives. One couple in particular attracted us, not only for the great respect and admiration we had for their
achievements but for the sheer pleasure of being in their company. They
were Dr. Samuel Williams, dean of Morehouse College and pastor of
Friendship Baptist Church, and his wife Billie, who at that time taught
remedial reading to black college students in South Carolina, a commute
of several hundred miles. Sam had been one of Martin King's teachers in
college and the two couples maintained a close friendship with each other.

    The dinner group had just begun meeting a few months before my
mother met Martin King and had not yet seen fit to include us women
in their get-togethers. Consequently, the little dinner party that Mother
was putting together for the Kings was to be my first experience with a
purely social biracial function. The anticipation of it titillated me in a way
I didn't like. I was too embarrassed by it even to mention it to Jack. I tried
to rationalize the feelings, telling myself that it was natural, simply a stage
one had to go through before reaching normalcy, but it bothered me
nonetheless. I wanted to tell people, to brag about it. When I could resist
the urge no longer I did mention it to a few carefully selected friends, only

[1]Rothschild, "The Atlanta Story," *American Judaism* 12, no. 1 (Fall 1967), JMR
MSS.

to discover that some of them had already entertained guests of both races in their homes together (usually physicians and their wives). They appeared to be as relieved as I was to have broken the silence about it.

Thus it was that the Kings and the Rothschilds first met as a foursome at the home of my mother, the not-so-little and not-so-old "lady in tennis shoes" who was born and raised in Columbus, Georgia. Jack and I planned to invite the Kings to our home soon afterward for a similar get-together, but circumstances, theirs and ours, interfered. Jack was getting ready to leave for his trip to Germany, and although none of us dreamed of it at the time, Martin was about to go to jail.

It happened while Jack was in Germany. Martin, as head of the Southern Christian Leadership Conference (SCLC), felt obligated to go along with his young followers when they determined to use direct action—a peaceful sit-in—against the policy of segregated facilities at Rich's, Atlanta's leading department store. When some of them were arrested he insisted upon going to jail with them, even though the authorities were trying to avoid taking him. That in itself would not have been too alarming, for the city and Fulton County authorities had proven themselves trustworthy. The problem arose when the not-so-liberal neighboring county of DeKalb got into the act. It had a charge pending against Martin for driving without a license, which DeKalb authorities used to have him removed from the city jail and brought to their own. From there he was transferred to the state prison at Reidsville, an institution well known for the brutality of its authorities and inmates. There Martin's life was in danger.

When I read the news I went immediately to the telephone to call Coretta. With Jack out of the country I didn't see how I could help, but at least I could offer sympathy and the willingness to help. I was surprised and gratified that Coretta took the time—had the interest, even—to chat at length that day with a newfound friend such as I. She did, however, and I hoped that in itself was of some comfort to her. We talked about our mutual problems as wives of outspoken clergymen and mothers of their children, who often suffered as a consequence of their father's activities.

It was then that Coretta told me about the problem she was having trying to explain to her daughter Yolanda—Yoki for short—why Martin was in jail. They hadn't prepared the child for it because they didn't expect it would happen quite so soon. She had heard the news in her car pool coming home from school. My heart skipped a beat when I heard that. Desperately groping for something helpful to suggest, I thought of how much Martin had been influenced by Mohandas Gandhi in India, and mentioned it to Coretta as a possible analogy to use in her explanation. She must have been amused at my well-meant naiveté, but she was too polite to laugh out loud. "Janice," she said, "this child's only five years old. She doesn't even know she's colored yet."

That was the beginning of my education in the realities of black personhood, in truly relating to some of the problems unique to the lives of minority men, women, and children. Our conversation made me think back to my own childhood, to the day when I was about Yoki's age, when I came home from school and asked my mother, "What is Jewish? Am I Jewish?" I remember that the answer she gave me was rather vague, not really satisfying, and I felt grateful that my own children had never needed to ask such a question. They grew up in a time of ethnic self-esteem that was just beginning to take root in the black community. Yoki and Marty—Martin III—were still too young to be hurt by the outside world. Until now.

The subject of helping our children grow up with a healthy self-esteem led Coretta and me into a discussion of another matter I hadn't considered. She mentioned that she was always on the lookout for pictures to show Yoki of black brides, models, or other black women in glamorous settings. The "Black is Beautiful" campaign may have been underway then, but it hadn't yet reached the awareness of most whites. I suddenly realized how I and many of my contemporaries had, as teenagers, been indoctrinated with the belief that willowy, pug-nosed, flat-chested blond was beautiful. It took Sophia Loren, an Italian of Catholic extraction, to convince us that Jewish was beautiful. Shortly after that conversation with Coretta I saw an ad in the *New York Times* featuring an adorable black child modeling a lovely handmade party dress. It was captioned, "Aren't you glad you have a little girl?" I cut it out and sent it to her for Yoki.

With Jack away I had no "inside line" to what was really happening in the community. From the accounts one could read in the newspapers most of us concluded that Richard R. Rich, chairman of the board of Rich's, was responsible for Martin's originally having been jailed. (His safe release and the circumstances under which it occurred are now a well-known part of history.)

Certainly Dick Rich was the key figure on behalf of the store in that dispute. Since Rich's led the way in setting policy for the retailers in Atlanta, those of us who wanted to see segregation ended bitterly resented what seemed to us to be his stubborn refusal to move ahead. I didn't go as far as to advocate boycott or tear up my credit card as many did, but I stayed away from the store for the duration of the impasse.

Those of us who knew Dick personally and knew his record of progressive action in behalf of the city were doubly puzzled and resentful. When Jack returned home from Europe he was besieged on all sides to "talk to Dick," who was a member of the congregation and, prior to this time, a good friend. Jack hesitated. He believed that it was a matter in which he was not qualified to advise and that it would do no good. When the situation was finally resolved he wrote a letter to Dick congratulating him and telling him that he had refrained from speaking to him about it earlier, as many had asked him to do, because he knew "that there was no more decent and liberal member of our community than you and I couldn't see how my voice could do anything but add to the problems with which you were faced and the struggle to find a solution to them." Despite this restraint on Jack's part, Dick made it clear that our friendship had ended. We never did learn why.[2]

The next six months flew by for us in our frenzy to effect the peaceful desegregation of our school system. Any attempt at a purely social evening originating with us was out of the question, although we did enjoy the considerable amount of socializing that we constantly engaged in, helter-skelter, wherever our various involvements called us. One of them, for Jack, was his twice-a-month evenings with the "dinner group," which finally got around to inviting the wives to one of its meetings. That invitation gave me the chance to meet Sam and Billie Williams.

By this time Jack and Sam had become close enough friends that Jack had no compunctions about sharing an ethnic joke with him. He did that evening; it was the latest "integration" story making the rounds among the liberal rabbis, and Sam was delighted with it. So delighted was he, in fact, that when he rose to open the general conversation around the table, he announced to everyone that "the rabbi" had a good story to tell. Jack, painfully embarrassed, tried to get out of it, but Sam persisted and the others urged him to go ahead. Finally he did—and to his great relief and surprise, the story was well received. Afterward, he told Sam how

---

[2]JMR to Richard R. Rich, 9 March 1961, JMR MSS.

embarrassed he had been, being coerced into telling an ethnic joke in mixed company. Sam agreed with him that normally it would have been in poor taste, but added, "it all depends on who's telling the story. There are exceptions to every rule, and in this case, you're it." Jack considered that one of the loveliest compliments he ever received.

By the time we finally got together on a date for dinner with the Kings, the following fall, I had gotten over my feeling of "strangeness," but by then Martin had become so famous that there was a new element of titillation involved. Our housekeeper, no longer Johnnie Mae but an older, more assertive type, was more excited about it than I at first realized. When I discussed the menu with her and designated for the entrée coquilles St. Jacques, which I always prepared myself, she contradicted me. Hands on hips, heels dug firmly into the kitchen linoleum, she announced, "Miz Rothschild, *you* may know very well what your fancy friends likes to eat, but *I* knows what colored preachers likes to eat. We are having barbecued chicken!" (*She* always prepared that.) Actually, we both ended up feeling like blue-ribbon cooks because Martin complimented her on the chicken and Coretta asked me for the recipe for the coquilles, which I had used as an appetizer.

Because we wanted to keep it informal and intimate we asked only two other couples, the president of our congregation and his wife, and another pair of very close friends who had not yet met the Kings. In the latter case the wife mentioned that her mother, a native of New Orleans, would be visiting her on the day of the dinner. I said to bring her, of course, and invited my own mother as well, but I had misgivings about how comfortable this elegant New Orleansean would be at an integrated dinner party.

When it was over I had misgivings instead about myself for having committed the sin of stereotyping. Not only was the lady, as well as her daughter, one of the truly genuine human beings in this world, she was also a fine musician—a fact I had forgotten. As our guests left that evening I overheard her and her daughter arranging a luncheon date with Coretta for the following week.

Two items of conversation from that evening are branded permanently in my memory. The first took place shortly after the Kings arrived, which was much later than the others. No explanation was necessary but Martin apologized anyhow and explained that they had been delayed trying to find our house. (The street was poorly lighted and the numbers hard to read.) They finally had to drive up to one of the other houses to inquire. As Martin told us this, he quickly added, "but we were careful not to embarrass you with your neighbors. I let Coretta go to the door so they'd think we were just coming to serve a party."

I still get a lump in my throat when I think of it.

The other dark memory is of our speaking of his growing fame and the growing danger connected with it. Someone asked if he was not afraid of another attempt on his life, following the near-fatal one he had sustained two years before. He tried to avoid answering by joking that he was having difficulty "keeping up with my reputation." When that answer didn't divert the line of questioning, Coretta said quietly, "We've thought of that. We know what might happen. If it's worth doing, it's worth the price we may have to pay." We thought of that reply constantly, as surely they must have done, throughout the six and a half years that followed.

Jack felt very strongly that the time had come, the school crisis having passed, to begin working on the human-rights problem where it really lay: "in the hearts of men," as he worded it. During Passover he preached on the subject, pointing out that the great Negro spirituals dealt with the same theme as our own festival: the story of the Exodus from Egypt. The current struggle for integration, he said, was not merely a matter of sitting in classrooms or at lunch counters. "We will never understand . . . unless we come to know it in its most basic terms—the human drive for freedom."[3]

Recognizing the need for understanding on both sides of the gulf, he addressed the problem from another point of view when he spoke to black audiences, as he did shortly after Passover that year at Atlanta's Interdenominational Theological Center. There he said:

> Here in the South, we have seen a kind of writhing agony—and I daresay these writhings of conscience take place among Negroes as well as whites. For what causes the agony is man's recognition of his own capacity to live up to the best of himself. And I am sure that there are Negroes, too, who choose a superficial equanimity and the preservation of the comfortable status quo. But I speak now only of the "white man's burden. . . . " What the law requires of them has shattered the very foundations of their lives. . . . How they wish it had

---

[3]Passover Sermon, "Yearning to Breathe Free," 20 April 1962, JMR MSS.

never happened—that they had never been forced to confront not alone the mores of their genteel society but, more soul-shattering, the good opinion they had of themselves as a decent, religious people.[4]

Speaking also of the gains recently made in Atlanta, he said that the trouble "with all this progress" was that it made the situation look much better than it actually was. He called it "superficial and grudging," as little as the law would allow because it existed "for all the wrong reasons."

"And we know that this is so," he declared. "That knowledge gnaws at our consciences and destroys the inner fibre of our being."[5]

It had been a very difficult winter and spring for Jack. His mother had been diagnosed as having metastasized cancer in December and died just before Passover. With no assistant rabbi and the congregation then numbering more than twelve hundred families, each trip he made to Pittsburgh to be with his mother was a problem for the congregation and a wrenching decision for him about where his greater duty lay. To make matters worse, I developed a lump in my breast, discovered the day his mother died, and both of us spent a frightened few weeks until surgery could be scheduled and we learned it was benign.

Relief was on the way, however. Rabbi Emeritus David Marx had passed away in the recent months and as a result the congregation could afford to engage an assistant rabbi. At Jack's suggestion it was decided to establish a policy of tenure for three years only, selecting candidates for the position from among those about to be ordained that year from the Cincinnati school. Jack went with the congregation's president to interview the men, and chose Stuart E. Davis as his—and actually The Temple's—first assistant rabbi. They marked the occasion with a service of installation followed by a reception soon after the Holydays the following October.

On Rosh Hashanah that year Jack spoke about happiness, pointing to examples of "one man's joy" being the sorrow of another. He began by citing the recent decision of the Supreme Court outlawing prayer in the public schools. This decision was a victory for those who believed as we did in strictly interpreting the principle of separation between church and

---

[4]Address to the International Theological Center, Atlanta, "Restoring Souls in a Shaken Society," 3 May 1962, JMR MSS.

[5]Ibid.

state, but it was a defeat for fundamentalists and other conservatives and evoked from them an uproar of complaint. Urging us to develop a view of happiness that would be attainable for everyone, he admitted that such would be possible only when persons were convinced "that there is enough of it to go around," and applied the idea to the racial struggle:

> Somehow, the Negro's demand for self-fulfillment brings unhappiness to the white man. He resists with all the power at his command. He perverts the law for his own purpose. He intimidates those who seek the full measure of their citizenship. He puts a woman's stocking over his face and shoots into a House of God, hat on head and cigarette dangling from his mouth to frighten and intimidate. He burns a cross crowned by a Negro's hat—a modern golden calf about which he cavorts with religious frenzy. . . . His female counterpart takes up her role as protector of "the cherished Southern way of life" by spitting once again on little children on their way to school.[6]

He then asked how persons could act in so barbarous a way, and answered his question with the true story of a sheriff in a small Georgia town. This sheriff, commenting on events in the civil rights movement, said in ignorant sincerity, "We never had no trouble here before. These nigras lived like we wanted them to for a hundred years—and everyone was happy." Jack commented that the sheriff, who obviously meant that all the whites were happy, had probably given the most honest answer yet heard on the subject, since he "never really understood how miserably unhappy the Negroes were." Adding that it was "a sorry quirk of human nature" that led persons to rest their own nobility upon the debasement of others, he concluded, "We must see whites and Negroes alike as the children of God—with the same needs, desires, ambitions, hopes. We must strive to understand that what drives us to seek the flowering of the human personality drives them as well. And what limits us, likewise limits them."[7]

That year our annual season of self-searching was punctuated with news from Oxford, Mississippi, where one lone black student, James Meredith, was attempting to register at the state university. His mere

---

[6]Sermon, "A Year of Happiness," 28 September 1962, JMR MSS.

[7]Ibid.

presence on the campus provoked a riot and bloodshed. The clergy of Oxford called for the observance of a Sabbath of repentance for this behavior
on the part of the townspeople, and the weekend chosen, by uncanny coincidence, happened to be the very weekend that we Jews were observing
our own annual Sabbath of Repentance. What an opportunity for a rabbi!
Sickened as he was by the cause, Jack gleefully latched onto it as a basis
for his sermon.

He began by castigating Governor of Mississippi Ross Barnett for
blaming the violence on outsiders, for selfishness in placing the sover-
eignty of the state above that of the nation, and for "callous playing upon
men's passions for personal gain." Asserting that prayers of repentance
were useless unless "by our acts we prove that we really meant it when
we said we were sorry," he noted sadly that in this case, "Mississippi has
some real atoning to do." Optimistically, he observed that it augured well
for democracy in America that the federal government had put all the
force of its resources behind the effort to keep one single black person in
the school of his choice, but he warned against complacency in the matter. Again challenging the religious community to take responsibility for
moral leadership, he declared; "If the church is going to be a significant
influence in our world, it had better start working on the issues of its own
day. It has received about all the help it can expect from official sources.
. . . Now it is up to us."[8]

Jack continued to stress that organized religion needed to make itself
heard on the moral imperatives involved in the racial struggle. On one
occasion the *Atlanta Constitution* quoted him as saying that the churches
and synagogues had been "woefully inadequate" in coping with the present social and moral issues, and that government officials should use their
prestige in rallying leadership in that quest. It would be another two years
before he would see any progress in this area. Gov. Carl Sanders would
ask him and others to suggest names of persons for appointment to a
committee for that purpose.[9]

There were still many Jews throughout the country, not just in the
Southern states, who disagreed with the premise that religious institu-

---

[8]Sermon, "Courageous Clergy in Mississippi," 5 October 1962, JMR MSS.

[9]Jo Anne Crawford, "Churches Only Partly Responsible in Moral Crisis, Leaders
Say Here," *Atlanta Constitution,* 15 June 1963, clipping in JMR MSS.

tions had a legitimate role to play in the struggle for human rights. Consequently, it was over the objection of a number of constituent congregations and the actual resignation of several, that the UAHC, in November 1962, opened its Religious Action Center in Washington, D.C. Although The Temple was not among those "seceding from the Union"—mostly due to Jack's influence over the years—he still felt the need to remind Temple members in a special sermon that autumn of the duties and goals to be furthered by such a center.

More than ever that year he was asked by colleagues in the North to address their congregations. Within a ten-month period in 1962-1963 he visited leading Reform congregations in Boston, Toronto, Minneapolis, and Westchester County, New York. He had already spoken in recent years at both of the principal Reform synagogues in Baltimore and in Cleveland, Pittsburgh, and numerous other cities. Wherever he went he stressed that Southern Jews, for the most part, were reacting "in a praiseworthy manner." For them, he said, "just not to join a white citizens' council is an act of heroism in some communities." He let his listeners in the North know that many Southern Jews had become active in the cause of human rights and that "almost without exception" they were willing to hear their rabbi speak out on the subject. Although the Southern Jew may be "uncomfortable, uneasy, even fearful," Jack told them, "he is essentially brave."[10]

While he staunchly defended what he perceived to be the majority of Southern Jews, Jack had little patience for those who contrived illogical and inconsistent excuses for their failure to become actively involved. He addressed that point with his usual logic in an article for the *Southern Israelite* in August 1963, entitled "No Place to Hide."

> No white American can evade any longer his personal involvement in the Negro's struggle for full citizenship. . . . The law guarantees equality—so he is involved as an American citizen. Every major religious organization has clearly stated its moral commitment . . . so he is involved as Christian or Jew. . . . How [the Southern Jew] wishes that Judaism didn't really say that. Or, since it does, that his national body or his own rabbi would stop reminding non-Jews of the

---

[10]Address, "Social Upheaval and Personal Peace" (first delivered as a Joshua Loth Liebman Memorial Lecture, Temple Israel, Boston), 6 April 1962, JMR MSS.

fact. . . . Yet, deep down inside himself he knows what is right and what isn't. . . . He can empathize with the members of another minority group. But still, he is white, and he lives among a white majority and, after all . . . he can't stick his neck out.

So the Southern Jew . . . more than all the other decent, God-fearing "moderates," equivocates and rationalizes. Above all, he joins his Christian friends (whose religion has also compromised them with uncompromising statements on the subject) in seeking to separate religion from life itself. . . . In recent days, however, he himself seems to have become less enamored of arguments such as these. . . . The Southern Jew seems ready to admit that this is an area in which religion cannot keep silent. . . . How, then, can he escape that feeling of Southern exposure that he wants so desperately to avoid? . . . He has devised a new philosophy which he hopes will provide him with the protective coloration he so desperately seeks. He now takes the stand that the struggle . . . doesn't really involve him as a Jew at all—it involves him only as an American! This position must be reckoned as one of the most startling pieces of evasion—and the most potentially dangerous escape hatch he has yet conjured up.

Does the Southern Jew really want to establish a dichotomy between his patriotism and his religion? . . . The Jew who has so bitterly fought anyone who dares accuse him of dual loyalty? Who has proclaimed himself "an American of the Jewish faith?" Who maintains—and rightly—that because he is a good Jew he can become a better American? Who with pride has asserted that the greatness of American democracy rests upon the Judeo-Christian tradition, part of which he shares? And now in order to avoid embarrassment and discomfiture does he seriously intend to present this new and damaging self-image?

For what is he saying? That there are two separate compartments of his life—one Jewish and the other American. . . . That when his fellow-citizens look at him, they must distinguish between him as a Jew and him as an American. He would have them blame his Americanism if he does anything they don't like—and credit his Judaism when they are pleased. But what if they come to the opposite conclusion—as well they may?[11]

---

[11]Rothschild, "No Place to Hide," *Southern Israelite*, Aug. 1963, undated manuscript in JMR MSS.

As always we had other facets of our life and work to deal with besides the civil rights battle. Jack was elected to the Board of Governors of
the Hebrew Union College-Jewish Institute of Religion. For years we had
agonized with its president, Nelson Glueck, over his difficulties estab-
lishing a branch of the school in Jerusalem. The building itself, destined
to be the first material presence of non-Orthodox Judaism in the Jewish
State, raised a furor within the Israeli Orthodox establishment and met
with untold numbers of delays and suspected sabotage. Finally completing it in 1963, Glueck scheduled a tour in order for members of his Board
of Governors to participate in the dedication and see Israel under his
guidance while they were there. Since it was he who had "followed the
trail of Abraham" in making the major archaeological discoveries in the
Negev, visiting Israel with him as our leader was a rare privilege and opportunity. We were overjoyed when The Temple board gave Jack leave to
use his expense account to go and to take me with him.

The trip was memorable for many reasons. Jack was honored in
being given a special part in the dedication ceremony, the prayer affixing
the mezuzah on the chapel. We were warmly received by President and
Mrs. Itzhak Ben Zvi at the official residence—the original one, which
looked more like a comfortable summer cottage than a chief executive's
mansion. And we delighted ourselves with the discovery that whereas our
American Negro spirituals were based upon the experiences of our ancestors in the Middle East, our present-day brothers in the Middle East borrowed the very same Negro spirituals to express their own longing for
peace, as well as their solidarity with the struggle for true freedom in
America. "When the Saints Go Marching In" seemed to be the favorite
that season. The Hebrew lyrics were different, however. The first line
translates, "When peace shall come." We later learned that Negro spirituals were especially popular at that particular time because it was the
week before Passover, and they were, in a sense, the carols of Passover.
Later, we participated in an unusual, impromptu Seder that one of the
couples on the trip with us quickly arranged for those of our party who
were stopping in Athens on the way home.

Back in Atlanta, Jack received another of those increasingly frequent
requests from other rabbis for an introduction to our friend, "the nice
young man who led the bus boycott." He was always happy to try, and
well received when he did, but met with less and less success as the direct-action movement gained momentum. To one such request he re-

plied, "I'm sure we can arrange a meeting with Martin Luther King if he's in town—which is rarely!"

That spring Martin had led the protest in Birmingham, faced the dogs and fire hoses turned upon him and his peaceful marchers by Public Safety Commissioner "Bull" Connor, and landed in the Birmingham jail. Jack received a copy of the now-famous letter written by Martin while he was imprisoned there and read it aloud to me with frequent sighs of appreciation. When he finished he commented wistfully, "I wish I could write like that!" The next day he wrote admiringly to Martin, saying, "It is without question the most moving and significant document I have yet read. . . . I hope you plan to give it wide distribution. I, myself, have taken the liberty of making copies available to Ralph McGill and one or two of my own interested laymen."[12]

Jack read the letter to his congregation as part of one of his sermons during the summer. Not everyone who heard the sermon agreed the letter was a masterpiece. Just recently I happened to see a report written by a member of our Temple choir to another Atlanta musician who was traveling abroad. He referred to the letter as "a tribute to himself from Martin Luther King" and commented "It was rather sickening."[13]

That was the summer of the Freedom March. Jack didn't go on it, nor, to the best of my knowledge, did he consider going. He knew that he was most effective in his own arena and that he could serve best by forgoing those "happenings" such as mass demonstrations, however important he knew them to be. He understood the fine distinction between outspokenness and flamboyance, and carefully avoided the kind of publicity that would reflect the latter. He never sought publicity for himself, neither did he hesitate or equivocate when members of the press asked him for a statement on a controversial issue (the only kind of issue he was ever interviewed about). The *New York Times* quoted him in regard to the Freedom March, reporting that "favorable mention of the march" had been made from several Southern pulpits and that Jack had said one of

---

[12]JMR to Martin Luther King, Jr., 10 June 1963, JMR MSS.

[13]Informal sermonette, summer 1963, no notes; Lowell Lehman to Hugh Hodgson, 6 August 1963, JMR MSS.

the results must be "the recognition by religious organizations of their responsibility to carry out the intent of the law."[14]

On Rosh Hashanah he again spoke of the Freedom March, basing his sermon on the familiar quotation of Rabbi Hillel, "If I am not for myself, who will be for me?" Too often, he observed, that portion of the quote was misinterpreted to mean "in order to be for myself I must be against someone else." That, he said, seemed to be the way many whites felt, now that black persons were finally demanding their full share of American citizenship. They felt abused by it, he said, "as though what the Negro seeks would decrease the white man's share in America, as though his being 'for himself' means that he is 'against you' . . . [but] it is not necessary to destroy another in order to safeguard self."[15]

Jack then related the story of the caged bird who says to its captors, "You see my food but you do not see my captivity." That, he declared, was the message of the Freedom March, the message that Martin Luther King so eloquently expressed on behalf of every black American. Jack told his congregation:

> He wants us to see his chains, his bars, his bondage. He wants out of his cage. He wants us to see him as a man—a child of God— with the same need for dignity and respect that we possess. This is what he told the nation and the world when he marched 200,000 strong and stood before the Lincoln Memorial. With dignity and fervor he spoke to the heart of his countrymen. Did you open your heart to let him in?[16]

On the Sunday morning after Rosh Hashanah we heard the horrible news that the 16th Street Baptist Church in Birmingham had been bombed and four young girls killed as they left their Sunday school room. Jack, near speechless with rage, immediately wrote a letter of sympathy to the pastor of the church and the following Friday night lashed out in fury in his sermon. Once more the obscene had occurred in the week leading up to our Sabbath of Repentance. In his sermon Jack asked,

---

[14]Irving Spiegel, "Clergymen in Many Cities Back Aims of the Washington March," *New York Times*, 2 Sept. 1963, JMR MSS.

[15]Sermon, "The Journey Through Time," 18 September 1963, JMR MSS.

[16]Ibid.

"What repentance is there for us in the murder of four children in a church?" Once again he placed the blame not only upon those who actually perpetrated the crime, but also upon "the politicians, clergy, all of us." Thundering that it was not enough to say we were sorry, he declared, "We must do something. Oratory is not enough."[17]

Temple members responded by opening their hearts and their checkbooks. Within two weeks Jack received a total of $3500 from 279 families, and more contributions continued to come in for weeks and months afterward. He forwarded it to the pastor of the church with a note saying he realized it could not "soften the grief nor allay the horror" of the bombing, but he hoped it would be of some use nevertheless.[18]

It meant a great deal to Jack to see the many letters and contributions that came from children in our religious school and from the young adults who had been students there. He thanked each of them individually and revealed in some of his letters facets of his personality that had not been seen in recent years.

His love for children, for example, and his knack for communicating with them shows up in the letter he wrote thanking two young sisters for their contribution. One of the children was only three years old at the time.

Dear Meg and Sophie:

I address the envelope only to Meg since I am sure that she will have to read the letter to Sophie. (I know that Sophie talks like a grown-up but I haven't heard any rumors yet that she can read!)

I think that this was the nicest gift that we have received for the Church in Birmingham, and I'm sure that they will think that . . . too. I have sent your letter along with your check and I have an idea that they may want to read it to the boys and girls of their religious school to show them that there are white children whose hearts are filled with love and concern for everyone, no matter what color their skins happen to be.

---

[17]Sermon, untitled (notes only), 20 September 1963, JMR MSS.

[18]JMR to Rev. John H. Cross, 27 September 1963, JMR MSS.

I am proud of you and shall continue to be proud of you as you grow and take your place in the life of our Congregation and Community.[19]

In a letter to a young woman off at college he let slip one of his self-deprecating half-jokes:

Dear Carol:

Every once in a while something happens that brightens my life and convinces me that my rabbinate has not been entirely wasted. Your letter was one of these events. It is heartening to know that I have been able to teach the message of Judaism to young people such as you.[20]

He would be even more heartened if he could see her today. She has put his teaching to work and become one of the most effective young leaders of the Atlanta Jewish community.

Our own children were fast approaching college age by that time, and we could only hope that we had led them to the same attitudes that we shared in regard to racial differences. Some of our friends went out of their way to shuttle their children back and forth across town in order to give them the experience of playing with the children of their black friends. We didn't, partly because the couples we knew, such as Martin and Coretta King, had children much younger than ours, and partly because we didn't believe in the efficacy of artificially created relationships. We trusted that Marcia and Bill would in due time meet young people of another race with whom they shared a common interest, and become friends with them in the same way that we had found friends in the black community ourselves.

They did, and sometimes with amusing results.

One day during the summer of 1963, the daughter of a well-known white activist friend of ours called Marcia to invite her to a spend-the-night party. She mentioned also that the girls planned to go downtown for lunch together the following day. When Marcia told her father and me of those plans we had some misgivings about her going. Knowing the

---

[19]JMR to Meg and Sophie Mantler, 25 October 1963, JMR MSS.

[20]JMR to Carol Zaban, 25 October 1963, JMR MSS.

hostess's mother as we did, we suspected that the party would be biracial and the purpose of going downtown for lunch was to test the policy of a department-store lunch counter. Having relied on osmosis rather than open discussion to convey our values to our children, we weren't sure Marcia was prepared for what she would encounter. At that point we felt awkward about discussing the matter because we didn't want to influence her against going but merely to know if she understood and was prepared for the possibility of confrontation. After a few oblique questions we let her go and hoped for the best. She returned the next afternoon, happily reporting that the format had been exactly as we suspected, that she had enjoyed it, and that nothing untoward had occurred.

The next morning I received a call from a member of the congregation whom I knew by name only. The conversation went something like this:

SHE: Mrs. Rothschild, I can't believe it, but one of my Christian friends told me she saw Rabbi Rothschild's daughter downtown having lunch with a Nigra.

ME: (*after a long pause during which I wondered if perhaps she thought that Marcia was not my daughter also*) Yes?

SHE: (*sputtering slightly*) Well, that couldn't be true, could it?

ME: (*with great innocence*) Why, yes. It could. Is there something wrong?

SHE: (*now really struggling for control*) Well, I couldn't believe that Rabbi Rothschild would let his daughter be seen having lunch with a Nigra. I'm just so embarrassed for my Christian friends!

ME: (*dripping with honey and honeysuckle*) Oh, I wouldn't be too worried about my Christian friends if I were you. If they hadn't learned any more than that at church they couldn't really be *very* Christian, could they?

End of conversation—but not end of incident. Jack delighted in recounting the story and this aftermath as an example of his board's reaction:

It brought an irate . . . letter of resignation to my Board. The letter received the usual treatment: Someone moved that it be accepted with regret. But someone else entered the breach. "Why with regret?" he wanted to know. And the Board—bless them—wrote a letter which said they were sorry the member had failed to "learn the lesson of Judaism taught by our rabbi in word and deed"—and agreed they would be happier elsewhere![21]

That was an extreme case, of course. So far as we knew no one else resigned because of his, or our, choice of friends. It was becoming rather popular, in fact, to agree with him. We didn't fool ourselves into believing that everyone who claimed to agree with him actually did, of course, but it was nice to know that the winds had shifted.

Jack summed up his attitude about such matters in the course of an article for the *CCAR Journal* a few years later. It tells, quite frankly, the "secret" of his success:

> Not all people agree with this rabbi—if they did, he wouldn't have anything to do. But I do believe that the manner in which problems are approached and the attitude of the rabbi in resolving them can go a long way towards lessening the pressures. It is my nature not to take myself or my life too seriously. . . . Sometimes a sense of humor will soften the hardest heart and the most irate tongue. . . .
>
> Many accomplishments have been made possible on the local scene simply because I—and others—ingenuously took them for granted and didn't make a *tzimmes* about them. "Doesn't everybody?" and the innocently raised eyebrow prove delightfully disarming and mightily effective.
>
> Of course, there are times when any rabbi is aware that he is treading on dangerous ground. There are occasions when he knows that he is right—and is willing to gamble that the cause will succeed because the cause is just. There have been such challenges in Atlanta, to be sure. I am proud to have had a small part in many of them.[22]

As Jack repeatedly told audiences in other parts of the country, the prime ingredient in Atlanta's ability to avoid the miseries suffered by many Southern cities during that period was the quality of its leadership. In 1962, after more than two decades of exemplary stewardship, Mayor William B. Hartsfield retired and handed the reins to another good and courageous leader, Ivan Allen, Jr. By that time the emphasis in the racial

---

[21]Rothschild, "One Man's Meat—A Personal Chronicle," *CCAR Journal* (1965). Original in JMR MSS.

[22]Ibid.

struggle had moved on from schools to restaurants and housing. The new mayor was greeted almost immediately after taking office with a crisis in blockbusting.

As vice-president of the Atlanta Council on Human Relations, Jack often received complaints from persons who disagreed with the actions of the council and with those of the mayor in helping to implement its recommendations. One of them came from a member of the medical faculty at Emory University, fearful lest the next target for blockbusting would be Druid Hills, the neighborhood in which he and others of the Emory community lived. He wrote to Jack because a newspaper report indicated that the council might use inflammatory tactics to accomplish integration there.[23]

Jack's reply to him reveals something of the way he and the council proceeded in their work and provides a prime example of the problems caused by careless newspaper reporters. He began by thanking the professor for the tone of his letter, admitting that it was "a welcome change from the anonymous variety plus telephone calls threatening not only me but my wife and children as well." He then explained how the story had come about. A UPI reporter had somehow obtained a copy of a paper prepared for a future meeting of the council. In it suggestions had been made regarding neighborhoods that were potential targets for future blockbusting and that therefore needed to be given attention in the coming months in order to avert possible trouble. The report had been taken out of context, as Jack explained:

> It was thought that perhaps by quiet counselling with people such as yourself who understand the problems involved there might be some way of preventing the mass exodus that so often takes place as a result of hysteria and the unscrupulous pressures put to bear by real estates owners, etc. The word "blockbusting" was never used. . . . The Atlanta newspapers in reporting the story used precisely the kind of scare technique that we—and you—would have been most zealous in avoiding.[24]

---

[23]Sam A. Wilkins, Jr., MD, to JMR, 15 December 1964, JMR MSS.

[24]JMR to Sam A. Wilkins, Jr., MD, 28 December 1964, JMR MSS.

Jack had been out of town when the story appeared and therefore had to do some research to learn what had happened. The newspapers apologized and published a follow-up story that attempted to correct the false impressions given by the original, but without much success. Incidents such as this taught Jack to be wary when it came to publicity.[25]

In early 1964 the demonstrations at restaurants were becoming increasingly bitter. Mayor Ivan Allen was doing everything in his power to persuade restaurateurs and hotel owners to change their "white only" policy voluntarily. At one point he called a meeting of these recalcitrant entrepreneurs and asked Jack to address them "from the moral point of view." In a disarmingly flattering introduction Jack referred to them as "intelligent and successful businessmen"—before delivering his main points.

> You throw up your hands in horror at the prospect of either a Federal or local public accommodations law. We don't need it, you say. We'll do it ourselves. But you don't—and you have no intention of doing it. You're just buying time. How, then, can you avoid helping make the passage of just such a bill inevitable? You deplore direct action, picketing, selective buying and all the rest. You say: we will work it out at the conference table. So you confer and appoint committees—and nothing happens because you don't really intend for anything to happen. But you know that your dalliance will bring about the very direct action that you deplore. Then you'll capitulate. After your city has been torn apart by dissension.[26]

He concluded that he had long since despaired of convincing them on moral grounds of the need for change but that they should at least recognize the practical grounds for such need.[27]

Shortly after that speech, in an address to the United Church Women of Atlanta, he said that although he didn't want to deprecate the real gains made, especially in Atlanta, much of the success looked better than it really was. Again he warned, "Until we are ready to make a soul-centered commitment, our best efforts will result only in the kind of 'to-

---

[25]Ibid.

[26]Notes on address to hotel and restaurant proprietors, ca. 1964, JMR MSS.

[27]Ibid.

kenism' that is so prevalent today. Thus far, we have erected a facade of equality that we know is a lie." He also reminded his listeners that the direct-action technique had come into use precisely in order to combat the perversion of such laws as the antitrespass law, which were being used to prevent black persons from exercising their civil rights.[28]

The direct-action groups had targeted for sit-in a popular New York-style deli-restaurant in a central downtown location. Its owner, Charlie Leb, fueled the confrontation by the manner in which he reacted to it; as a result the young student demonstrators vented their spleen in ways nasty but nonviolent. (We heard that they had left the restaurant interior in shambles, and there were rumors that some of the students had deliberately relieved themselves on the restaurant floor.) Leb had them arrested on charges of trespassing. Reports of the ensuing trials indicated that the excesses of the students had been counterproductive to their cause. Court procedure tended to be unusually strict and judgments harsh. It was during one of these trials—that of a white girl, daughter of a retired general in the army—that Jack had his chance to fulfill his life-long dream: "reincarnation" as a trial attorney.

One evening, just as we sat down to dinner, he received a frantic phone call from a woman identifying herself as the wife of a history professor at Spelman, the predominantly black women's college in Atlanta. She said her husband had been taken from his classroom that morning to testify as a character witness for this student and had ended up in jail himself for contempt of court. The caller added that she herself was seven-months pregnant, a stranger in town with a two-year-old, and—quite understandably—upset.

Jack was anxious to help but couldn't understand why the woman had called him, until he asked her. "Because I'm Jewish!" she answered, as if it were the most natural thing in the world to find a Jewish professor at Spelman (actually, it wasn't that unusual, but we weren't aware of it at the time). The distraught housewife had simply looked in the yellow pages for a rabbi and found Jack. He said he would do what he could, took her telephone number, and promised to call her back.

---

[28]Address to United Church Women of Atlanta, "Crisis and Decision in Today's South," 1 May 1964, JMR MSS. Also delivered in Rochester, New York, 28 January 1964.

He never got to eat his dinner that night. First, he called the attorney in charge of all the civil rights cases, a man whom he knew well and who likewise knew him. The lawyer advised him that the case was hopeless: the professor had made a gratuitous statement to the effect that Southern courts were known to try to impugn the witness, an unwise remark to have made in any court but most foolhardy in that particular one, presided over as it was by the irascible and unpredictable Judge Durwood T. Pye.

Jack remembered Judge Pye in a more pleasant light. The latter had seemed fair and sympathetic in his dealings with the first of the Temple-bombing trials. Since Jack thought he had an approach that would soften Pye's heart toward the loquacious professor, he told the attorney he would meet with him that evening in order to work out a strategy.

They must have conferred into the early hours of the morning, for I didn't hear Jack come in. As he left for work the following day he mentioned something about pleading the professor's case himself and commented "probably we'll both end up in jail." (Times like these made me less enthusiastic about his sense of humor.)

That afternoon he returned grinning like a ten-year-old with his first straight-A report card. He had succeeded so well that the defense attorney offered to put him on staff any time he wanted to switch professions. When he recapped for me what he had said to the judge, it sounded very much like Portia's plea from *The Merchant of Venice*. He began with words like "Your Honor . . . I'm not questioning your action. . . . Justice is your department. But, Your Honor, I'm not a judge, I'm a rabbi, and just as justice is your department, so mercy is my department." His real problem had not been in persuading Judge Pye to forgive the professor, but in persuading the professor to ask for forgiveness without saying anything else.

While the professor was restored to his growing family without further mishap, the student whose exemplary character he had come to defend was not so lucky. She drew the maximum sentence of six months in jail, one year on the public works, and a one-thousand-dollar fine—with bond set at fifteen thousand dollars. However indiscreet he may have been in voicing it, the professor's opinion of Southern courts was accurate.

Of all the Southern rabbis who had shown courage during the civil rights struggle, the one whom Jack admired the most was Charles Mantinband, who had served in Mississippi and later moved to Longview, Texas. During the sit-in period, Mantinband had written to Jack asking his opinion of sit-ins and of several other matters pertaining to current problems. Jack wrote him that the demonstrations had been planned to coincide with the visit to Atlanta of a UN subcommittee coming to investigate the conditions, and while they were "nothing to compare to what happened in Oxford or Birmingham" they were "bad enough" and might very well have been worse. He continued:

> I have objected rather strenuously to the tactics that were employed and therefore am somewhat persona non grata with the movement. To begin with, I object to the objectives. S.N.C.C. set out to "destroy the image of Atlanta" . . . by creating an impression that the Atlanta police were as brutal as the Birmingham police and that there was no difference between them and any other Southern law enforcement officers. I have long held no brief for the "image of Atlanta" and have said repeatedly that the image is better than the fact. But I don't see the purpose of undoing what little has been done by deliberately exacerbating the situation.[29]

Jack added that in general he believed the demonstrations were valuable because almost nothing had been accomplished without some sort of pressure, but that they tended to be disruptive and were sometimes "unnecessarily extreme." He thought the sponsors of the demonstrations made a tactical error in permitting such disruptiveness but conceded that, on the whole, they had made "comparatively few mistakes in a very delicate situation."[30]

Charlie Leb was not the only owner of a popular eatery to resist desegregation. Most famous of the lot was Lester Maddox, who parlayed his fame as a segregationist into a term as governor. Upon our arrival in Europe that summer, Jack and I were embarrassed to see that a Brussels newspaper had devoted a quarter of its front page to a picture of Maddox brandishing an ax handle at a black man who had asked to be served at his fried-chicken establishment.

---

[29]Rabbi Charles Mantinband to JMR, 3 February 1964; JMR to Mantinband, 10 February 1964—JMR MSS.

[30]Ibid.

We encountered personal difficulty with still another, more formal Atlanta restaurant, Fan and Bill's, which was located across from the city's finest hotel at that time and, consequently, a great favorite with visiting celebrities. One day during the period when the mayor was trying so hard to achieve open accommodations voluntarily, I received an invitation to a luncheon being held there by the Women's Division of the Atlanta Jewish Welfare Federation. Before blowing my stack I double-checked my facts by calling the restaurant to make a reservation. I received the utmost courtesy, too much, in fact. We didn't go there often enough for the maître d' to have known us. I supposed he might have remembered us as a result of our having been there with Isaac Stern a year or so before. In any case, he was only too happy to reserve a table until I mentioned, as if in afterthought, that one of my guests was black, and added casually, "That's all right, isn't it?" He snapped, "No, it is not!" and slammed down the telephone.

I called Jack, then the Federation office to tell the director, then the women who were chairing the event. Jack agreed with me that the luncheon should never have been scheduled for that restaurant but doubted whether anything could or would be done about it. The others, all favoring open accommodations themselves, couldn't see what was wrong about holding the luncheon there. Each began by reminding me, "It's for Israel," and ended by saying, "You may be right, but it's too late. There's nothing we can do about it now."

There was, of course, something that could be done and somebody did it. (Not I, although most people thought I did.) Someone—I can only guess who it was—had the good judgment to call the nationally known journalist who was scheduled to speak at the luncheon and tell him of the situation. He didn't have to be told that most likely, student demonstrators would learn of the affair and have a field day with the attendant publicity. He couldn't take the chance, so he canceled. The luncheon itself then had to be canceled. I hope that it didn't prevent anyone from contributing properly to the Federation or to the United Jewish Appeal that year, but if it did, then so be it. For me morality begins at home.

My vigilantism was not without its price. A few weeks later, Isaac Stern gave another concert in Atlanta, and we went backstage afterward to say hello. He asked us if we could join a supper party that was being given for him later, and as we eagerly agreed, he sent the hostess over to confirm the invitation. We thanked her and because the dressing room was becoming crowded, said we'd leave and meet her at her house. "Oh, no," she corrected. "We're not going to my house. I've reserved a table at . . ."

It was *that* restaurant! We had to tell her the reason why we couldn't go there. She understood, and even apologized for not being able to change the plans at that point (which really was too late, since other guests were already on their way). The real problem came when we had to tell Isaac Stern why we weren't going to join him. He was so angry when he heard about the restaurant's policy that *he* didn't want to go there either. We had to plead with him not to spoil the party (and ruin our friendship with the hostess) by refusing to go.

Looking back on it, an unusual number of events that occurred during those years had something to do with lunch or dinner. There was a beautiful luncheon Coretta gave at her home on one day's notice, when she learned that a friend from California would be in town for just that day. She invited twenty of us, did the cooking herself, and appeared as calm and unruffled as she does on television today. Martin helped out by driving the children's car pool at noon and even took time to sit down and visit with us for a while afterward.

There was the all-day seminar on "Rearing Children of Good Will" sponsored by the National Conference of Christians and Jews, on which Coretta and I served as panelists. The keynote speaker at lunch was a child psychiatrist, herself a mother. She invited Coretta and me to have lunch with her a few weeks later (at one of the downtown restaurants that *had* voluntarily complied with open accommodations) and lured us both into confessing our misgivings about how well we were raising our own children. (Her advice was to relax and have faith.)

Jack was serving at the time on the board of the UAHC. An incident at the opening dinner of the 1963 board meeting in Washington, D.C., demonstrated to us how little our friends in the North understood our relationship with our black friends at home. There were members of our congregation present as well as representatives of other Southern congregations. During dinner our chairman learned that Martin King was in the same hotel preparing to address another group later that evening and asked Jack to invite Martin to stop by our meeting en route to the other one, just to say hello. Jack did, and returned with Martin, who followed him in but only part way to the dais. Martin had spotted me sitting at a table some distance away and had detoured to greet me with the customary buss on the cheek. Jack and I were pleased at the attention and thought no more about it. Afterward we were puzzled and then dismayed because friends from the North gathered around to praise me for my "courage." They were surprised that I would let Martin kiss me in front of members of our congregation! Jack and I tried to explain that we treated all our friends in the same manner regardless of who was looking.

Shortly after, Jack was given the honor of introducing Martin at the UAHC Biennial Banquet in Chicago. He was thrilled at the prospect and annoyed but not disturbed by rumors that some of the Southern delegations planned to walk out. He described his feelings in an article for the *CCAR Journal*:

> Sometimes, I suppose, I am genuinely naive. When I was asked to introduce Dr. Martin Luther King, Jr. at the Union Biennial, I was honored and flattered. Not only is Dr. King one of the great men of our generation, but we happen to be personal friends. I honestly didn't know that I was agreeing to undertake a revolutionary assignment—not until I began to hear all the talk about walk-outs and the like. But the members of my own congregation accepted it as an honor, too, and were almost annoyingly complacent about my part in the whole proceedings.[31]

None of us remained complacent as the evening progressed, however. It had nothing to do with walkouts; if there were any we didn't see them. The three thousand people crowded into that enormous ballroom waited as eagerly as we to hear what Martin would have to say, and the list of "greetings" bringers was so long that we began to wonder if he would ever get the chance to say it. The last of the speakers to precede Jack at the lectern remained there for some forty-five minutes, during the second half of which he was drowned out by the objections of an understandably impatient crowd.

I went from clammy to catatonic worrying about how Jack would be able to recapture the attention of such an audience. By the time he came to the lectern to give his introduction it was 11:30 P.M.. He had edited his carefully prepared remarks so that they would occupy only a fraction of the time allotted him.

---

[31]Rothschild, "One Man's Meat—A Personal Chronicle."

The audience quieted down immediately, indicated its appreciation of him, and welcomed the speaker we all had come to hear. Martin apparently appreciated Jack's words, too, for he asked for a copy of them. They read, in part:

> Who of us, watching the historic Freedom March can ever forget the full-throated roar of love and respect that greeted one man as he took his place at the speakers' rostrum? Such a spontaneous emotion left no doubt that here stood the acknowledged leader of his people in their struggle for human dignity. Here was their spokesman who—like a prophet of ancient Israel—had fearlessly confronted the society of his day with its failures; he had sought to rouse men to a vision of their own nobility. He had become at once the still, small voice within and the not-to-be-stilled, impassioned voice crying aloud for the freedom and dignity of every man. The wild thunder of sound assured him of his place in their hearts and in the hearts of great numbers of Americans whatever hue their skin might be.
>
> But not in all. For this man has not been always and everywhere so enthusiastically received. Just as in Isaiah's day, so are there in our own those: "who say to the seers—see Nothing, and to the prophets—Never tell us what is right, Speak to us pleasant words. . . . Get out of our way. . . . Let us hear no more of the Holy One of Israel."
>
> But he would not "get out of their way." Nor would he cease reminding them of the presence of the Living God and what that God required of them. Not when they threatened him nor yet when they put him into jails. And jails have been his home often enough to lend some credibility to the oft-told tale that he is one celebrity who has given out more fingerprints than autographs. Undaunted by the virulence of those who hate and fear him—and equally unmoved to arrogance by the adulation of those who honor him, he has worked with quiet stubbornness and exalted patience to preach his message of equality and justice for all men. With serene courage and dedicated idealism, he has never forsaken his faith in an America, righteous and just, an America which will yet fulfill its promise as a land indivisible, with liberty and justice for all. He has earned his place as the moral leader of our social revolution.[32]

---

[32]Introduction of Martin Luther King, Jr., UAHC Bienniel, 20 November 1963, JMR MSS.

Soon after we returned from that convention Jack preached a sermon entitled, in part, "Is Atlanta Ready for Greatness?" A year later we had the chance to find out. When we heard the news that Martin had been selected to receive the 1964 Nobel Peace Prize, Jack said immediately, "The city ought to do something to honor him." He said it to me, and he also said it to some of his friends in the black community.[33]

In mid-November Ralph McGill wrote Jack, describing a visit paid him by a delegation of black leaders. They proposed having a dinner to honor Martin as soon as possible after he returned from the ceremonies in Oslo. They wanted Ralph, Jack, Archbishop Paul Hallinan, and Dr. Benjamin Mays to chair the event. What they had in mind was an early dinner at one of the hotels, followed by a public meeting at the city auditorium, with celebrity entertainers presenting the program. They wanted to make it a fund raiser for the Southern Christian Leadership Conference, the organization Martin headed.[34]

Jack enthusiastically agreed to co-chair the event but argued against the proposed format. He wanted to see the city honor its first Nobel laureate, give a gala banquet for him undiluted by any ulterior purpose. They finally conceded and went with him to discuss the matter with Mayor Ivan Allen. Ivan liked the idea and offered to take it to the "power structure," the small group of top financial leaders who really called the shots in Atlanta. Nothing of any consequence ever took place in the city without their endorsement.

The power structure did not look favorably upon the proposed dinner, but Jack and the committee decided to go ahead with it anyway. Ivan said he would help. By then it was the beginning of December. The earliest date the affair could be scheduled was 27 January. Even then, there was little time to make the necessary arrangements with a proper eye to detail.

One day after meeting with the group Jack casually asked me what I thought would be an appropriate gift to present to Martin at the banquet. "Not silver," I said immediately, assuming Coretta had little time to bother with housekeeping and therefore would not want more silver to keep clean. "What about a piece of Steuben?" I suggested.

---

[33]Sermon, "Is Atlanta Ready for Greatness," 15 November 1963, JMR MSS.

[34]Ralph McGill to JMR, 13 November 1964, JMR MSS.

The next day Jack came home from still another meeting with the committee and told me, "They like your idea and want you to attend to getting it." When I asked how much had been budgeted for the gift Jack quoted a modest figure but told me not to worry if whatever I thought appropriate cost more than the allotted amount. They had tried to keep the cost of individual tickets to a minimum so that as many of Martin's followers as possible could afford to come. Ivan had assured them that he would be able to obtain any extra funds they needed to "do things right."

While we were talking about it I reached for a pencil and on the back of a discarded envelope sketched out an idea I had. It was a dogwood blossom—symbolic of Atlanta, "the dogwood city," but also significant to Christianity and the Prince of Peace. Jack composed the inscription: "Dr. Martin Luther King, Jr.,—Citizen of Atlanta, Recipient of the 1964 Nobel Peace Prize, with Respect and Admiration, January 27, 1965." I couldn't believe that the two of us, "ordinary people," were sitting there in our own living room putting together something connected with the Nobel Prize for Peace.

My excitement gave way to anxiety when I considered how to go about placing the order. Steuben's only outlet in the Southeast at that time was Rich's. Aside from the inappropriateness of ordering Martin's gift from the establishment that had been the first to send him to jail, Jack had warned me against letting any information about the dinner leak out to the press. I decided to call Steuben directly and tell someone in charge, confidentially, what needed to be done.

A vice-president of Steuben listened patiently while I described what we wanted, and suggested that a crystal bowl would be useful as well as ornamental. Then he asked me when we needed to have it ready. When I told him we wanted it in Atlanta a few days before 27 January, there was a long silence. "I don't know about that," he said finally. "It's now only two weeks until Christmas, and then our workrooms are shut down for two weeks. Let me talk to our copper engravers and see if they'll do it that fast."

I thanked him and asked about the price. He hesitated to give one, even an estimate, because he had doubts that he could carry out the order. At my insistence, however, he did. It was considerably more than the budgeted amount. While he spoke to his artists about doing the work, I spoke to Jack about paying for it. "Call Ivan," he said, so I did. True to his word, the mayor promised to provide the extra money if we needed it and told me to go ahead with the order.

As it happened, we didn't need his help. When the Steuben executive told his artists what we wanted—and, more importantly, who it was for—they readily agreed to work overtime if necessary to complete it on schedule. Furthermore, the company lowered the cost so that it fell within our budget. As for delivery, they vowed to get it to The Temple on time "even if we have to charter a plane to send it in."[35]

The charter wasn't necessary. Within two weeks we had a photograph of the bowl with a scale sketch of the engraving. We approved it and received the finished piece, by normal delivery, five days before the date of the dinner. In the interim it remained locked in Jack's study at The Temple.

What happened next is history. The power structure learned that the little group of white clergymen and black establishment members, with the help of the mayor, were proceeding with the dinner without their approval. They were surprised but not persuaded to support it until Coca-Cola allegedly dropped a hint that it could move its home base elsewhere if Atlanta proved an embarrassment to its Third World operations. Meanwhile, FBI Chief J. Edgar Hoover carried on his vendetta against Martin to the point of having his agents spread rumors that there would soon be an exposé of his alleged "sexual infidelities." They tried to persuade Ralph to pull out on the grounds that his support would embarrass the paper and even visited Archbishop Hallinan, who was very ill and in the hospital, to try to persuade him to do the same.

Ralph had to keep a low profile in order to remain effective, but his influence with the people—or person—who really held the power in Atlanta is probably responsible for the business establishment's about-face. With him restrained and the archbishop sick, Jack had to serve as chief spokesman to the general public on behalf of the dinner committee. He had excellent assistance in the paperwork and other details from an enthusiastic team headed by Don McEvoy, regional director of the National Conference of Christians and Jews, and Helen Bullard, public relations executive and former campaign director for Ivan Allen.

---

[35]Author's conversation with James A. Thurston, December 1964.

Despite precautions, the New York press heard rumors of the affair well before Christmas. One of the reporters called Jack at home on a weekend to get the story. Jack wasn't yet prepared to release it so he suggested to his caller, "Why don't you ask your fellow journalist, Ralph McGill?" Jack didn't normally pass the buck, but in this case he knew Ralph could handle it better than he, especially if he didn't intend to reveal anything at all.

The first stories to appear in Atlanta were published by the *Atlanta Constitution* on 29 December. One was a reprint from the previous day's *New York Times*, the other an article written by a local reporter. The former brought out all the negatives. It mentioned that about one hundred of Atlanta's leading citizens had been sent letters inviting them to be sponsors of the dinner and that very few had responded. (How many people answer their mail promptly during Christmas?) It also revealed that several of those responding had refused, "including one banker who strongly stated his objections." (The banker was notoriously outspoken in regard to most matters.)

The local reporter printed the scene in brighter hues. He quoted the mayor, the vice-mayor and the mayor emeritus, each with an upbeat statement differing little on the surface but—to those of us who knew the men and knew the city—revealing subtle nuances that expressed the various attitudes of those white citizens supporting the event. With the incumbent, Ivan Allen, it was courtesy and caution. With Bill Hartsfield, who had epitomized the very soul of the city over such a long period of time, it was decency and civic pride. With Sam Massell, the vice-mayor who later became mayor—and who was a lifelong member of The Temple—it was determination and faith. He echoed the feelings that Jack and I shared when he said he thought it would be "inexcusable" if Martin Luther King's hometown refused to honor him, adding, "I'm convinced that we will."

Unfortunately, Martin became involved in an attempt to unionize one of Atlanta's major industries in the weeks just before the dinner. Many of the striking employees were members of his own congregation, so he felt doubly obligated to support them regardless of the ensuing publicity. It stirred up some carping conversation and probably gave those who wouldn't have come to the dinner anyway a further excuse for their attitude, but that was all. By that time we no longer doubted that the dinner was going to be a success.

At first Jack and the others had not set their hopes too high. They had been confident of getting 500 people to attend and were prepared to be content with that number. Later they raised their goal to 1,000. When that many tickets sold out a full week in advance, they pulled out an additional 71 to take care of the press and members of the King family and closed the reservations the following day. The maximum number of persons the largest hotel facility in town could accommodate, 1,250, had been reached. From executive suites all over the city, secretaries began to call members of the committee begging them to "please find just two more tickets for Mr. _____." Ironically, one of the calls to Jack was made on behalf of Dick Rich, who had already subscribed but wanted additional reservations. Jack tried to accommodate but couldn't. He even called "Daddy" King, Martin's father, thinking perhaps the family had some tickets they weren't going to to use. They didn't. When Jack called, Daddy King was out looking for more himself! The hotel managed to stretch its facilities to take in a total of 1,390 persons for the dinner, and still more than 1,000 had to be turned away.

Despite the forecast of rain for that evening the only cloud on our personal horizon on 27 January 1965 was the announcement by the Klan and Charlie Leb that they intended to picket outside the hotel where the dinner was being held. They carried out their threat, but no one noticed except the reporters and the police, both in the line of duty.

Jack had come home early that afternoon in order to rest. Since he was to chair the dinner itself he wanted to be in peak condition. Marcia and Bill were to attend with my mother, who wouldn't have missed it for anything, so they had to get their homework done during the afternoon. I was just about to wrap up the day's work myself when the telephone rang. It was Coretta. She wanted to know what I was planning to wear, a long dress or a short one.

I couldn't believe it. It was the first time I had ever heard her voice any concern about such trivial matters as clothes. I told her I planned to wear my "uniform" for formal dinners: a long black skirt and whatever top seemed best at the moment. She continued to discuss the question, still undecided as to what to do. I was puzzled. After almost an hour's conversation I finally realized what was bothering her. She was afraid that if she wore an elegant long gown it would embarrass members of their congregation who couldn't afford to be dressed as nicely as she. In my opinion, they would *shep naches* (derive great pride and joy) from seeing her dressed that night more glamorously than anyone, and I told her so. At that point it was so late that both of us had to hang up and begin dressing.

Everyone inside the hotel holding room was bubbling like champagne, sparkling and beautiful. Even Archbishop Hallinan, who had left his hospital bed just long enough to attend the dinner, looked buoyant despite his mortal illness. When Martin and Coretta arrived we felt as if we should be throwing rice, so joyful was the mood. I noticed she was wearing a long gown, but it wouldn't have mattered. The expression on her face that night made her more beautiful than anything she could have worn.

We knew to expect a crowded ballroom and we knew to expect a barrage of reporters and cameramen, but we never could have imagined the crowds, the lights, and the cameras that we actually encountered as we made the long walk to our places at the head table. The vast room was so tightly packed that we had to squeeze sideways between the tables to reach our destination. Friends reached out to touch us as we passed, just to let us know they were there. The applause was so loud we couldn't hear what they were saying.

I was seated directly above the table reserved for the King family, so I had the pleasure of conversing with them from time to time. I knew Mrs. King, Sr., from her visits to The Temple for our sisterhood's annual interfaith programs, and knew her to be normally exuberant, but never as she was that night. She kept repeating, as if she had to keep hearing it to believe it, "To think that this could happen in our lifetime! The grandson of a sharecropper!" The tributes from the white establishment in Atlanta seemed to mean more to her even than the prize itself.

Jack opened the festivities with a greeting that paid tribute to Martin and the entire assembly. He told the persons who were there that their presence affirmed their concern for the cause to which Martin had dedicated his life, and that in honoring him they honored themselves as well:

> You attest the truth that goodness and righteousness do reside
> in the human heart. You give the lie to the canard that prejudice is
> always stronger than decency, that hate is more powerful than love.[36]

---

[36]Opening remarks, Atlanta Dinner honoring Martin Luther King, Jr., 27 January 1965, JMR MSS.

Then he spoke of Atlanta, telling his listeners that by their presence they also honored their city:

> You—rich and poor, Jew and Christian, black and white, professional and lay, men and women from every walk of life—you represent the true heart of a great city. You are Atlanta. You—and not the noisy rabble with their sheets and signs now slogging sullenly the sidewalks beyond these doors. Here is a truth we must resolve never to forget. Let none of us ever again fear to summon this truth so simply, so eloquently and so forcefully brought home to us tonight by our presence here.[37]

After dinner there were a number of speakers, each paying tribute to Martin from a different aspect of his achievement. When it came time for Jack to present the bowl to him, he began by telling a story from Jewish tradition. It was the legend of Adam, watching the sun go down on his first day on earth, and terrified lest the darkness, which he had never seen before, should last forever. God tells him to take two stones, the rock of Despair and the rock of Death, and rub them together. Adam does so, and the friction causes a spark to ignite, starting a fire. Thus man first produced light for himself. Jack connected this story to Martin's own accomplishments:

> We are coming to understand that our hands, too, must seize the cold stones of Darkness and Despair and from them strike the flame that will guide mankind from the gloom of despair to the radiance of hope. We pray that together you and we—and all decent men everywhere—may bring dignity of soul, nobility of heart and tranquility of spirit to every child of God—and thus ensure brotherhood and peace in all the world.[38]

As he handed the gift to Martin he concluded with a reference to the bowl and the appropriateness of its being crystal:

> You epitomize the glowing hope of light restored to a world stumbling in the darkness of hate, because you symbolize the chal-

---

[37]Ibid.

[38]Presentation of bowl to Martin Luther King, Jr., 27 January 1965.

lenge to all men that they become God's helpers to assure the dawn
of a more radiant day.[39]

Martin responded with the eloquence that was uniquely his, speaking of the peaks and valleys of life, phrases made all the more poignant
for many of us by the gnawing intuition that much too soon one of those
peaks would become a precipice and this remarkable young man would
be with us no more.[40]

When he finished speaking the audience rose as one to applaud
what he had said and what he had done. Instinctively, without waiting for
the benediction, everyone joined hands in the cross-armed symbol of
brotherhood and sang, "We Shall Overcome." If there were any dry eyes
in the room as that benediction was being pronounced, we couldn't see
them through the tears of joy in our own.

Afterward, amid much hugging and kissing and hand touching
across the table, Jack and I posed for still more pictures. This time the
photographer was our son Bill. Of all the photographs we have of Jack and
Martin, and a few of Coretta and me, the only one we have of the four of
us together is the one Bill took that night with his brownie camera.

Martin later wrote a letter of appreciation to Jack echoing the feelings both of them had expressed at the dinner: "I must confess that few
events have warmed my heart as did this occasion. It was a testimonial
not only to me but to the greatness of the City of Atlanta, the South, the
nation and its ability to rise above the conflict of former generations and
really experience that beloved community where all differences are rec-
onciled and all hearts in harmony with the principles of our great
democracy."[41]

He declared that Jack's presentation was one he would treasure "as
a light of encouragement for the many dark and desolate days of struggle"
that he knew must lie ahead. And he added in a handwritten postscript:

---

[39]Ibid.

[40]Address by Martin Luther King, Jr., Atlanta Dinner in his honor, 27 January
1965, Martin Luther King, Jr., Papers, Martin Luther King, Jr., Center for Nonviolent
Social Change, Inc., Atlanta, Georgia.

[41]Martin Luther King, Jr., to JMR, 8 March 1965, JMR MSS.

"P.S. I will never forget the great role you played in making the testimonial the great success it was."[42]

Jack had indeed worked hard to insure that the dinner was successful. His reward was in the accomplishment itself, and in the satisfaction derived from knowing that "his" city had proven herself truly ready for greatness. If he was disappointed in not receiving credit for his part in it in the reams of copy that described the event in newspapers and magazines, he never said or indicated so in any way, even to me. But there were some who did notice and express their disappointment. Archbishop Hallinan wrote to him from his hospital bed to thank him and to compliment him on "the magnificent program . . . and my admiration at your handling of the whole affair." He also spoke of the press coverage, especially that of *Time* magazine, which he considered "most inept and inadequate." He continued, "You were ignored, in fact the whole Catholic-Jewish contribution was passed over. . . . It is not a question of credit; it is a matter of factual record. This affair would not have come off at all had it not been for you, the Negro religious and academic leaders, & the Catholic cooperation."[43]

---

[42]Ibid.

[43]Archbishop Paul J. Hallinan to JMR, 9 February 1965, JMR MSS.

CHAPTER EIGHT

BITTER HARVEST

If any one event can be judged the peak of a career as broad in interests and goals as Jack's, the dinner for Martin Luther King would be it. For Atlanta, even more than for Jack personally, it was a triumph, yet neither he nor his fellow Atlantans fooled themselves into believing that the gains had been solid. Jack knew it would take many years and many battles more before true victory would be won. None of us, though, foresaw the great crop of bitterness that was to come.

Jack had detected the sowing of that harvest since the start of the decade and had repeatedly warned against it. In his sermons he had pointed to the "rumblings of impatience" in the black community and told his listeners that they existed because "of our unwillingness to move at all" toward the goals of a free society.[1] When President John F. Kennedy was assassinated in 1963, Jack saw it in the context of a larger sweep of events. Although it was not directly related to the racial struggle, it was, he said, "the climactic act which made it impossible any longer to ignore the signs." At our congregation's annual joint Thanksgiving service with Glenn Memorial Congregation that year, only a few days after the tragedy, he told the worshipers:

> There is an ugly mood in America that we have fostered—a mood of hate and suspicion. It culminates in lawlessness which is made more terrifying by our own callousness to its presence. . . . We have abdicated our leadership to the violent, the hate-possessed, the scorners of the law. . . . We can no longer luxuriate in the comfort of silence.[2]

Speaking soon after to a Rotary club, he warned:

> Time is running out for us. . . . The Negro is becoming more impatient and less willing to wait quietly and peacefully for the fulfillment of glib promises smoothly made but that we don't really mean to keep. . . . Moderate leaders are being goaded into action by younger, more impatient voices. . . . Only the blind can fail to see . . . that the noble experiment is no longer as strong as it once was.[3]

When a colleague asked him, in 1964, what he thought of the Civil Rights Act then being debated in Congress, he replied that while he didn't expect it to cause "any miraculous turn for the better," it would provide a legal base for many of the demands "which the Negroes rightfully make." He believed it would set the direction for people and "serve as a backstop."[4]

---

[1]Sermons, 1961-1962, JMR MSS.

[2]Sermon delivered to Glenn Memorial Congregation, Atlanta, "Using God's Gifts," 28 November 1963, JMR MSS.

[3]Address to North DeKalb Rotary Club, Atlanta, "In My Brother's Shoes," 12 March 1964, JMR MSS.

[4]Rabbi Charles Mantinband to JMR, 8 April 1964; JMR to Mantinband, 14 April 1964—JMR MSS.

The same rabbi asked him if he thought there would ever be a black political party, and if he thought blacks had anything to learn from the Jewish experience. He answered the first question with the following thought: "Somehow we've always been able to avoid the forming of political parties for specific reasons. . . . Anyhow, I think that the Negro leadership is much too astute ever to fall into the trap of forming a minority party which would have little chance of success as far as tangible achievements might be concerned."[5]

As for blacks benefiting from the Jewish experience, he said he had always been skeptical of making that comparison. Besides the obvious physical differences, he noted, Jews had always sought equality while maintaining their uniqueness, their right to "equality without uniformity." He believed that blacks preferred to have their differences forgotten and "go unnoticed in the total community." He didn't see how, with such a difference in goals, it would be useful to employ the same technique in trying to achieve them.[6]

For Rosh Hashanah, 1964, he wrote one of his strongest sermons on civil rights. He called it "A Love Affair With Life," but its title was the only element in it evoking images of sweetness and light. He began by noting that the preceding "long, hot summer" could not have been avoided unless we had been willing to forgo forever "the promise and the dream of American democracy." He praised the newly passed civil rights law, observing that the only means for escaping it were "secession, which seems to have been settled at Appomattox," and the subversion of law and order. Such subversion, he reasoned, would destroy the fabric of American life and bring about "the very police state the segregationists accuse us of becoming. . . ." It was time, he said, to move from "the safe trenches of the muted moderate"; the Civil Rights Act had engendered a climate in which that could be done. He warned against wasting the opportunity, declaring that "no amount of double talk can excuse the individual white man from treating the Negro as an equal and accepting him as a partner in the life of our society."[7]

---

[5]Ibid.

[6]JMR to Mantinband, 14 April 1964, JMR MSS.

[7]Sermon, "A Love Affair With Life," 6 September 1964, JMR MSS.

He so feared the implications of the forthcoming presidential election that in the same sermon he broke his long-standing self-imposed rule and spoke out against one of the candidates. Although he did not specifically name Barry Goldwater, he said:

> The radical right has become the rallying ground for all those who believe that a coalition of minorities has stolen this country from them and has betrayed it to its enemies. It offers simple answers to complex problems. . . . But the greatest danger for us lies in ignoring the emotional impact of such a position. . . . The easy promise of "pie in the sky" becomes the rallying cry for vast numbers of unhappy people who are unable to face realistically the inevitable risks of living in a modern world. . . .
>
> We face, for the first time in my memory, a challenge to our way of life, to the future of our country, to the principles of American democracy. I am not so much afraid of the trigger finger that, shooting from the hip, will set off The Bomb. I am mightily concerned with the slow attrition of our ideals and the gradual altering of our goals. I do not want an America whose face is scarred by the hustlers of hate, whose hands are bloodied by the cutting off of full citizenship to any man, whose heart is shriveled by its own unconcern for the poor, the aged, the underprivileged. And above all, I must resist the reach for power sought by dividing this country into an oversimplified issue of white versus black.[8]

After Jack preached the sermon it was published and distributed to congregations throughout the country. After reading it, one of his colleagues in the North wrote him, "I loved your 'Love Affair With Life.' The difference between your sermon and mine is not only in approach. It took no courage to preach mine."[9]

Although he always appreciated such praise, Jack didn't believe that what he said or did required great courage. When soon after delivering his sermon he and two others were honored by the Southern Regional Advisory Board of the ADL for their bravery in the civil rights battle he responded in his typical fashion. He told the story of my reprimanding him for not having the downspouts on our house painted before the Tem-

---

[8]Ibid.

[9]Rabbi Ely E. Pilchik to JMR, 29 September 1964, JMR MSS.

ple bombing, and said that *that* (risking my anger) was something requiring true bravery on his part.

While Jack had never considered participating in any of the demonstrations himself, and had at times voiced some reservations about the wisdom of Jewish organizations participating as such, he seemed somewhat regretful that he had not joined the Selma March in the spring of 1965. So many of his colleagues from the Northeast had participated and stopped off in Atlanta between flights, that for a while I thought Jack was running a shuttle service between our house and the airport. Each time he visited with one of them he came home looking slightly wistful. One especially scholarly friend stayed overnight with us on his way back to New England. I thought I knew him fairly well, but I had never seen him as exuberant as he was then. Jack, who knew him far better than I did, was astounded. "I thought he never left his ivory tower!" he remarked in amazement.

Jack was undoubtedly still thinking of the march a few weeks later when he was approached to write an article for the *CCAR Journal* about his experiences in the civil rights struggle. At first he hesitated to accept the assignment. He was afraid that whatever he said would be interpreted as an attempt to excuse himself for not having gone to Selma. Finally, however, he must have realized that the chance was worth taking.[10]

In the article he applauded the fact that so many clergymen did go to Selma, and called it "a long overdue statement of deep spiritual commitment." He predicted that the march would bring about the passage of a voter registration bill and praised it for having "roused the conscience and shocked the sensibilities" of Americans who had not yet been moved by "the virulence of hatred that seethed in Southern souls."[11]

He also praised the clergy for finally having become aware of the need to involve itself "in a more direct way than preaching sermons and attending conferences," and welcomed members "to the field of battle," saying he hoped they would not see "this single, dramatic act" as the climax of their involvement. He didn't want them to withdraw "in the mistaken belief that the war is won." Above all he hoped they would not

---

[10]Rabbi Daniel Jeremy Silver to JMR, 10 March 1965, JMR MSS.

[11]Rothschild, "One Man's Meat—A Personal Chronicle," *CCAR Journal* (1965), JMR MSS.

confuse their own need for fulfillment, which he understood and in no way meant to deprecate, with the "continuing need for the less dangerous, less dramatic acts."[12]

While his latter statement could have been interpreted as an excuse, it was a true expression of his feelings and his considered judgment in regard to his own ability to continue serving the cause. In a further comment on the demonstrations he said he questioned the wisdom of staging so many, particularly after the brutal murder of two peaceful participants during the Selma march. He believed that, like the case of the boy who cried "wolf," the frequent use of such tactics vitiated their effectiveness in cases where they might have served some purpose. While the Selma march had been effective, he said, the sympathy march in Atlanta had been "something less than meaningful."[13]

The horror of Watts could be seen on our television screens that August as Jack was considering the content of his sermons for the forthcoming Holydays. He wondered if viewers were becoming inured to such scenes of violence. Warning against such inurement in his New Year's sermon, he paralleled it to what he imagined must have been the attitude of the inhabitants of ancient Pompeii. The Pompeiians, he believed, had probably been warned by repeated minor eruptions of Vesuvius and sloughed off the larger danger with a casual "You learn to live with it." That adaptability, he predicted, could be the source of our ultimate doom. We had better start declaring our unwillingness to adjust to evil.[14]

Making clear that he in no way condoned the explosion at Watts, he did try to analyze and explain what had caused it. He repeated the reasons why black Americans were unable to contain their frustration. He reminded us that they see their freedom "not as a gift bestowed by the white majority" but as a right of their own citizenship. To those who would ask indignantly why the people of Watts would riot after so many gains had been made, he answered:

> For generations, the Negro had been kept completely segregated. He was invisible, hopeless, and helpless. Such total frustration

---

[12]Ibid.

[13]Sermon, "Pulpit Potpourri," 28 May 1965, JMR MSS.

[14]Sermon, "To Lie Down In Peace," 26 September 1965, JMR MSS.

does not explode because it cannot explode. It stagnates and disintegrates into total futility. Frustration expresses itself only when there is hope unrealized and promise unfulfilled. We have, at last, given the Negro hope—but held it always tantalizingly away from him. We have promised much—and delivered little.[15]

To those who blamed the spate of lawlessness on the leaders of the direct-action movement, he pointed out that it was not the blacks who had advocated disregard of the Supreme Court decision, who had bombed churches and synagogues, hurled fire bombs and shot bullets into the homes of innocent people.[16]

"Who were the night riders that murdered Lemuel Penn and Viola Liuzzo?" he asked, referring to the two killed on the Selma March. "Who killed the three civil rights workers in Mississippi and hid their bodies in a dam? Who beat Rev. Reeb to death and shot another minister in the bright light of day? Who rioted to prevent the admission of a Negro student on Southern college campuses? And who has escaped punishment for every single act?"[17]

Again he reviewed the facts. For three hundred years, with beatings and violence, whites had fostered an atmosphere of savagery and had spurned blacks as animals. They established a society based on fear, he said, and as the curtain of fear lifts "it reveals a stage set with pure hate." He noted that the expression of hate had thus far been "only sporadic," and added, "We have been lucky. James Baldwin's warning of 'The Fire Next Time' seems not so remote a possibility after all."[18]

Despite the situation, however, he believed we would now have to ask black Americans to discipline themselves still further in order to achieve their goals. It would not be an abandonment of the dream of total victory and "Freedom Now," but a move to solidify the gains already made and perhaps to make the "now" come sooner.

---

[15]Ibid.

[16]Ibid.

[17]Ibid.

[18]Ibid.

Just think—all the vast energies, the selfless dedication, the tremendous discipline directed to taking advantage of the new found opportunity to vote, given over to education and social advances! To ignore the stumbling blocks placed in their path . . . and to prepare themselves for that promise of full equality now within their grasp! Not to be discouraged or frustrated by the futile sniping of a few—as they have not been turned aside by the murder and pillage even up to now.

What then? Would such a course of action change the hearts of men? Would Negroes thus command a new respect for themselves as children of God—even as we whites think ourselves to be? Perhaps yes—and if not, at least they can stand before us and say "We have tried. God knows we have tried. We could not win in peace. You have driven us to war."

I do not know if we can in all reason expect such discipline. Certainly it is more than we have shown ourselves capable of. I do not know whether we whites have it in ourselves to respond even if it is there. But I do know that only by such an act of will can we and they achieve a society of peace and security in our beloved land.[19]

While he was no more optimistic on Yom Kippur, ten days later, his use of metaphor was apt. He opened his sermon with a reference to the first flight of the astronauts circling the earth, quoting the description that one of them had given of the world looking so peaceful from outer space. Hurricanes, he had said, were of no concern to them until time to reenter the earth's atmosphere. We, too, Jack said, would like "to ride our space capsules around the globe safely insulated from the real world."[20]

As the racial revolution began to draw away from the aid of white liberals, other aspects of the social revolution began to concern Jack and his fellow rabbis. Drug abuse, increased intermarriage, Vietnam and the growing draft resistance by idealistic young men, all translated into tragic, personal problems that persons needing guidance and support brought to the rabbis. While these problems didn't reach Atlanta as soon or in quite the volume that they reached Northeastern communities, Jack did deal with his share of them, and he agonized over every one.

---

[19]Ibid.

[20]Sermon, "The Immoral World and Moral Man," 5 October 1965, JMR MSS.

Jack had always considered himself "a seeker of peace," and he sympathized with those who came to him for help in filing as conscientious objectors. Although he rejected much of the philosophy and most of the behavior espoused by so-called peaceniks, he understood the complexity of American involvement in Southeast Asia and deplored the simplistic demands to immediately pull out all the troops as much as he feared the "drop the bomb" solution advocated by hawks. As the tragedy evolved, however, he most feared the tendency toward a neo-McCarthyism that he noticed as extremists on each side tried to suppress the opinion of the other. He even saw in his own congregation a revival of that old syndrome that made some of its members mortally afraid to express an opinion contrary to that of the majority. Again he warned us against making second-class citizens of ourselves by our unreasoned fear and refusal to use our rights as citizens. He reminded us that by suppressing free speech to combat communism we not only strengthened communism's determination to survive but weakened democracy. By perceiving Vietnam only within the narrow context of winning or losing a war, he said, we were forgetting that we could win the war but lose our souls. He advocated finding a peaceful solution even if the terms were not tantamount to an American victory.[21]

Although he did agree to serve as a sponsor of the *Pacem in Terris* (Peace on Earth) convocation in Atlanta, he was far from pleased with its results. Afterwards he expressed these feelings to the chairman of the sponsoring committee:

> I am tremendously disturbed over the present psyche of America—its hysteria, its unwillingness to countenance dissent, its ready equation of any opposition to the present policy of our government with Communism and/or treason. Such one-sidedness ill becomes a democratic people and I deplore it. But I equally deplore the utter refusal to recognize any right or good in the U.S. policy—either in act or intention—by our own citizens. Such an attitude also exemplifies a closed mind and a totalitarian prejudice. I deplore the superpatriotism and jingoism that insists our country is always right but the only acceptable alternative is not that it is always wrong.[22]

---

[21]Sermon, "The Right to be Wrong," 14 January 1966; Sermon, "The Jew in the South Today," 16 January 1966—JMR MSS.

[22]JMR to Rev. John R. Yungblut, 17 December 1965, JMR MSS.

When it came to intermarriage, Jack had always insisted that each rabbi should be responsible for his own decisions rather than be bound by any hard-and-fast prohibition against it set forth by the CCAR. (The CCAR was not a hierarchical authority—it therefore could not make any of its laws binding. However, some rabbis wished for it to prohibit intermarriage in order to use that ruling as a cover for their own decisions.) Generally, he was opposed to performing marriages between Jews and unconverted Gentiles and did so only in those rare cases where exceptional circumstances convinced him that it was right. After several experiences in which his judgment had been proven wrong, he hardened his own rule and refused to perform them at all. He cited as his reason the statistics—as well as his own experience—which showed that most of those marrying unconverted Gentiles either did not remain Jewish themselves or did not inspire their children to remain Jewish. He did not consider it his duty, he said, "to preside over the dissolution of Judaism."

It was about that time when he discovered, somewhat to his surprise, that his colleagues in the Northeast when approached in regard to an intermarriage could no longer assume that the word implied "interreligious." While Jack was never called upon to perform a biracial marriage, he and the congregation did welcome more than one biracial couple into their midst. A single woman who is black joined the congregation in the sixties and became one of its most devoted workers, eagerly sought out for membership on various committees of the sisterhood. She arrived seeking conversion, which Jack and his assistant, Rabbi Richard Lehrman, were reluctant to perform because they were afraid she didn't understand all the ramifications of "Jewishness." When, during one of their consultations on the subject, she happened to mention that her mother was Jewish, the two rabbis looked at each other, smiled, and breathed a sigh of relief. Latching onto the technicality of matrilineal descent, they told her, "You don't *need* to be converted if your mother was Jewish! You're Jewish already." It wasn't a matter of welcoming her into the congregation—they had already done that. Their problem was one of moral responsibility for performing the conversion.

By the end of 1966, both Marcia and Bill were away at college. We knew we were as vulnerable to the problems of the day as any of the couples who came to Jack for comfort and support about their grown children. Both of us had formed our opinion of the Vietnam war during the years while Bill was still a child, or so he seemed to us, and the possibility of his having to serve there had never entered our minds then. Now it seemed as if the war would drag on forever. The likelihood of his being drafted was near indeed. We knew he opposed the continued fighting there, and we worried about what course he would choose if the awful decision actually confronted him. However, we were among the lucky ones. The draft lottery was established during his senior year at college and his number was high enough to insure that he wouldn't be called.

We had more reason to be confident that our children would avoid the other special pitfalls of those fateful years. Not that we were so naive as to believe intermarriage could not happen—we were more realistic than that. What we did believe was that both Marcia and Bill were so deeply committed to Judaism that regardless of who they married, they would insist upon their children being Jewish. That was all that mattered to us. At least, so we had always believed. Now, however, there was a new factor to be considered. How would we react if one of them decided to marry someone of another race?

One night at dinner, which had suddenly become a tête-à-tête for us on most evenings, I insisted upon discussing the subject with Jack, who did not really enjoy introspective conversation. When I asked, "How would you feel?" he shifted the burden of answering onto me, since I had introduced the subject. I had been thinking about it for a long time and had reached a decision—or, rather, a determination. "We'd have to realize," I said, "that the problem would be ours, not theirs. They would have faced it already and resolved it for themselves before deciding to get married. It would be up to us to make the adjustment."

Jack stared at me long and hard. Finally—and with absolute finality—he replied, "I guess you're just more liberal than I am," and went back to eating his dinner. I never brought up the subject again.

If his liberal tendencies were waning it was due not to encroaching reactionism but to approaching age. Both of us noticed it in other ways as well. His physical stamina was not what it once had been, nor was his flexibility of thought and action. Attacks of kidney stones and back pain, which had plagued him occasionally since the early fifties, now occurred more frequently. He never wanted to be fussed over when he was ill, only to be left alone, but he did consult a physician whenever the situation warranted and followed orders without complaint. His ever-ready sense of humor came to the rescue now as his calls to our internist, a good friend and former neighbor, Dr. James I. Weinberg, became ever more frequent. After describing his symptoms, he would say, "Tell me, Jim. Do I have 'Learn-to-live-with-it' or 'It's-going-around?' "

He was not so sanguine about the mental symptoms of aging he observed in himself. While I had not noticed any symptoms, and doubted that anyone else had, he began to feel that his ability to find the exact word to use in a sermon or controversial discussion was declining. It infuriated him—and no wonder, considering the phenomenal vocabulary he'd had at his disposal for most of his life. I tried to reassure him. Even in his supposed decline, his ability was still far better than most.

For the past ten years I had worried about his health, for he worked with little respite under extraordinary pressure. What I had feared was instant collapse. What occurred was early burn-out. It was our personal bitter harvest from seeds sown.

The summer of 1966 we had gone to Europe for another meeting of the World Union, and for the first time saw for ourselves the scorn and hostility toward America that we had heard of, but had not seen on our past travels. Graffiti on walls, anti-American Sunday speeches in Hyde Park, unfriendly hotel clerks in Paris, American flower children by the hundreds painting or singing for thrown pennies in the streets of Amsterdam and Copenhagen—all portrayed an image of our country and countrymen that we found distinctly unsettling.

Conditions in Sweden gave us additional reason to question our inherent belief in the superiority of the American way of life. We visited housing projects with facilities to care for the elderly without segregating them from the rest of society. We saw child-care centers that had long been established for, and used by, families of all economic levels, not only those in which the mother was forced to work and had no other alternative for the care of her preschool children. Also we had the unfortunate opportunity to sample Sweden's socialized health-care system—unfortunate not because of the system but because of the extremely painful symptoms that forced Jack to use it. The doctor on duty made a house call to the apartment of friends who had invited us for lunch. He came quickly, served cheerfully and effectively, and presented us with a bill far lower than we had any reason to expect. Had we been tax-paying Swedish citizens, we were told, there would have been no bill at all.

Our return home was even more discouraging: the Georgia gubernatorial campaign was in progress. By a peculiarity of voting procedure that has since been rectified, the segregationist restaurateur Lester Maddox had won the Democratic primary—opposite a conservative Republican, Howard "Bo" Calloway, whom many believed to be as reactionary as Maddox, though far more polished and acceptable to the urban upper middle classes. Liberals, dreading the prospect of four years under the leadership of either candidate, mounted a write-in campaign for former Governor Ellis Arnall, an attorney who had proven himself over the years as a fair-minded, responsible leader. Those who knew Jack had assumed he would support the write-in. While there was no mistake as to which candidate he preferred, the actual placing of his vote was another more complicated matter. He feared, along with many others, that a vote for Arnall would in effect be a vote for Maddox. On the other hand, he couldn't determine a viable alternative. Even staying away from the polls, he felt, would help Maddox as well as be morally wrong, an abdication of responsibility as a citizen.

Never had I seen him so distraught over making a decision. Finally, after weeks of agonized soul-searching, he decided to vote for the write-in. Meanwhile, so many members of the congregation had spoken to him, asking for guidance in making their own decision, that he felt obliged to give them an answer now that he had found his own. He did, by means of his regular column, "Between Us," in *The Temple Bulletin*.[23]

Calloway supporters, who had been trying all along to win him over, now pressured him even more to meet privately with the candidate and thereby, in one-on-one dialogue, they hoped, to satisfy himself that the Republican was the better choice. Finally, he gave in and did so four days before the election. Jack left the meeting still disagreeing with Calloway on basic issues but convinced that as governor he intended to serve "all the people of the State, not out of paternalism but with sincere respect for their worth as human beings."[24]

Now Jack faced an even thornier problem. Having broken his own rule to make public his choice in advance of an election, and now having made a different choice from the one announced, was he not morally obliged to announce that change? He had no time to spend in indecision.

[23]Rothschild, "Between Us," *The Temple Bulletin*, 3 November 1966, JMR MSS.

[24]JMR to The Temple members, 4 November 1966, JMR MSS. A copy of this letter is attached to Howard H. Calloway/JMR correspondence, 3-4 November 1966.

Accordingly, he wrote a letter to all members of the congregation saying that each of us "has a moral commitment that transcends the satisfying of his own conscience" and that therefore he could not perform an act that "might serve to place the reins of government in the hands of Mr. Maddox and those with whom he has surrounded himself."[25]

Just as we feared, Maddox won the election. Recrimination was rife among all factions of those who had opposed him, each blaming the other for having "swung the vote." Jack's letter to the congregation, received on the eve of the election, brought an avalanche of response to his desk, almost all of it praising his courage but by no means agreeing with his decision. In reply to one critic he said, "I do not claim infallibility. Even at this late date I'm not sure whether I was right to change or not. I only know that as a basically honest person I wrestled with my soul and at one time came to one conclusion and at a later time came to another."[26]

On the following Friday night he told his congregation that he had never before experienced a campaign engendering the bitterness and animosity that this one had. He attributed the degree of bitterness to the fact that people were torn by their own uncertainties, angry because they could not rest comfortably with their own decisions. He himself was no exception.[27]

The peaks and valleys of Jack's life came close together in those days. He had little time to reflect on the election before leaving for Richmond, Virginia, where he had been invited to address the Conference on People, Religion and a Changing Virginia. More than one thousand religious leaders of all denominations heard him say there that it was the shame of the religious community that it had involved itself in the social revolution "only to accommodate, rarely to lead." He accused them, collectively, of being "just another defender of the status quo, another institution trembling at the threshold of change," and then gave them a distilled dose of the medicine he had been dispensing to his congregation over the past two decades. He added a list of recent statistics to support

---

[25]Ibid.

[26]JMR to Adalbert Freedman, 21 November 1966, JMR MSS.

[27]Sermon, "Vox Populi—Which People and Whose Voice?" 11 November 1966, JMR MSS.

his accusations but declared that one didn't need them to realize the extent of failure in achieving truly integrated education:

> Even when we succeed in placing bodies—white and black—in
> the same school building, after the horror of tire chains and baseball
> bats on the backs of little children, we are still faced with the prob-
> lems that only we as religious men and women can solve. . . . such
> human problems as integrating Negro children into the class-room,
> the lunch-room, the activities room and the playground . . . creating
> an atmosphere warm enough that Negro children can sit at ease in
> class and put their minds to the business of learning; that they need
> not be concerned about the hostile hall they must traverse when the
> next bell rings. . . .
>
> I believe that the time has come for men to feel indignation at
> their failures and wrath at the indecencies that some of them per-
> petrate on others. I believe that until we are able to summon forth a
> righteous anger we shall never catalyze the teachings of our religious
> faith. And until we do apply them we shall never forge a world pleas-
> ing to God—or to man.[28]

Jack came home from Virginia not knowing whether to look upon
the glass of progress as being half full or half empty. His speech had been
accepted with great enthusiasm, both by the audience and by the local
press. On the other hand, it could only have been discouraging to realize
that after so many years of saying the same things, the same things still
needed to be said. He was especially discouraged by the defeat of a new
civil rights act designed to promote open housing and to help protect civil
rights workers. It seemed to him as if we had actually gone backward in
the field of social justice that year.

In his "wrap-up of events" sermon that year he attributed the re-
versed trend to the white backlash and said that we Americans "had better take a good look at ourselves." He compared the "crystal night" of the
Nazi Holocaust to the burning and bombing of Negro churches in America, the Nazis' use of lead pipes and guns to that of white Southerners
beating up Negro children. He asked, "What has happened to our image
of ourselves as decent, loving, warm-hearted people? What of our

---

[28]"Changing Educational Patterns," from the Virginia Conference on the Role of
the Religious Community, *Presbyterian Outlook* 148, no. 44 (5 December 1966): 5-6,
JMR MSS.

vaunted American principles of equality and democracy?" He noted the
rise of "Black Power" and asked how we can deplore the use of it "if we
constantly and malevolently deny the black man a share in a white-pow-
ered kingdom of God on earth?"[29]

Even interfaith relations, so long on the upgrade, seemed to be slip-
ping that winter. Through the assertive directorship of Don McEvoy, the
National Conference of Christians and Jews had made giant leaps in in-
tergroup relationships in our area. The Catholic church, led by the saintly
but human Archbishop Hallinan, had fostered Christian-Jewish dialogues
(and more importantly, friendships) to the point where we really did feel
like brothers and sisters. Jack was frequently asked to write articles for the
Catholic publication, the *Georgia Bulletin*, and had become very close
friends with the archbishop, whom he admired immensely. Bad as things
were in other aspects of the social revolution, we had reached the stage in
interfaith relations where we had all but forgotten the days when "Brotherhood Month" meant searching for understanding between Christians
and Jews.

Not so in 1967. That February we had a fresh example of anti-Semitism to consider, and from a most unlikely source. A highly qualified
teacher about to receive her doctorate from Emory University was denied
a teaching position at Agnes Scott College because she was Jewish. Jack,
asked to prevail upon the president of Agnes Scott, whom he knew and
had worked fruitfully with in the past, did so. Much to his amazement,
he learned that it was a long-standing policy of the school to engage only
professing Christians for its faculty. He was even more astounded when,
having brought the matter to the attention of Agnes Scott's board of trustees, the board reaffirmed the policy.

The teacher easily found employment elsewhere, but the incident
caused Atlanta Jewish leaders to reconsider how much progress had really
come about during the past decade or two. A few years before, some Atlanta dentists had accused the Emory School of Dentistry of anti-Semitism. The university officials had looked into the matter, examined the
evidence, and moved quickly to correct the wrong. Agnes Scott authorities did eventually change their policy to eliminate the bias, but that they
upheld it at the time was deeply disturbing.

---

[29]Sermon, "And Now Tomorrow," 6 January 1967, JMR MSS.

Jack spoke of the incident in a second "brotherhood" sermon for 1967. Commenting that all the so-called progress might be "merely the misleading frosting on a still lethal cake of explosive hatreds," he said that the school had the right to institute whatever policy it wished but that he questioned the wisdom, morality, and implications of such a policy. Then he dissected, point by point, the position paper issued by the trustees in defending it, exposing the illogic and bias implicit in it. The greatest offense committed by the writers of the policy, he declared, was the concept of "Jewish contamination" that it fostered and that, by implication, could invite a return of "old-style" anti-Semitism.[30]

We enjoyed a euphoric respite from such matters for a few weeks that spring while we prepared for the weekend celebration of the congregation's one hundredth anniversary. I had written a history of the congregation, which was published in hardback and distributed just prior to the anniversary. Jack and I each appeared on television in connection with the celebration, and generous space in the print media was allotted to it. Maurice Eisendrath, UAHC president, came to make the main address on Friday night, and because of our close friendship, his wife Rita came with him to help us celebrate.

The anniversary banquet on Saturday night was sparked by entertainer Bert Parks, who had grown up in The Temple and whose Atlanta family still belonged. On Sunday afternoon a commemorative service was held for the community at large, and the congregation presented the city with a gift of money to be used for an annual award in human relations. It was a memorable weekend, and for us personally a good tonic to sustain us for the disappointment that lay ahead.

Within days of our celebration we heard the first rumblings of approaching war in the Middle East. When Gamal Abdel Nasser closed the Straits of Tiran and we feared for the very survival of Israel, Jack did his best to persuade his Christian colleagues to speak out on Israel's behalf. He had little, if any, success. It disappointed him that men who had shown such courage and forthrightness in the struggle for racial justice could not now summon the same force of character for a Jewish cause. We did, of course, receive from Christians individual expressions of support during the weeks of crisis leading up to the Six Day War—both

---

[30]Sermon, "Straws of Hate in the Winds of Love," 10 March 1967, JMR MSS.

from politicians and private citizens. It was only the religious establishment that seemed unwilling to declare itself.

During the six days of fighting Jack took part in the effort to raise
funds for relief in Israel. When Dr. Benjamin Mays heard of the fund-
raising effort he wrote to Jack saying he wanted to participate and asked
where to send his check. While his was hardly typical of the general reaction on the part of Negro leaders, it was most encouraging and
appreciated.[31]

Thrilled as we were with Israel's stunning victory, we realized that
the battle to solidify Israel's gains in world opinion had only just begun.
This was an area in which we could help. Jack began by inviting about
twenty of the city's most prominent Christian ministers to a luncheon to
meet and hear from the consul general of Israel to the Southeastern
United States, Zeev Boneh. They came away enthusiastic, most of them
interested in organizing a tour to visit Israel together as quickly as possible. One of them, a Baptist, wrote Jack afterward, thanking him and
saying, "You not only contributed to Israel but to the religious fellowship
of Atlanta by having that group together. I came away feeling closer to
that group than to a lot of Baptists whom I know—and would like to
change!"

The trip did not come about, but it wasn't due to lack of interest on
the part of the ministers. The government of Israel was not yet ready to
deal with visitors of that nature on such short notice, and the necessary
delay would have scheduled the tour too far into the busy months of fall
for them to get away. Jack and I busied ourselves with putting together a
tour from the congregation, however, which did take place the following
January.

One longtime goal of Jack's was reached during the early months
of 1967, and gained momentum through the summer: the establishment
of the Community Relations Commission (CRC), appointed by the
mayor and officially sanctioned by the board of aldermen. The twenty
men and women named to the commission chose Sam Williams as its
first chairman and Jack as vice-chairman, a happy combination in view
of their many years of working together and enjoying each other's
company. The commission began by holding hearings in neighborhoods

---

[31]Dr. Benjamin E. Mays to JMR, 8 June 1967, JMR MSS.

where existing conditions threatened to spawn trouble. Jack always returned from the hearings angry and frustrated. He and the other whites
who served on the CRC, who had thought themselves aware of the inequities of city services in these neighborhoods, now were made truly
aware. Listening to the testimony of persons who actually lived in housing with faulty sanitation, on streets untended and often unpaved, with
no recreational facilities available to their children—he and the other
white clergymen became determined to transmit their new awareness to
the members of their congregations.

Jack predicted that there would be massive demonstrations in Atlanta if we did nothing about the "unkept promises and deliberate delay"
in giving these poorer neighborhoods their share of tax dollars for necessary improvements. More important to him was how the long-time
practice of diverting tax dollars away from the poorer neighborhoods was
affecting those neighborhood's schools. Now the city neighborhoods
with the most children had the fewest schools. It had been obvious that
the crisis was coming. Jack condemned the school board for having chosen to ignore it until it became acute, and for then trying to solve it by
instituting double sessions.

In his sermon for the Day of Atonement that year, Jack lashed out
at these inequities. He said it should be obvious that a four-and-a-half-
hour day could not provide the same quality of education as a six- or
seven-hour day could; by thus reducing it, he said, we were shortchanging
the very children who needed it most. Double sessions created another
problem as well:

> Parents work—many of them in our kitchens. They leave their
> homes in the early morning hours to fix our breakfasts and tend our
> children. Who watches over theirs? Double sessions leave hundreds
> of teenagers to their own devices for most of the school day. . . . They
> roam the streets and stand on corners. . . . And the relief offered by
> the Board? Only after great pressure from many quarters were the
> members willing to admit that the problem existed at all. Now they
> respond by proffering another kind of freedom of choice. Those
> whose parents elect the option may apply for transfer to a less
> crowded school but with no transportation provided. This places a
> financial burden on those who can least afford it. In addition it places

hundreds of teen-agers in the heart of the city as they transfer from
one bus to another.[32]

Restricted neighborhoods, he pointed out, lay at the base of all these
problems. An attempt was then being made to establish a biracial neighborhood in southwest Atlanta. Some members of our own congregation
were involved in it. Sadly, Jack observed that their efforts were being frustrated. "One open area is not enough," he said. "It creates only a new—
and somewhat better ghetto, but a ghetto nonetheless."[33]

Even more discouraging was a spate of recent remarks indicating
anti-Semitism among members of Martin Luther King's Southern Christian Leadership Conference (SCLC). Always direct in manner, especially
with friends, Jack wrote to Martin as soon as these incidents were called
to his attention, saying how important it was that they discuss the matter.
He said he could not believe that these men's alleged statements could
represent the position of the SCLC, "particularly in the light of your
many speeches in which you have publicly made clear not only the complete absence of any prejudice in your own heart but an empathy and a
sympathy for Jews whether in the United States, in the Soviet Union or
in Israel."[34]

Martin responded with a five-page letter explaining those incidents
whose details he knew. The gist seemed to be that the men had been
quoted out of context and that one of the spokesmen (though Martin
probably didn't realize it) did harbor some deep latent anti-Semitism.
The letter is particularly interesting in that it expresses so eloquently and
so honestly, as friend to friend, the point of view from which blacks—
even those who are most sincerely good friends of Jews—judge the actions and reactions of American Jews. Interestingly, one of the spokesmen
alluded to in the accusation (not the one I suspected of anti-Semitism)
was Andrew Young—the present mayor of Atlanta—who as ambassador
to the United Nations a decade later raised even greater question among
Jews as to whether or not he was anti-Semitic. Had Jack been alive at that
time he would certainly have spoken out to and for the beleaguered am-

---

[32]Sermon, "Soul Searching or Soul Scratching?" 13 October 1967, JMR MSS.

[33]Ibid.

[34]JMR to Dr. Martin Luther King, Jr., 7 September 1967, JMR MSS.

bassador, whom we personally knew to be as unbiased as his former leader
and mentor, Martin King. In his letter to Jack concerning the accusations
of anti-Semitism, Martin confirmed specifically his confidence in Andy's
attitude toward Jews.[35]

Later in the fall of 1967 Jack again found it necessary to remind his
congregation that religious organizations—specifically the Union—had a
right and an obligation to address the issues of the day. People were more
afraid than ever to speak out, especially about the war in Vietnam. Jack
led gently into his admonition with some examples of how some of our
biblical forebears had dealt with the same problems we face today. He
quoted Isaiah on condemned housing, pockets of poor in the midst of
plenty, police brutality, and discriminatory immigration policies. He
cited Ecclesiastes on economic injustice. As for peace, he had only to
point to our prayer book. In every Sabbath service we pray for peace and
ask that we be made "the messengers of peace and our country its advocate in the council of nations."[36]

Then he attacked the oft-voiced idea that representatives of religious organizations should not speak out because they lacked expertise to
do so on such matters:

> Of course they do not speak as specialists—they're not scien-
> tists and they're not economists and they're not military experts—
> but they are religious men and women who are vitally concerned with
> the world in which they live. . . . Maybe the reason we have so utterly
> failed to resolve these problems . . . is just because we have left them
> too long to the experts, to the generals and the politicians and the
> economists. . . . Maybe what we need is the dedicated, fearless voice
> of religion. . . . To seek to still the voice of the spirit on such matters
> as the disgrace of sprawling slums and the degrading poverty that
> exists in them just because Washington has passed an Economic Op-
> portunity Act and thus poverty becomes political is to me ridiculous
> and specious. To silence our voices on the overriding issue of world
> peace simply because we are engaged in war borders on the ridicu-

[35]Martin Luther King, Jr., to JMR, 28 September 1967, JMR MSS.

[36]Sermon, "To Make Our Voice Heard," 10 November 1967, JMR MSS.

lous. When should we seek peace if not when there is an existence of these circumstances?[37]

In his year-end sermon Jack noted the happy news of the world's first successful heart transplant and commented that the world itself seemed to need such surgery. Especially concerned that the war in Vietnam had "torn at the heart of America," he listed some news items of recent days:

> There must be something wrong with America when its highest officials must be smuggled into a meeting where they are scheduled to speak to avoid angry mobs who disagree with them, when the President of the United States must virtually sneak off to attend the funeral of a Catholic prelate, where steps of buildings are painted with human blood—and where the head of the Selective Service advocates that those who oppose the nation's policies should be punished by being drafted first.[38]

He concluded that the gap between what we are and what we once had hoped to become had widened and deepened, our hearts had worn out, and we were kept alive "by injections that only keep us kicking and jerking in spasms of discontent."[39]

When the President's National Advisory Commission on Civil Disorder issued its report later that winter, Jack referred to it as "a bomb that exploded over America" and warned that we must wake up lest we sleep through the destruction of our nation. Noting that the commission had found racism to be the real cause of the present disorder in America, he asked his listeners to consider honestly their own attitudes and determine where their own racism began: was it sitting next to a black person on a bus, eating beside him in a restaurant, having their children go to school together? Jack enumerated each step of drawing closer with those of other races, concluding with visiting in each other's homes and living next door to one another. He then noted that the commission's report "questions our own decency and humaneness" and asked if it did so without justi-

---

[37]Ibid.

[38]Sermon, "Does the Word Need a New Heart?" 22 December 1967, JMR MSS.

[39]Ibid.

fication. If justified, he asked, "what can we do about it?" and "are we willing to do anything at all?"[40]

Life was not a solid block of work and gloom during that time, Jack's sermons to the contrary. His love for baseball had revived when the Braves were moved to Atlanta, and we occasionally had an opportunity to see them play. During one of his incarcerations at the Catholic hospital—this time for back pain—he discovered that one of the sisters was an ardent baseball fan but had never seen a live ball game. Soon afterward he told the manager of the Stadium Club about her and added, "I may be calling on you for help. . . . As soon as I get permission from the Archbishop, I'm going to take her to a ball game."[41]

While he rarely attended football games he enjoyed them whenever he went. He always looked forward to being invited to give the opening prayer at one Georgia Tech game each season. There was more fun to this assignment for him than merely watching the game. It always intrigued him to compose prayers in the terminology of the game or professional group for which he was offering the invocation. His efforts at the Georgia Tech games never went unrewarded by at least one letter or call of appreciation. One of those, in the 1967 season, came from the man whose home we had considered buying twenty years before. Not only did he compliment Jack on his prayer at the game, he expressed his appreciation for Jack's leadership and courage throughout the years, and reiterated his wife's earlier statement of "disappointment" in their neighbor's anti-Semitism. It was a case of the past coming back to encourage rather than to haunt.[42]

Jack needed all the encouragement he could get that fall and winter: the darkest days were still ahead. Through February and early March he watched with anguish as his friend Archbishop Hallinan declined sharply in what all realized was a losing battle with death. He died on 27 March 1968. Jack served as one of his honorary pallbearers and mourned deeply, as did many others. It was a tremendous loss for the city. For us it was a tremendous personal loss as well.

---

[40]Sermon, "Separate But Unequal—Is Money Enough?" 8 March 1968, JMR MSS.

[41]JMR to Edward Glennon, 18 May 1967, JMR MSS.

[42]John J. Partridge to JMR, 6 November 1967, JMR MSS.

Two weeks later we sustained a second terrible loss, one shared by the entire world. We were watching the evening news when we heard that Martin King had been shot at a motel in Memphis. Although the initial reports left hope that he was still alive, our inner radar told us otherwise. Within minutes someone called from one of the local television stations to ask Jack to come down for an interview about his association with Martin. After he left I saw the television coverage of Coretta, with Mayor Ivan Allen and his wife accompanying her to the airport, being turned back by the news that it was indeed too late, that Martin was already dead. No sooner had her image left the screen than Father Noel Burtenshaw, secretary to the late archbishop, called to say he was coming to pick up Jack and drive with him to visit her. I planned to go with them, but when Jack came home he insisted that I stay behind. He had heard reports of rioting in some other cities and was afraid there might be trouble in downtown Atlanta as well. Martin and Coretta had deliberately chosen a new home on a street surrounded by pockets of very depressed neighborhoods. One could not reach it without going through at least one of them.

By then it had begun to rain heavily, as if the heavens matched our mood. I worried far more about the possibility of trouble than I would have if Jack had let me go along. As the two men went out to the car I called after them to be careful. Noel made me even more apprehensive, albeit with the cheer of his Irish humor, when he called back in his charming brogue, "Oh don't ye worry. Now we've lost the two o' them in two weeks, we can't afford to be takin' any chances with your husband."

The two men returned safely. They had encountered no disturbance on the way. Coretta, they reported, had been sitting alone in her living room, calm and contained as ever, and apparently very glad to see them. She had embraced them both and spoken easily with them for the short while they were there. She told them she planned to go to Memphis on the following day to bring Martin's body home.

I planned to visit her on Saturday afternoon, after she returned from Memphis, and Billie Williams had mentioned the possibility of visiting her then also. My cleaning man, Travis Sims, who was black, overheard me discussing it on the telephone with Billie. When I finished he told me, "If Miz Williams don't go with you, I'm takin' you there myself. Ain't safe for no white lady in a convertible to be drivin' through them neighborhoods today."

His concern was touching and I appreciated it, but I was also happy that Billie could go with me and that there was no need for alarm in reaching Coretta's house. We passed a few stores with broken windows, but that was all. Even the teenagers we saw clustered on several street corners appeared reasonably docile.

Coretta wasn't at home, but Billie and I had a chance to visit with each other. During the course of our conversation she said something about seeing me at Martin's funeral the following Tuesday. When I told her that Jack and I had not been invited—and admittance to the church was by invitation only—she said that she was certain one had been sent and asked Sam to check on it. He, too, was certain we were meant to receive one—and was dumbfounded when he inquired and found that we weren't. Apparently there were so many celebrities to include that Ebenezer Church could hardly contain them all, and the family understandably needed to leave room for members of the church and those close friends who had known Martin all his life. No arrangements were made for Atlanta's white clergy.

That we understood did not make us any more amenable to the idea of milling around in the streets with what promised to be an enormous crowd. The funeral had already begun to take on the characteristics of a media event. Jack especially wanted to hear the service undisturbed, and both of us preferred to pay our last respects to Martin in a setting more conducive to quiet contemplation than standing in a mob on Edgewood Avenue. For that reason we decided to stay home and watch it on television.

So many visitors were arriving in Atlanta for the funeral that telephone committees were at work requesting private accommodations. No one called us until 10:30 Monday night, when two friends of Bill's from Yale telephoned to say they were stuck downtown with no place to stay. We told them to come to our house, and we bedded them down in Bill's room. At about 4:30 the next morning the overhead light in our bedroom was turned on. It was Bill. He and a carload of students had decided at the last moment to drive down to Atlanta. They had left New Haven after their morning classes and driven all night to arrive in time for the funeral. Bill wanted to know who was sleeping in his bed—and where he and his fellow travelers should go to get some rest before their early-morning race to find advantageous places in the crowd outside the church. They had already stopped off at my mother's house in order to drop off the female member of their party, who would sleep there. After a few more hours sleep, I made breakfast for the unexpected houseful and confidently assured them that a hearty dinner would await them on their return. "Sorry, Mom," Bill said. "We appreciate it but we're going to have to hit the road right after the funeral to get back to New Haven in time for class tomorrow."

Jack and I looked at each other in despair. No matter how we tried, it seemed we were not going to be able to avoid completely the carnival atmosphere that was evolving around this tragic occasion. Happy as we were to see Bill, we would have preferred to see him and his friends under different circumstances. During the break in television coverage between the service at Ebenezer Church and the one that followed on the grounds of Morehouse College, I telephoned the delicatessen, ordered a mountain of sandwiches, pickles, and Coca-Colas, and Jack went to pick them up. The kids stopped long enough afterward to gather their gear and the food, and were off in the proverbial cloud of dust.

The following Sunday afternoon we paid our final respects to Martin at a city-wide memorial service conducted by the combined clergy of Atlanta and held at the Episcopal Cathedral of St. Philip. The young Catholic prelate who had been serving as assistant to Archbishop Hallinan was chosen to give the memorial prayer. Then a newly elevated bishop, he is now Joseph Cardinal Bernardin, Archbishop of Chicago.

The ministers chose Jack to deliver the eulogy. In it he asked when mankind would learn that the dream of truth and justice and human dignity could not "be delayed or stayed by the wanton killing of the dreamer." Martin Luther King, Jr., had died, he said, because he dared to challenge white America to fulfill the ideals of its own democracy and because men "cowered before the sound of their own conscience." He reminded the vast crowd of whites assembled there that unity, not divisiveness, had been Martin's goal and noted bitterly the "crowning contradiction" that he who had lived "by the olive wreath" should be "destroyed by the sword." It would indeed be a desecration of his memory, Jack declared, if this tragedy became the signal "for the very acts of violence that he sought with all his power to prevent." While he could understand the "impotent rage . . . the need to strike out in fury" that gripped the black community, Jack said, the only fitting memorial to Martin would be a firmer dedication to his teachings and a greater determination to achieve a united America "which will offer justice and dignity and equality for all its citizens." Then he spoke of the challenge that confronted white America:

> Now, at long last, we must set about changing not the laws of America but the hearts of Americans. Do we reject the potential Apartheid that threatens to take over our land? Then we must be willing to admit the Negro into the structure of our white society. Do we deplore violence? Then we must be willing to remove the cause of violence—the frustration, the denied hopes, the unfulfilled dreams that we have nurtured in so many hearts. "I have a dream," once cried Martin Luther King. Now that dream is dying in too many souls. And it will continue to grow ever more dim until we dream the same dream—and set about making it a waking reality.
>
> For the America that we create shall be his lasting memorial— if it be a land of domestic tranquility, a land of opportunity for all, a land of justice and love and righteousness, a land where a man does not lift up sword against his neighbor but where each sits under his own vine and under his own fig tree and there is none to make him afraid.[43]

A portion of the eulogy was carried on national television that evening. Maurice Eisendrath saw it in New York and wrote to Jack the following day to compliment him. He also commented that if the country "does not now move to implement the programs and meet the needs for which so many of us have been pleading, the situation is hopeless."[44]

In his reply Jack said he felt ambivalent about the sincerity of response shown in the funeral and the mourning. "It was an outpouring of guilt," he ventured, "but I'm not sure whether it is going to have any lasting effect or positive result."[45]

He was more optimistic in his response to a member of the congregation who had written saying that locally "we were intimidated by phone calls and we experienced fear . . . which has now turned somewhat to indignation and in general being angry with oneself for allowing the fear to take place." However, the writer had added that, in his opinion, we At-

---

[43]Memorial address for Martin Luther King, Jr., "Martin Luther King, Jr.—A Memorial," 5 April 1968, JMR MSS.

[44]Rabbi Maurice N. Eisendrath to JMR, 8 April 1968, JMR MSS.

[45]JMR to Rabbi Maurice N. Eisendrath, 12 April 1968, JMR MSS.

lantans had made a "good show" superficially. Jack told him that he had
been aware of some of the "actions of intimidation and threat" that went
on in the community and did not condone them. He also knew of incidents that had occurred in the black community but believed that the decision made and kept by the news media not to report them had been a
wise one. Then he added:

> On the other hand, I believe also that it is true that "Atlanta
> responded with dignity, decency and genuine sorrow." The efforts
> made by many of the downtown churches to house and feed thou-
> sands of visitors, of the volunteer car pools and chauffeur service, the
> genuine sorrow that was manifest in a large part of the community
> was I think real as was the interdenominational service which I had
> the privilege of participating in at the Cathedral of St. Philip.
>
> You are right, however. We still have a long way to go and there
> is a great deal of hypocrisy in our attitudes. Until we can change
> men's hearts it will do little good to change laws which their hearts
> refuse to persuade them to obey.[46]

The trend of events continued to discourage Jack. An increase of violence, callousness, and indifference by much of the population when
confronted with human need, and further decline of dedication to American ideals, caused him to say that he could see "among the haves only
smugness and anger over the disturbing of their tranquility." He was horrified that housewives were finding it necessary to take lessons in handling firearms, and that cities were buying tanks and weapons carriers,
and even types of paralyzing gases. He felt strongly that the ultimate protection of our cities was to be found "not in armored cars but in a righ-
teous society," and that the aim of a democratic society was "not to quell
riots but to fulfill rights, not to cool the ghetto but to transform it." So
disturbed was he by the state of events that he even failed to find his tra-
ditionally upbeat ending for that sermon during May 1968. He
concluded:

> I fear for the American dream. Not King's dream—but our
> American dream of one nation, indivisible with liberty and justice for
> all. I fear for what the foundering of that dream is doing to us—hard-

---

[46]Charles J. Altman to JMR, ca. April 1968; JMR to Charles J. Altman, 6 May
1968—JMR MSS.

ening our spiritual arteries, brutalizing our natures, making us a cruel
and heartless people. I fear that unless we are able to change—and
change quickly—this noble experiment will fail. A land called America will survive—but it will not be the America we set out to create.[47]

We went to Israel again that summer for the meeting in Jerusalem
of the World Union. After a week's vacation at Caesarea Jack departed for
another invitational tour of Germany. I stayed on to do some vignette doc-
umentaries of everyday life in Jerusalem for an Atlanta television station
and met him in New York at the end of the two weeks. The vacation
helped relax Jack physically but did little to lift his spirits. It had been sad
to visit the divided city of Berlin so soon after rejoicing with the residents
of Jerusalem in the miraculous reunification of their own city. He spoke
about it in one of his Holyday sermons that year. While he described Israel in terms of optimism and joy, he saw the Berlin wall as a symbol of
pessimism and despair.[48]

In his Rosh Hashanah sermon he lashed out against hypocrisy, saying Americans suffered from "psychic schizophrenia." He declared that
there was so vast a gulf between what we believed and what we did that
large segments of our society had simply given up on us.

> We believe in ethics but its absence in the business world has
> become a national scandal. We stamp our letters "Pray for Peace" but
> vilify anyone who works for it. We maintain that we're a nonviolent
> people but advocate the right of every man to own a gun to use
> against anyone he disagrees with. We preach morality—but we don't
> practice it. There's nothing wrong with our values. The trouble is that
> we don't really mean it when we set them up as our goals.[49]

Obviously, there were no easy answers. He did not imply that he had
found any. He criticized the government for its continued policy of bombing in Vietnam and the antiwar extremists for their obscene behavior in
pouring blood on draft records and burning the American flag. He condemned the growing separatism in the black community but reminded

---

[47]Sermon, "My Fears for the Soul of America," 10 May 1968, JMR MSS.

[48]Sermon, "To Light the Darkened Joy," 22 September 1968, JMR MSS.

[49]Ibid.

us that we had "unquestionably" earned it. This last was an especially sore point with him. He deeply resented the current trend by blacks to reject all that he and so many other whites had spent their lives working and striving for. Noting this trend he asked bitterly if he would now be forced to choose "between a new Black Power militancy which is just as racist as the Klan ever was" or a withdrawal from the battle because "any moderation stamps me as an Uncle Tom."[50]

Again he could find nothing hopeful with which to end his sermon. The best he could do was admonish us not to use the fact that we weren't wanted as an excuse to opt for withdrawal and ignore the problems. "They are ours to face," he concluded.[51]

Jack was honored at two public dinners that fall. At the first, which took place in September, the National Conference of Christians and Jews presented him with its Herman L. Turner Clergyman of the Year Award. That Dr. Benjamin Mays, whom he liked and admired so very much, had been the only previous recipient of the award made the occasion even more meaningful. Dr. Mays made the presentation to Jack before a full assembly of friends, black and white.

Representatives of the different church groups and leaders of the political life of the city brought greetings and words of tribute, all of which fell happily upon our ears. One, however, we had to admit, stood out as an exceptional tribute, because it described exactly the kind of rabbi that Jack most wanted to be. Protocol had demanded that the new archbishop, Thomas Donnellan, bring greetings on behalf of the Catholic community, which he did with warmth and enthusiasm. Since Donnellan had so recently arrived in Atlanta, however, and knew Jack only slightly, Father Noel Burtenshaw had been asked to say a few words relating to the close association that Jack had had with the late Archbishop Hallinan. He ended:

> Let those of us who think that our place is solely in the sanc-
> tuary, watch him at work in the halls of our political leaders. Let
> those of us who think that our words must be uttered solely in pul-
> pits, listen to him in committees. And especially let those of us who
> think that to bend the knee is sufficient, watch him in action. The

---

[50]Ibid.

[51]Ibid.

motto of the monks of Saint Benedict might well be his—*laborare est orare*—to work is to pray.[52]

Whether in Latin or in Hebrew that was Jack's idea of piety.

The second honor Jack received that fall was the Abe Goldstein Man of the Year Award from the Anti-Defamation League of B'nai B'rith. Something happened in the intervening weeks, however, that caused the mood of this dinner to be much different from that of the other. In early November he had spoken at a meeting of the Hungry Club, a group of prominent black businessmen and professionals that met regularly for a luncheon sparked with discussion of current issues. Many of the members were Jack's friends, men with whom he had worked harmoniously for years in the civil rights struggle, men for whom he had great respect and whom he thought had equal respect for him. Nevertheless, he must have realized that he would be treading on thin ice with his remarks that day, for he prefaced them with the following apology of sorts:

> There was a time when you and I would have been in perfect harmony in our joint efforts to achieve dignity and equality for Black Americans. Perhaps we still are—I hope so. . . . I want freedom for all Americans—and I want it now. But I am convinced that the way to achieve those goals is not to destroy the fabric of American democracy.[53]

He then told them basically what he had been telling his own congregation in regard to his objections to separatism. While insisting that he understood "the justifiable scorn which greets any plea for patience," he declared that he could not accept any form of apartheid, even a voluntary one, as a solution to the inequities existing in American society. Granting that it might gain the black man his self-respect, he reasoned that it would not gain him the respect of the white American because "it would relieve him [the white American] of the responsibility to face his own conscience." Not that he expected blacks to be concerned about the

---

[52]Father Noel C. Burtenshaw, tribute to JMR, delivered at NCCJ Clergyman of the Year dinner, 25 September 1968, JMR MSS.

[53]Address to the Hungry Club, "Promise Denied and Hope Fulfilled," 13 November 1968, JMR MSS.

spiritual well-being of whites—to clarify his point he spoke of the age-old challenge confronting Jews:

> I am of a people, small in number and weak in power, whose only claim to greatness has been its willingness to be the conscience of mankind. Reviled and persecuted, decimated by pogrom and holocaust, we have still maintained our visibility and sought to obey the rabbinic dictum: "Separate not thyself from the community." I would urge upon the Negro a similar commitment.[54]

In a further argument against apartheid he advocated working toward a unified America by putting into action "all the positive and constructive programs, which become . . . a source of strength, self-reliance, self-respect and self-confidence." Such was the kind of black power he believed would bring about the changes necessary for an integrated society. He added:

> Such power does not despair of our society as the best it can get and beg for concessions. It calls for Black Americans to mobilize their full power, range it alongside the strength of that segment of White America that shares its dream of the future, and together fight the battle to transform our society and make it in reality what it professes to be in theory.[55]

He concluded by stating unequivocally his objection to the current effort to exclude him and other Jews from the battle they had so long fought and so ardently espoused as their own. As always, he was blunt and honest.

> I don't like being told it's not my fight. It is. . . . As a Jew, I have a commitment to justice and dignity and equality. And as a Jew, I am not going to forgo my religious commitment in the face of black separatism any more than we Jews withdrew from the battle in the face of white segregationism.[56]

---

[54]Ibid.

[55]Ibid.

[56]Ibid.

Jack's candor gained him little thanks. He was hissed and booed for the first time in his life and came away realizing that his words had been unconvincing. As he commented to another white who had heard the speech, "This may well indicate that it is too late for us any longer to convince the Negro community of our determination and sincerity."[57]

Only one of the black publications, the conservative *Atlanta Daily World*, reported the speech in anything resembling a favorable light. The worst consequence of the speech, however, was the apparent ostracism placed upon us by our black friends. Not one of them showed up for the Anti-Defamation League dinner two weeks later. Even Sam and Billie Williams, whom we knew would not desert us for such a reason, had to be elsewhere that particular evening.[58]

Black anti-Semitism became more virulent during the winter months, militants at Southern universities were making "nonnegotiable" demands for separate dormitories, James Foreman issued his "Black Manifesto" calling for a half million dollars in "reparations" from churches and synagogues and recommending the overthrow of the United States government, the massacre at My Lai became known to the public (which generally reacted by refusing to believe it), and practically everyone we knew, it seemed, was buying a gun, being burglarized, and wiring their houses for protection. Jack said he didn't know whether to laugh or cry at such a state of affairs. I pleaded with him to have an alarm system installed in our house, and he reacted to the suggestion with the same disdain he had exhibited in the early sixties when all of our friends were frantically building bomb shelters. He had said then that it was unseemly for human beings to live burrowed into holes like rodents and that he would have no part of it. Now he deplored turning our homes into armed fortresses.

As if in ghoulish déjà vu, a new crisis confronted the public schools of Georgia. Reaction to it in the state legislature was similar to that towards the earlier crisis. It concerned busing and the Court order to desegregate school faculties. A bill had been introduced in the legislature calling for abandonment of compulsory attendance rules as a means of

---

[57]See note 53 above; JMR to Howard Hurtig, 18 November 1968, JMR MSS.

[58]"We Agree with Rabbi Roth[s]child," *Atlanta Daily World*, 16 Nov. 1968, JMR MSS.

circumventing the Court order. Jack commented disgustedly, "As if Georgia schools are not bad enough already, and their products ill-prepared enough to meet the challenges of a modern society!" He attacked the current argument that ill-prepared black teachers would lower the standards of the previously all-white schools, by reminding his listeners that our sins had come back to haunt us. After all, who had systematically prevented them from becoming better prepared? Besides, he reasoned, if the true purpose of education was to prepare children for life, then their heightened understanding of the human situation gained as a result of having such teachers would amply compensate for the little bit of extra time they would need to catch up on their arithmetic![59]

Our cup of personal sorrow continued to fill that winter as our friend Ralph McGill died suddenly, on 3 February, of a heart seizure. Again the city mourned, as much for a great and good spirit as for the extraordinary editor and columnist it had lost. We knew we would not likely find again so strong a voice for justice as his had been.

By the end of 1969 our euphoria over Israel's victory in the Six Day War had been dissolved by the acts of terrorism occurring across the Jordan Valley. Jack had gone to Israel during the winter on a mission with the United Jewish Appeal, and I went twice, in the spring and in the following fall, on writing assignments sponsored by the Israel Ministry of Tourism. Each of us returned to write and speak glowingly of what we found to be the quality of life there, notwithstanding the constant threat of terrorism and open warfare. When Jack preached on the subject, though, he had to admit that he detected "growing seeds of pessimism and hopelessness" within American Jews in regard to Israel's problems. He told his congregation that we American Jews had both the need and the obligation to visit Israel and reminded us that we would be safer there than on the streets of our own cities. He commented on the one-sidedness of world opinion, which was currently blaming Jews and Israel for the arson committed upon the El Aksa mosque by a deranged Christian from Australia, and charged each individual with the duty to become an active defender of Israel by learning enough to be able to refute on the spot the lies promoted by Arab propaganda. Furthermore, he said, he was convinced that the time had come for American Jews to speak out against

---

[59]Sermon, "Soul Searching or Soul Scratching?"

the inequities perpetrated upon the Jews of the Middle East "even when—especially when—our own country is a party to those inequities. . . . It is time that we spoke out for justice and decency for our own brethren—and to our own government."[60]

One means of furthering that goal occurred to him when the consul general of Israel asked him to suggest a Christian clergyman who might benefit from an invitation to visit Israel as the guest of the government. Jack thought immediately of Sam Williams, whom he knew would benefit from the trip, and whom he knew also, confidentially, was designated to be the next recipient of the Clergyman-of-the-Year Award. Since the invitation from the government of Israel was likely to be repeated over the next few years, Jack thought it would be a good idea to tie it onto the NCCJ award. The only hitch was that the government could not supply the overseas transportation. Jack solved that problem by prevailing upon Harry Dwoskin, the generous Jewish co-chairman of the Atlanta NCCJ at that time, to donate sufficient funds to send the recipient and his wife to Israel for as many years as the Israeli government renewed its invitation.

We were thrilled that Sam and Billie were given the trip, even more delighted that they chose to take it in the spring, when we planned to be there ourselves attending the CCAR. We met them in Jerusalem, went with them to some of our favorite places, attended Sam's lecture at the Hebrew University, and shared honors with them at a party given by our mutual dear friends, the former consul-general in Atlanta, Shimon Yallon, and his wife Ilse. Billie by then had become a television personality, appearing as co-hostess on the local version of the "Today Show." When we returned she invited me to join her on the program to show some of our slides and to discuss the trip. As a result, we thought of a plan that would promote good will at home and toward Israel: we would organize a tour of Israel for the following Passover and Easter, integrated racially and religiously, with the two of us as leaders.

Our brochures were at the printers the following September when, on the eve of the Jewish Holydays, Sam went to the hospital for what was to be a relatively simple operation. He was reported to be recovering satisfactorily. On Yom Kippur, when Jack went into his study to rest between

[60]Sermon, "Victory of the Spirit," 12 September 1969, JMR MSS.

the morning and the afternoon service, he received the awful news that Sam had died—of complications resulting from the surgery. There were no words of consolation for Jack at the news of this bereavement. We could hardly find words to proffer comfort to Billie.

Again the entire city mourned for one of its greatest spirits, one of its strongest, most forthright leaders. There were some who thought that Jack should take his place as chairman of the Community Relations Commission, but Jack did not agree. He believed that a black person ought to be in the top position and recommended another clergyman, former Executive Director of the SCLC Rev. Andrew Young. Andy took the job and held it until he left to represent his—and our—district in Congress two years later.

Although the death of other close friends and the deterioration of his own health caused repeated sadness in the years that followed, the death of Sam Williams in October 1970 seemed to symbolize the misery and frustration of that period, which someone else once characterized as "a slum of a decade." Worst of all was the gut feeling that so much of it could have been prevented. As Ralph McGill had observed in regard to the bombings of The Temple and the school in Clinton, Tennessee, a decade earlier, it was the harvest of seeds sown.

CHAPTER · NINE

CELEBRATIONS

Happier times were on the way. They would be of short duration, but we did enjoy them, and Jack would know for certain that his work had been appreciated.

Rosh Hashanah of 1970 had marked the beginning of his twenty-fifth season as rabbi of The Temple. He took note of it in his sermon, indulging in one of his rare displays of nostalgia. He laced his message with reminders of how far he and the congregation had progressed with each other, but included words of moral uplift for the future as well. Much of what he said referred to Israel. It was hard to imagine what our life would be like without Israel, he declared, adding that it "has kept us faithful to our heritage and been our salvation as Jews as surely as we Jews have played a part in ensuring its survival as a Jewish State." That statement alone probably represented the greatest change that had taken place in the congregation during his quarter century of leadership.[1]

Jack also spoke of our growing sense of security as Jews in America. He recalled the calm courage shown in the time of the bombing and the overwhelming support of our Christian neighbors. He spoke of civil rights, not with the goading admonitions that characterized other sermons on the subject but with gentle and genuine appreciation for having been permitted to be as outspoken as he had been throughout the years. When he mentioned the storm that had broken over the sisterhood's insistence upon holding a luncheon with a nonwhite speaker in 1955, a titter rippled across the crowded sanctuary. "You laugh—now," he said, realizing that many of his listeners were too young to have been aware of it at the time. "It wasn't funny then." He continued:

> I tell you this because it epitomizes a long journey we have made together. . . . because after twenty-five years you deserve to be complimented for your patience and your courage. I am not unaware of the discomfiture and uncertainty that I may have caused you. . . . Yet you never once denied me the right to speak. . . . You never threatened me with dismissal for my stand. And much more than that, large numbers of you accepted my interpretation of Judaism as your own and stood with me in those early days when to be in the forefront of the fight was often neither comfortable nor safe.[2]

Even on such a sentimental occasion he could not end without briefly referring to the fact that the battle was not yet won completely. The backlash—both black and white, he said—threatened to undo whatever gains had been made during all those years. Then he returned to nostalgia, concluding his sermon with a prayer of gratitude to God for having been permitted to spend so large a portion of his life as rabbi of that congregation, and offering it his strength and his devotion in the years to come.[3]

---

[1]Sermon, "Past, Present and Future," 30 September 1970, JMR MSS.

[2]Ibid.

[3]Ibid.

Although he had not yet begun to admit it to me—and perhaps not even to himself—he had little strength left to give. The pain of repeated bouts with kidney stones and slipped discs over the past fifteen years, though not life-threatening in themselves, had taken their toll in terms of energy and now began to interrupt his work more frequently and with increasing severity. More and more he mentioned retirement—casually, in conversation with his colleagues and old friends from other cities, and with me. He steadfastly insisted that he intended to retire at the earliest opportunity—age sixty-five—and hoped he would be able to travel for the first six months in order to give his successor an easier time of it than he had had when he first came to Atlanta. Beyond that he refused to plan, or even to conjecture what he would do with his life after retirement. The most he would say was that he would play golf three times a week instead of two.

I worried a lot about that attitude because I knew how unrealistic it was, and I couldn't understand how someone as reasonable and practical as Jack could think of preparation for retirement only in terms of financial readiness. It became almost an obsession with me, trying to make him discuss it seriously. Once I pushed him too far and he closed the subject permanently by saying, "Maybe I won't have to decide. Maybe I won't live that long."

Whether that was a premonition or merely a deliberate attempt to shock me into silence I couldn't determine. He had always been keenly aware of the twelve-and-one-half-year age difference between us, and in the early years of our marriage made a point of telling me repeatedly that I would probably outlive him by many years and should expect to make a new life with someone else. I never let myself dwell on that possibility but I did realize the need to develop a basis for a future on my own, outside the aegis of his career. I strongly believed that both of us needed to do so well before his retirement. It occurred to me that he might be inspired to consider a secondary career for later life if he could test retirement with a sabbatical leave. He had never had one, never asked, and my guess was that no one among the congregational leaders had ever thought of it. I made certain that someone would in the weeks ahead.

Between Rosh Hashanah and the observance of his anniversary at the time of the congregational meeting in April, we could sense that something special was afoot. Jack knew only that his close friend from college days, Rabbi Sidney Berkowitz, had been invited to be the speaker on Friday night, that Pauline Berkowitz, whom we loved as much as we did her husband, would come with him, and that the annual meeting itself would take place at a formal gala banquet.

I was privy to slightly more information because parts of the surprise for him required assistance from me. Rabbi Philip Posner, his assistant, was creating a special worship service for the occasion, composed of quotations from Jack's own sermons. He asked me to help him with it so he would use the ones most meaningful to Jack. Also, several members with professional stage experience were preparing a musical "roast" for the entertainment at the banquet, and they needed anecdotes for their script.

In addition, Marcia and Bill—both of whom, happily for us, were living in Atlanta that year—conspired to invite several couples of our closest friends from distant cities. Jack expected to see his sister and brother-in-law, Jean and Calvin Levinson, of course, but when he walked out onto the bima that Friday night and saw others dear to him from Detroit, Chicago, and Pittsburgh sitting in the sanctuary with us he was truly flabbergasted.

The evening had begun with a lovely Shabbat dinner at the home of J. Kurt Holland, president of the congregation, and his wife Carolyn. At The Temple the sanctuary was filled as if for the Holydays, and not only with members of the congregation but with friends both Jewish and Christian, white and black. Afterward they greeted us at an elaborate reception in Friendship Hall. The arrangements committee had thought of every detail, even to engaging a photographer to record the reception.

After services on Saturday a close friend of the family gave a luncheon for us and our out-of-town guests. An avid horticulturist who specialized in orchids, he had stopped off at our house before the luncheon to deliver—literally—a carload of orchids as decoration for the buffet supper we were giving for the board on Saturday night.

Sunday morning the children of the religious school held a special assembly in Jack's honor and presented him with a gift of trees planted in Israel; they had raised the funds for the trees from among themselves. This act touched him most deeply of all, for the religious school was still the aspect of his work he loved the most.

The banquet that evening was held in the newest and most elegant hotel ballroom in the city. It was also the largest, and it was filled to capacity. Just before the dinner was served all of us received a surprise.

Jack's assistant-to-be, Alvin Sugarman, and his wife Barbara had been flown in for the occasion, their appearance saved for the most auspicious moment. Alvin was more than just another assistant to Jack. A native Atlantan, he had been confirmed at The Temple, had taught in its religious school, and when he considered studying for the rabbinate had been advised and encouraged by Jack, who secretly hoped that he would not only become his assistant but that he would one day become his associate and perhaps successor. He and Barbara were already a part of our Temple "family" even though he had not yet been ordained.

The entertainment was sensational. I had expected it to be very good because I knew the talents of the men and women who were working on it, but it exceeded even those expectations. Both Jack and I were overwhelmed with the warmth and enthusiasm of the performance, as well as with the professional quality of it.

As I had hoped, the congregation gave him as an anniversary present the six-month sabbatical that would enable us to live and study in Jerusalem. In addition, those individuals who would have given personal gifts were encouraged instead to contribute to a single check that would help defray the cost of the trip that everyone knew we wanted to take. It was so generous that we were able not only to travel to Israel via the Orient, seeing a part of the world we never expected to be able to visit, but even to book the first leg of the trip on first class. I considered first-class travel an almost obscene extravagance, but Jack insisted that the gift had been intended for him to use to provide a pleasure he would not otherwise have had, and this was the pleasure he chose. That did seem odd coming from a man who had never before shown the slightest interest in personal luxuries, but I didn't complain. I thoroughly enjoyed the treat of being pampered all the way from Atlanta to Tokyo.

While I boned up on eastern-hemisphere geography and made the travel arrangements, Jack finished his end-of-the-school-year duties. After twenty-five years and a tripling of congregational membership these duties included a lot of june weddings. During one of the ceremonies he came so close to blacking out that he had to ask for a chair and complete the ritual sitting down. As soon as it was over we rushed him to the hospital, only to discover that what we had thought to be a persistent virus bothering him over the past few weeks was actually an infection caused by a kidney stone. In the past his kidney stones had been excruciatingly painful but not life threatening. This one had caused no pain at all but was far more dangerous. For the first time also he had to have it surgically removed.

We planned to leave Atlanta two days after Yom Kippur and return the week before Pesach. Two days before Yom Kippur our surgeon discovered that a recently formed lump in my breast, though benign, seemed "ominous"; he believed it was dangerous for me to leave on such a prolonged journey without having it removed. Without giving me time even to go home and pack, he cleared his schedule for the afternoon, sent Jack home to get my things, and had me on the operating table within the hour. The next day he checked, decided that all was well with me, and told Jack to take me home so that he wouldn't have to worry about me leaving the hospital on Yom Kippur. He saw me in his office on the day after, gave me a package of bandages and the name of a doctor in Honolulu in case of emergency, and wished us a bon voyage. The next morning Marcia drove her father and me to the airport, all of us in utter disbelief that, after all of the problems, we were actually on our way.

Jack was excited beyond even his capacity to describe it. He had written in his last column for *The Temple Bulletin*, "The very names of the places we shall visit leave me unbelieving and breathless: Japan and Singapore, Hong Kong and Bangkok, Rangoon and Kathmandu, Benares and Agra, Udaipur and Jaipur, Teheren and Isfahan. The dream of a lifetime." Once again he thanked the congregation for "having made the dream come true." We tried to share it in part through letters to be used as columns for subsequent issues of the bulletin and with a series of slide lectures after we returned.[4]

Although one segment of our adventure proved harrowing, most of it was delightful and all of it exciting and interesting. Our friends the Yallons were living in Tokyo then—Shimon serving as economic minister in the Israeli Embassy—and through them we were able to meet members of the Jewish community. Shimon even prevailed upon Jack to give a talk at the community center. He also sent along greetings to all of the Israeli ambassadors on our route, which enabled us to meet them and gain some special insights into Israel's relationships with countries in that part of the world.

---

[4]Rothschild, "Between Us," *The Temple Bulletin*, October 1971.

The World Union had alerted its contacts in the Far East that we would be coming through, which resulted in a charming young woman in Hong Kong writing Jack to ask if he would speak at the synagogue there. He did, and while it didn't do much for Progressive Judaism (the people there seemed perfectly content with their own, undefined brand of Judaism), we benefited greatly by making friends with the promoter and her family.[5]

Jack spoke again at the synagogue in Bangkok, but by pure accident. The chaplain-rabbi was away servicing troops in the north, and by chance the officer in charge was a native of Atlanta whose relatives belonged to The Temple. These relatives had written him that we were coming. It was a pleasant surprise because we were there on Shabbat and had not expected to find a synagogue in Thailand.[6]

In Burma and Nepal we didn't look for synagogues or anyone with connections in Atlanta, but we did enjoy our contacts at the Israeli embassies. In both countries the sightseeing was fascinating, although the feeling of "Big Brother Watching" in Burma detracted from our pleasure in being there.

India was the most fascinating of them all, partly because of its size and the variety of its culture, and partly because of the persons we met there. Through acquaintances at the American Embassy and the Ford Foundation in New Delhi we met members of the Indian Jewish community who lived in the capital, and attended services with them on Friday night. It seemed very strange to be saying our traditional prayers in a congregation where the women wore saris and where most of the worshipers bore all the physical characteristics we normally identify as "Indian." It seemed stranger yet the following Friday when we worshiped in the famous Paradesi Synagogue in Cochin, home of the exotic colony—whose members are known as "white" Jews—that dates its arrival in India from 72 C.E. Because throughout the centuries they have not intermarried with other Indian Jews they have retained their Western features. Their appearance seemed all the more incongruous in view of some of

---

[5]Marcia Lewison to JMR, September 1971, correspondence discarded while traveling.

[6]Photograph, 5 November 1971, Rothschild private collection.

their oriental customs, such as removing their shoes before entering the synagogue.

In Bombay we encountered the only Progressive—or Reform, as it is known in America—congregation in Asia outside of Israel. The World Union had told the members we were coming, and they arranged a meeting at which Jack could speak to them. They seemed thirsty for contact with the rest of the Jewish world. Bombay at that time had the largest Jewish population in India, about fifteen thousand individuals, with eleven synagogues. Interestingly, the national president of every world Jewish women's organization with an affiliate in India belonged to this congregation.

The harrowing part of our journey began after we left Bombay, while we were in Rajasthan, the beautiful "wild west" area on India's frontier with Pakistan. Ever since our arrival in the country three weeks earlier we had been reading and hearing rumors of imminent war with Pakistan. Now it began. We were in Jaipur, Jack back at the hotel nursing a feverish cold and me sightseeing at the legendary pink palace, when we heard the first air-raid sirens. No one seemed to pay any attention to them—except me. Air-raid drills, I recalled, indicated that one should take cover when the sirens sounded. I was more than a little disturbed that no one, my guide included, seemed to know anything about where to take cover.

The hotel was under blackout orders, as was the entire city, because Jaipur was in the path of the Pakistani planes trying to bomb installations to the east of us. We were scheduled to fly out the next evening and make connections in New Delhi for our flight to Tehran. When we telephoned our friends at the American Embassy they told us to go in the other direction, back to Bombay, because all international flights to or from New Delhi had been canceled. We had no choice. We had to go to New Delhi to pick up all of our winter clothes, which we had left at the hotel there while we traveled in the south. Since it was doubtful that our flight would even land in order to pick us up in Jaipur, we decided to hire our guide to drive us to the capital the next morning. On the map it looked like a drive of only a few hours. With clogged roads full of foot travelers, animals, and army convoys it took all day—without air conditioning and with few, if any, functioning shock absorbers. We arrived in New Delhi, which was also under blackout orders, just after dark and were lucky to get the last available room at the Oberoi Hotel, where we had left our clothes. The travel agency gave us little hope of getting out by plane in less than a week.

Two days later, with Jack's health steadily worsening, I indulged in a most dramatic performance. As a result, the travel agency found us a flight to Bombay. Jack rushed to the international ticketing counters while I took care of the luggage. By luck he was able to get us the last two seats on a flight to Tehran that night.

The airport was mobbed, and became even more so as the afternoon hours wore on. We went upstairs to the restaurant to wait in relative comfort: it had a modified form of air conditioning. Friends from the congregation where Jack had spoken came to visit with us for a short while, making sure to get home before the blackout began. They told us that there had been enemy planes and rocket fire over the city the night before. Their news left us worried as to whether our scheduled flight would get in or out that night. Our fears were not lessened by watching from the restaurant window as planes did land and take off—in complete darkness.

Our plane did take off that night but not without a harrowing five-hour delay in which the pilot waited for permission to enter Indian air space and to land. Jack, always one to persist in getting information about flight delays, had the advantage of having been ticketed by one of the many Jewish employees of Bombay's travel industry (we had been treated royally by others on our earlier visit to the city). In this way he was able to keep up with the minute-by-minute changes in the situation. As nerve-wracking as these news flashes were, the advantage was questionable. Some of the other passengers remained peacefully asleep, sprawled out on the benches and even on the floor. Many had been waiting for days to get out of India.

At about 2:30 the next morning we were quietly summoned along with the other passengers and led through security out onto a pitch-black runway in complete silence. We felt as if we were boarding a ghost ship. As we buckled our seat belts we prayed silently, thankful to have come so far but mindful of the risk that lay ahead: taking off in the dark. Some of the passengers who had boarded at the flight's origin in Australia didn't even wake up until we were alerted for landing in Tehran. As for us, we were so exhausted that we, too, were able to sleep for a few hours. It had been a very frightening experience, made worse by the knowledge that our own government's continued support of the Pakistanis was so resented by the Indians that, had the war gone badly for them, all Americans in India would have been in danger.

Whether due to the circumstances under which we arrived or not we never knew, but Jack and I did not feel well disposed toward Iran. It was the only country we visited in which we felt no warmth at all from the people we met. In the light of more recent history I suspect their own malaise had something to do with it. Thus, we were relieved and delighted to get "home" to Jerusalem.

Through our friends the Yallons we had been able to rent the apartment in Rehavia belonging to Professor Gershom Scholem, the noted authority on mysticism, and Mrs. Fanya Scholem. It contained their fabulous library, reputed to be the largest private collection in Israel, and we were honored and thrilled at the prospect of being its guardians for three months. We immediately registered for classes at a nearby *ulpan*, where we studied conversational Hebrew three mornings a week, and we also telephoned all of our friends to invite them to help us celebrate our twenty-fifth wedding anniversary at the end of the month.

"Playing house" in Jerusalem was the experience of a lifetime for me. Grocery shopping, entertaining friends for the traditional "coffee" on Shabbat, enjoying our membership with the Israel Museum, attending concerts and lectures at the Hebrew University, taking buses instead of taxis, pretending that we were really Jerusalemites—I reveled in it, thorns and all. Jack took the problems of everyday life in good stride, viewing the unaccustomed inconveniences as adventures and enjoying the ambience of Jerusalem friends and life-style as much as I did. He did not "plug into" it as I did, however. Every time I stepped out the door, it seemed, I stumbled into another project that absorbed me. Not so with Jack. He espoused several causes that he believed he could help on our return to Atlanta, and he was interested in taking a number of side trips to see areas of special concern at that time. However, he never felt the enthusiasm for immediate involvement that I felt and that he customarily showed for causes at home. On most afternoons he seemed perfectly content—eager in fact—to stay in the apartment and read or study for the next morning's class in conversational Hebrew.

We recognized that his attitude was due initially to his health problems, but we didn't realize the extent to which they had affected his outlook and energies. The virus picked up in India plus the tensions involved in getting out of that country plagued him for weeks afterward. Two of

our Jerusalem friends who were physicians noticed that after several
weeks he hadn't gotten any better and insisted that he go to the hospital
for tests. They also gave him some medication that helped him, but he
no sooner defeated one ailment than he developed another: severe headaches. For his headaches he consulted a specialist at Hadassah Hospital
who diagnosed the problem as extremely high blood pressure and put
him on medication to reduce it. Despite everything, he agreed that our
time in Jerusalem was well spent and, like me, was planning our next visit
before we had finished the one we were engaged in.

While we were there I received an invitation from the German government, similar to the last one Jack had received, to visit Germany as its
guest for two weeks on our way back to Atlanta. Jack had instigated the
invitation, having spoken to the consul-general about it before we left
home. I didn't really want to leave Israel—ever, let alone two weeks before
we were scheduled to leave—but knowing how much Jack wanted me to
have the opportunity he had enjoyed on the previous two occasions, I
didn't dare refuse. Now it was I who lacked enthusiasm. Though I tried
sincerely to fulfill my obligation as a guest journalist, preparing interviews
and taking many rolls of photographs, I was never able to bring myself to
write a story or prepare a slide lecture on the experience after we returned
home. As a fitting climax to a journey undertaken with such a negative
attitude, I developed the worst cold of my life halfway through it and
spent the last few days in bed with very high fever, in a miniscule room
in a Munich hotel without room service.

What might have been a disastrous ending for a marvelous six-
month journey turned instead into a spectacular finale as we reached Atlanta. Considering the state of my health after the long flight from Frank-
furt and the short one from New York, I thought I was hallucinating
when, walking from the plane into the Atlanta terminal, I thought I heard
voices singing Israeli folk songs. When they became louder as we approached I mentioned it to Jack. He, too, had heard them and thought he
was only imagining it. When we arrived at the gate we saw that it was no
illusion. It was Marcia, Alvin and Barbara Sugarman, and the entire Temple Youth Group. They had been singing and doing Israeli folk dances in
the hall just outside the gate area for the past hour while they waited for
our flight to arrive, much to the amusement of passersby, no doubt. Holding aloft "Welcome Home" signs, they sang and applauded (we warned
them not to hug or kiss us because of our contagious condition) and es-

corted us through the terminal to a waiting limousine while a liveried chauffeur attended to our luggage! That part of the surprise had been solicited from a member of the congregation who owned a limousine service and had generously contributed it to the "cause." Jack, who had said repeatedly after the initial celebration that "nobody—but *nobody*—ever had a weekend like this!" now exclaimed in utter disbelief that there could be no homecoming to equal this one. I think he finally knew they loved him.

He returned to his duties, diligent as always but never to regain for more than a moment the fire or enthusiasm that had marked his past work. Wonderful as it had been, the sabbatical had come too late in his life to serve its customary purpose of rest and rejuvenation. For him it was a taste of retirement that only made him more impatient for the real thing.

Although we didn't realize the large part his state of health was playing in his lethargic reaction, we could see several other contributing factors. For some years he had noticed the changing trends of Judaism, as in the mores of society, and he had no desire to deal with them to any extent. Even the ones he applauded in theory, he demurred at implementing: for example, incorporating the Sephardic pronounciation into the worship service. He admitted that it was logical to use the Sephardic pronounciation, since Hebrew had become a popular living language and that was the way it was pronounced in conversation, but he couldn't bring himself to change. After a lifetime of pronouncing Hebrew according to the Ashkenazic style he was afraid of embarrassing himself by lapsing into "Ashkefardic" on the pulpit.

Another example was the reinstatement of the bar mitzvah service into the ritual of the congregation. On past occasions when the question had come before the board, the members had agreed with him that the ceremony of confirmation had replaced the bar mitzvah in Reform tradition. Furthermore, they believed that the impact of confirmation on young people would be lessened if bar and bat mitzvahs were allowed to supercede it by being performed at an earlier age. Now the board thought otherwise. Jack had seen their decision coming and did not contest it. He merely insisted upon guidelines that would help insure that the ceremonies remained "more '*mitzvah*' than 'bar' " and established high standard requirements for each candidate to fulfill before becoming eligible for the rite.

Civic, national, and international problems continued to evoke his anger and response, but not the vigorous, outraged action of his former days. After the massacre of Israeli athletes at the 1972 Munich Olympics, there was some question as to our collective safety. Alleged plots by Arab students at Georgia Tech had been reported. Happily nothing came of them. Jack had denounced the terrorism and the lack of concern over it indicated by the continuation of the games. His Christian colleagues in Atlanta expressed their sympathy and outrage instantly, publicly, and without having to be urged to do so.

A few months later Jack and I together participated in our first and only protest march. It was for Soviet Jewry and was in response to the Soviet's recently imposed "head tax," which placed unattainable prices on exit visas for professionally trained persons. The Jewish students planned it as a protest against the appearance in Atlanta of one of the Soviet ballet troupes. Still as disinclined as ever to participate in such activities, Jack agreed with other adult leaders that the presence of adults was necessary in order to insure discipline.

The only time he demonstrated, with regard to topical issues, the old feisty spirit that had characterized his previous involvement was in January 1973. An evangelical movement called Key '73 had come onto the scene. Its avowed purpose was to bring the "unchurched" into the fold of Christianity, but because it threatened to sweep the country into a frenzy of conversion Jack and other Jewish leaders feared that it would trigger a revival of virulent anti-Semitism. Consequently, they did everything they could to show reasonable Christian leaders—all of whom seemed to favor it—why we Jews felt it was potentially dangerous. The movement did not take hold, but its failure to establish itself could hardly have been due to persuasion by the rabbis. Jack, who in the past had always been able to explain his point of view, failed completely to gain the understanding of his own good friends among the Christian clergy of Atlanta.

For years he had admitted that he smoked too heavily, but made no visible attempt to stop. On one occasion when Judge Jephtha Tanksley invited him to serve on the Georgia Committee on Youth, Smoking and Health, he had responded honestly: "I do believe that the young people who take up smoking in light of the new knowledge about its dangers are endangering their health and are stupid besides. However, I have a moral problem. . . ."[7] On several recent occasions his smoking in the car had bothered me so much that I had had to ask him to stop. On 19 May 1973, we were at the head table at a public dinner where the smoke from his cigarettes so constantly blew into my face that it began to nauseate me. I mentioned it to him and he moved his chair back so that the smoke would no longer blow in my face, but he continued to smoke throughout the evening.

When we came home he commented that he too felt slightly nauseated and wondered what we had eaten that would have caused it. I tried to explain that my nausea was not caused by anything I had eaten, but he paid no attention. At about one o'clock in the morning he said he had chest pains and called Jim Weinberg. His willingness to disturb a doctor at that time of night made me realize it was serious. Jim told him to go to the hospital immediately *with me driving the car.* That he permitted me to do it—he detested being driven anywhere by anyone, especially me— gave me further cause for concern. His tolerance for pain was so high that for him to behave in such a manner meant that the pain must be extraordinary. When he urged me to go through a red light at a blind intersection I became really alarmed.

Jim brought a fine cardiologist onto the case with him and they told us that Jack had suffered a coronary with a "medium" amount of damage. Jim's first words to Jack when he saw him the next morning were, "You've just smoked your last cigarette."

"Okay," Jack replied, and then asked, "Until when?"

"Until ever," Jim told him, "if you want me to take care of you."

Jack never smoked another cigarette, but the damage was already beyond repair.

We were inundated with attention—from physicians, hospital staff, friends, members of the congregation, even by the public at large. One of Jack's innumerable get-well cards came from the Jewish inmates at the Atlanta Federal Penitentiary. A friend who worked for a local television station contributed to much of the attention. He had called Jack at his office that morning and, suspecting that something was wrong because of the vague answers Eloise was giving him, had asked if Jack was seriously ill. When he learned that he was he had the news broadcast on his station

---

[7]JMR to Judge Jephtha C. Tanksley, 25 January 1968, JMR MSS.

at noon on the first day of Jack's stay in intensive care. The broadcast brought on the flood of attention instantly. It presented some problems for me, but the support it engendered made them well worth it. It was wonderful having friends constantly looking out for my own health and welfare during those first terrible days of sitting outside of the intensive care unit.

When Jack was permitted to move into a private room he complied with the orders that banned company (except for the doctors, who always ignored such rules and came in to chat even when they had nothing to do with the case) and even enjoyed himself watching television all day for three weeks. It was the time of the Watergate trials, and they were wonderfully entertaining if watched with a sense of humor. Jack was disappointed that for this first time in his career he would be unable to finish training and bless those being confirmed, but he didn't complain or try to wheedle the doctors into letting him out before they judged it advisable. He was also very disappointed that he couldn't attend the CCAR, which was meeting that year in Atlanta. Both of us had looked forward to hosting our friends for the first time in our beloved home city, but it wasn't to be. By the time they met, in late June, Jack was out of the hospital. Although he was still restricted to visiting with small numbers of persons, a few of his closest friends did come out to see him.

He followed doctors' orders, even taking the required walks, which he hated to do other than on the golf course. At the end of the summer we had permission to drive to the beach for a week's vacation, with me doing the driving. He stood it for the first hundred miles and then took over—on the grounds that "if Jim knew how much worse it was on my heart to have you drive he'd say it was okay." Actually, that instance marked his only infraction of doctors' orders, which surprised them as much as it did me.

Jack was "set free" to resume his duties on a limited basis as of the Holydays, and told merely to "take it easy." What rabbi could take it easy on Yom Kippur, 1973? We heard the news of the attack on Israel as we were leaving for services that morning. When Jack left the sanctuary to rest between services he tried to get some information by telephone but since it was Saturday none of the switchboards at the newspapers, radio or television stations were open. We decided to walk over to the NBC affiliate, which was located diagonally behind The Temple and wait at the back door until an employee with a key arrived and could let us in. That strategy worked, and we read the telexes coming in, but we didn't learn very much.

The next day Jack was summoned to a meeting of the community leaders to discuss emergency aid for Israel. That he let me drive him there and stay with him should have told me something about the way he was feeling. Both of us had difficulty keeping out of the controversial discussion that took place, but we managed to do it—I, because I had no business being at the meeting and Jack, because he knew he had no business letting himself get angry. We were disturbed because each speaker seemed to place a priority on his or her organization's interests rather than on Israel's immediate needs. Somehow they managed to cut through their self-interests, however, and stage a huge and successful fund-raising rally for Israel two days later.

Shortly after, we left for a vacation in the south of Spain—with the permission of Jack's doctors, of course. We had timed our return so as to be back in New York on the eve of the UAHC Biennial. Maurice Eisendrath was retiring from the presidency of the union at that convention and was slated to take up new duties as president of the World Union. We looked forward to being with him and Rita for the joyous occasion.

Instead we attended his funeral. He collapsed and died the night before the convention opened. We were so distraught and so concerned with the awful shock Rita had sustained, that we hardly thought about ourselves at all. If Jack felt any physical pain or strain he didn't mention it.

We had hardly settled down at home again before the Jewish world suffered another great loss. David Ben Gurion died in Israel. While his death was not a personal bereavement for us, it did require more of Jack's energy because he was the rabbi designated by the community to give the eulogy at the community-wide memorial service for Ben Gurion. It was a bittersweet experience, holding the service in The Temple, with The Temple's rabbi preaching the memorium, quite a dramatic and welcome change from former days. But it took its toll on Jack.[8]

Another situation arising at The Temple caused him even greater stress. It was a delicate matter involving a member of the staff, and he and Alvin had to keep it absolutely confidential in order to protect innocent parties. It was a very difficult time for both of them.

---

[8]Eulogy for Ben Gurion, 9 December 1973, JMR MSS.

In the midst of this stressful time, in mid-December, there was a week in which Jack was called upon to officiate at four funerals, all of them for friends, one a very special, beautiful woman who had died during surgery. Then came the worst blow of all. He returned from The Temple that afternoon distraught and went directly to the telephone to call Miriam Freedman, Eloise Shurgin's sister. He explained while he dialed the number that Eloise had been very ill all day and refused to see a doctor or go home early. Another member of the staff insisted upon driving her home at the end of the day. When Jack reached Miriam on the telephone he received the terrible news that his warning had come too late. Eloise had collapsed and died on her way into her house.

Under those circumstances we were hardly surprised, though terribly upset, when about a week later Jack developed angina pains. Jim Weinberg was out of town for the winter holidays, but before we went to Spain he had warned Jack that he might experience angina and had told him how to deal with it if the situation arose. Jack took the nitroglycerine and called Dr. Harold Ramos, the cardiologist who had been treating him since his coronary in May. Dr. Ramos had him come to the office for tests, found nothing beyond the angina itself, and sent him home with orders to get plenty of rest.

With Alvin also away on winter vacation and The Temple office in complete chaos since the death of Eloise, Jack couldn't stay away from his desk altogether, but he did make an effort to slow down. The weeks before and after Christmas are reasonably quiet ones for rabbis because no meetings are scheduled then, so he could stay home in the evenings. But the pains persisted. He went back to see Dr. Ramos after several more days of frequent and intense pain, and again his EKG indicated no reason to hospitalize him. On our anniversary, 29 December, he was still suffering, so we canceled our plans and stayed home for the evening. We stayed home the entire weekend but the pains persisted.

On Monday, 31 December, the pains were so bad that he stayed home, rested, and later called Dr. Ramos again. This time he asked me to drive him to the doctor's office, which he had not wanted me to do before. Again the EKG failed to register anything alarming, but Dr. Ramos decided to hospitalize him in order to observe him and enforce complete bed rest. He assured both of us that there was no indication of immediate danger.

Typically, Jack refused to get undressed and into the hospital bed
until he made arrangements for someone else to perform the wedding he
had scheduled for the following day. With Eloise gone and Alvin out of
town, the task took several telephone calls to accomplish. Then he was
concerned about the first meeting with his confirmation class, which was
scheduled for the end of the week. "In case I don't get out of here in
time," he told me, "you know where my notes are. Be sure you tell Alvin."
    Finally he went to bed and submitted to treatment. By evening the
pains had left him for several hours—a much longer pain-free interval
than he had had in several days—and he wanted me to go home. It had
been pouring all day, and even in better weather he wouldn't have wanted,
on New Year's Eve, for me to drive home any later. He tried to talk me
into calling someone to pick me up for the party we had planned to attend, but I refused. He finally persuaded me to go home, however, by
turning on the television and reminding me that he intended to spend the
evening watching the football game. I kissed him and left at about half
past six.
    Staff members from the hospital called me at a little after ten
o'clock to say that I should come back, he'd "taken a turn for the worse."
I wasn't fooled by the euphemism. Marcia was out of town but Bill, home
on vacation from law school, had left word where he could be reached. I
called and told him to meet me at the hospital.
    Dr. Ramos met us as we came off the elevator, tears streaming down
his face. It had been a massive coronary. Instant and irremediable. Jack's
room was next door to the coronary care unit, and attendants had responded on "red" signal. Nothing, they said, could have saved him.
    Bill notified Bob Lipshutz, who was the president of the congre-
gation, and then drove me home. I called the family from there. Before
I had finished friends started to arrive, most of them still in their formal
clothes. We were told that as the news spread the parties at the Standard
Club and elsewhere began to thin out and shut down. Many of those who
left stopped off at our house on their way home.
    Jack had imbued our children and me with his philosophy—the
teaching of our Jewish faith—enough to help us accept his death as a part
of life and resist the temptation to dwell upon its untimeliness. By his
example he had taught us to see humor in the worst of circumstances.
This ability did not desert us then. Undoubtedly some who came to offer
condolences were shocked at our compulsion to recount anecdotes that

made us laugh. If we offended them we are sorry. We know—as we knew then—that Jack himself would not have been offended.

A few years before he died Jack had been invited by the students at Hebrew Union College-Jewish Institute of Religion to address them at one of their Sabbath services on his activities in the civil rights struggle. He was greatly pleased. In view of the widening generation gap, he considered it particularly flattering. In order that the students might understand what motivated him to involve himself as he had, he began by describing what he saw as the role of a rabbi.

> A rabbi must himself have a deep dedication and a pervading commitment to the ideal of equality and dignity for all men. He must be prepared to involve himself in every facet of community life that will translate that commitment into the minds and hearts of those he would lead. Assuredly, he must do so with patience and forbearance and tact but there must never be the slightest doubt about what he believes or where he stands. . . . It is the rabbi's responsibility to teach his congregation—and to let Christians know—what Judaism has to say on the great moral issues that confront mankind. . . . There is great joy and satisfaction to be derived from the changing attitudes of large segments of . . . society and from the knowledge that one may have had a small part in effecting that change, and that what once had been a lone and lonely voice has become one with a swelling chorus. . . . What seemed impossible then, has partly at least been achieved. That is something—but not nearly enough.[9]

In concluding he reflected about himself, candidly as always:

> There is grave danger in personal reminiscence. . . . Some of my colleagues—especially in the South—will maintain that it was all too easy in Atlanta, a more progressive and enlightened community than many others, and that given such circumstances they would have been able to accomplish more than I here and I less than they there. Perhaps all of them are right. I only know what I have done. I wish it had been more.[10]

---

[9]Sermon to HUC-JIR, Cincinnati, "A Rabbi in the South," 9 January 1970, JMR MSS.

[10]Ibid.

INDEX

One Voice

Designed by Margaret Jordan Brown
Composition by MUP Composition Department

Production specifications:
    text paper—60-pound Warren's Olde Style
    endpapers—Multicolor Antique Thistle
    cover (on .088 boards)—Holliston Roxite B 53548, linen finish
    dust jacket—100-pound enamel, printed two colors, PMS 296 (blue)
        and PMS 552 (light blue), varnished

Printing (offset lithography) by Omnipress of Macon, Inc.
    Macon, Georgia